TITIAN
THE MAGNIFICENT

By Arthur Stanley Riggs

The Romance of Human Progress

The Spanish Pageant

VENUS AND ADONIS

TITIAN
THE MAGNIFICENT

and the Venice of His Day

By

ARTHUR STANLEY RIGGS

*Officer of the Royal Order
of the Crown of Italy*

THE BOBBS-MERRILL COMPANY

PUBLISHERS

NEW YORK · INDIANAPOLIS

First Edition

"Pretium non vile laborum"

CONTENTS

LIST OF ILLUSTRATIONS

List of Illustrations—Continued

TITIAN
THE MAGNIFICENT

Introduction

MANKIND seems to be divided into three general classes: those who make history, those whose intelligence and industry applied through the different arts, sciences and letters record it in cultural progress, and the vast, always inert mass that dully follows routine and complacency.

Of the two active groups, the so-called makers of history are clearly the inferiors. They are usually sadistic extroverts who smash, buy or bluster their way to individual material power. Alexander, Caesar, Charlemagne, Napoleon and, in our own time, Hitler, are examples. All had to learn the hard way that they accomplished nothing of immortality for themselves beyond an evil reputation, created only infinite misery. None of them ever realized he was but the animate tool destiny employed to inspire those other, stronger, often nameless, men who drew marvelous achievement and progress from the history-makers' murderous activities.

Today we see how Hitler, attempting world-domination, backed by the weird notion of a super-race, failed. Gradually we shall all see how his diabolical wickedness inspired science to achieve more wonders than the world ever saw before in any similar period of time. Safer, faster, more comfortable transportation by air, with the practical annihilation of time and distance; astonishing new plastics; hitherto unknown foodstuffs and unknown methods of preserving them; vastly improved general communications—these are but specimens. The man in the street neither knows nor cares

1

who is responsible for these things and scores of others. It is nothing to him that they grew out of the sharp necessities imposed by total warfare. Why should it be? They represent merely a phase of the material progress he has been taught to associate inseparably with "the American way," and his comfort and convenience are served, so they are a matter of course to him. Why should he pause to consider that the men who thus, by their constructive activity, record imperishably the destructive futility of war, are the real makers of history, its true constructors and engineers?

Some men from the moment of birth appear, in the light of later analysis, to have been destined to grow in creative genius at the same rate as that displayed by their countries. As the country, so the man; or perhaps the antipode is true, since countries but reflect the impact of mass thinking inspired and rendered effective by individuals. We have seen several such periods in history. Not the least of them was the Renaissance in Italy. It was no sudden, divinely inspired, unanticipated ebullience of the hitherto dormant Italian genius. Far from that, it was the cumulative effect upon Italy and through it upon the world of more than six hundred years of struggle, sweat, agony, daring and profit. The money-lenders, ship-builders, merchants, brokers, agents, explorers, soldiers who built up overseas trade and colonies, brought the rich pollen of alien thought and habit into the Peninsula, and fertilized with it an almost dead flower. The result was an astonishing hybrid full of color and fire and eternal youth. The men who smashed out the conquests from which the Renaissance derived were merely the tools. The true history of the period lies neither in the battles won nor in the trading colonies strung like beads on a chain all the way to the Crimea, but in the calm genius that developed logically from Giotto and Dante to the Bellini, to Titian, and carried on through them to Rubens, van Dyke and their heritors.

Of all such men Titian in many ways was the most fortunate as well as the sanest and most gifted. Yet everything in the man's personal history is so cool and balanced we see the real picture of him and what he was only when we view him as a gleaming, sharply cut cameo, standing out in white relief against the turgid background of his times. Seen as a part of them, sunk intaglio-fashion into them, as most historians of art have seen him, he is blurred of line, lacking in depth, ineffective. So it is the intent of this book to show him as a cameo, at once a product of his background of the time and of the Venetian State, yet entirely distinct from both while expressing with his matchless color and inexhaustible imagination the fullest conception of Venetian glory and supremacy ever permitted to any individual.

Titian was born in the most fortunate possible hour for his own good. The full glory of the Renaissance was dawning—that period reaching from the last quarter of the fifteenth through the first quarter of the seventeenth century which Senator Molmenti has called the epoch of "The Splendor." True, Venice was doomed, her decadence well begun; but none read aright the clear signs of the times; none recognized her spiritual bankruptcy and steady descent toward the most cruel of all fates for a serene city-state: unimportance.

On the surface the era was full of significance and promise. Great discoveries followed one another with amazing frequency. Venice sat preening herself at the zenith of her power, wealth and prestige. The Lion of St. Mark was never more arrogantly conscious of his place in the world without a rival, never was more contemptuous to his enemies, never more patronizing to all others. Venetian argosies shuttled between the lagoons and distant Russia with almost the regularity of modern train schedules. Wealth, foreign products, eminent strangers, talent and genius poured into the proud and populous city on the piled-in mud flats, ministering ostentatiously to the Republic in what Symonds has aptly called the most insolent display of genius and wealth in the service of a supreme State the world has ever seen.

The age was one of discovery and conquest that opened wide the portals of the European mind and flooded the continent with resources never before imaginable by any save the mightiest of princes. But it had another side also. In 1453 the Ottoman Turks led by Muhammad II captured Constantinople, tore down the Cross, raised the Crescent, and began that gradually increasing, expanding pressure that eventually squeezed Venice, Genoa and Pisa completely out of their vast colonial holdings and a diversified and lucrative export-import trade that reached all the way from Italy to the shores of the Sea of Azof. Three scant years after Constantinople surrendered, following a siege that still makes the pulses hammer, the German city of Mainz in 1456 produced the first Bible in type, with Johan Gutenberg as the reputed first printer of any book. "The art preservative" had been found, and history suddenly became no more a matter of expert penmanship and dubious memories.

Two decades later Titian in 1477 opened his eyes upon a glowing world still lusty and glorious notwithstanding it carried in its heart the seeds of corruption that was eventually to destroy it. Not even the wisest and most thoughtful of the Venetians appear to have realized that their ancient culture, deep-rooted in the traditions of Greece and Rome, had turned weedy and was choking with its superficialities every vestige of piety, sapping patriotism by its exaggeration of love for the classical, and, by thus distracting attention from the true life of the people, was paving the way with deadly certainty for the new tyranny eventually to pour down over the Alps and make the ruin complete.

We see all this today. Venice thought not at all of it then. The bright lad from Pieve di Cadore was a scant fifteen years old when the most momentous of all epoch-making discoveries transpired with the completion of the first voyage of Messer Cristoforo Colombo of Genoa. On and on goes the roster. The list of the creative spirits of Italy of the period is a veritable Golden Book. Great men of many nationalities achieved prodigies of genius and disaster—Columbus discovered the new world in the mists of the Unknown; Cortéz conquered Mexico with a handful of Spaniards; Vasco da Gama found the route to India and El Cano sailed completely around the world; Gutenberg invented printing from movable types; Aldus Manutius revived the Greek classics and gave the world volumes from his press that are collectors' items today, every one. A complete catalogue would include literally hundreds of names, cover every field of human activity. It was a day when money flowed like blood, blood like water. Passion, pride, arrant prejudice, luxury, display, traditionalism, all the foibles and vices of an aristocratic ruling class whose hates, ambitions, loves and accomplishments shot the fabric of Venetian life through with scarlet and gold, were the ambient into which this child of supreme genius was born and by which he could not but be profoundly influenced.

To endeavor to breathe life again into some of all this is my purpose. Art criticism in itself serves a useful aesthetic purpose for training and for the awakening of the individual to the logic of beauty. But here we have a human problem quite as much as an artistic one. I cannot add much by way of criticism and comment of significance to the critical studies of years by men who have spent their lives upon Italian art. But Titian has been thus far neglected as a great human being, an astonishing phenomenon of his time. In so far as I may succeed in disclosing glimpses of his humanity and greatness in contrast with the characteristics and events of his glorious century, I shall have contributed something. It may perhaps add modestly to the general public enjoyment of his art by throwing new light upon it, making it come closer to the non-technical minds of those many who recognize beauty but do not always analyze its expression, yet who wish earnestly to bring it ever nearer in a spiritual intimacy that spells complete satisfaction.

I cannot bring to a close the work that has absorbed me for more than six years without justifying my attempts at simplification of Titian's story, and my omissions of much detail of infinite sorts. Many of these details concerned Venice. Some applied to Titian's technical methods and so had, to my mind, no proper place in a book written for the layman. Some were fragments only, bright bits of mosaic concerned with men or events but, as mosaics, however glamorous, out of place in a canvas such as this. The addition of any or all of these would have lengthened the volume unduly. Too much of a good thing goes a very long way indeed.

The omissions of artistic interest are another and very different matter. Probably more words with less meaning have been solemnly written in the name of art by self-announced pundits than about even politics or religion. Irksome repetition has been mistaken many times by every professional critic-historian for fresh information and clarified exposition. In a textbook that is to be expected. In the schoolroom it is essential. But once the effective principles and manner of the Venetian School had been as clearly expressed as possible, it seemed to me there was small profit in iteration to an adult audience reading for enjoyment and information rather than for study. Except in cases in which some hitherto unstated technicality appeared vital, simple description and comment were unquestionably the wiser and more interesting purpose.

With such a vast number of paintings by Titian to consider, every one of them worthy of study for itself, a decision had to be made regarding the ones to be omitted here. Obviously they could not all be described in the text. For purposes of comment and comparison only those canvases were selected which are so outstanding they attract universal acclaim, those connected with special circumstances of importance or unusual interest in the painter's career, those which reveal his growth and technical progress, and those of such rich and lucent beauty—as the *Venus* in the United States National Gallery in Washington—they catch away our breath by the sheer poetic enchantment of spiritual loveliness and completely satisfy our aesthetic needs. I have tried, to state the matter in different terms, to do here precisely what Titian so masterfully accomplished: to give as richly colorful, precise and evocative an impression of my subject as he gave of each theme of his; not at all to attempt a stodgy realism which would include much of neither interest nor value, and whose mass of detail would serve only to confuse the reader and obscure the perspective. Like Giorgione, I have recognized the individual, tried to make him live in my picture, and shown him against a background which sets him off to advantage without ever offsetting him.

I hope the errors in chronology are reduced here to a minimum, but I cannot be sure of it. I shall be grateful for any corrections that may be sent me, provided they are accompanied by complete documentary references to make a thorough checking practicable. With every one of the critics and historians apparently making mistakes in both facts and dates, it is extremely difficult for the biographer and historian to be certain he has not lapsed into similar irregularities and produced further confusion. Every date and fact in the text has been checked for accuracy with anxiety and care. If notwithstanding all my efforts mistakes have crept in, as they no doubt have, I tender the reader my apologies and ask his indulgence.

It will be noted that I have appended no bibliography. The reason is that save for a collegiate monograph or two of no importance, not a single original book on Titian has been published in English so far as I know since 1877, about seventy years ago, with the two exceptions of Ricketts and the English translation of Georg Gronau's German life. The two monumental volumes of research by Crowe and Cavalcaselle, Gilbert's bulky quarto on Cadore, and the often contemptuously dismissed and very dry earlier biography by Northcote are the only substantial sources in English, dating

from 1830 to 1877. Besides these I have read carefully and anno-
tated most of the Italian and French basic chronicles and com-
mentaries on both Venice and Titian; made some use of such older
English authors as Ruskin and Walter Pater; examined the modern studies of art by Claude Phillips, Berenson, Byll, Davies and
others; and consulted the fragmentary references to be found in
the Italian books of Edward Hutton, Cecil Headlam, Thomas
Okey and others. No layman reading for enjoyment and not especially equipped as a linguist and student can take the time or make
the effort for such a study. Moreover, no single work gives a fully
rounded presentation of the subject. My entire effort has been to
present, framed in my own view, the clear, accurate within reason,
consecutive story of one of the world's most remarkable men, written so simply and straightforwardly the reader will gain a fresh
impression of a giant of accomplishment and be able on looking
at his works to see in them more than might otherwise be readily
perceptible.

To Mr. Ben Abramson, president of the Argus Bookshop, I wish
to express my hearty thanks for his courteous permission to quote
from his just-published study of *Leonardo da Vinci,* by the great
Austrian neurologist, Dr. Sigmund Freud, of which, at my request
before the book was issued, Mr. Abramson kindly sent me a set
of galleys. I am most grateful also to Messrs. Charles Scribner's
Sons for their kind permission to use quotations from Edwin
H. Blashfield's edition of Vasari's *Lives,* and to the indispensable Library of Congress for co-operation in putting at my disposal its vast store of source material without which this book
could not have been written at this time. I am also deeply indebted
to my old friend Dr. David M. Robinson, of the Greek Department
at Johns Hopkins University, for his generous correction of the
text of Cassiodorus' letter, and his personal translation. Dr. Robinson did not, in fact, use the Latin text I sent him, drawn from
Sansovino, but the Mommsen version, to be found as Letter 24,

SELF-PORTRAIT IN MIDDLE AGE

THE BIRTHPLACE OF TITIAN. THE VECELLIO FAMILY HOME ON
THE PIAZZA DELL'ARSENALE IN PIEVE DI CADORE

Photo by the Author from a Sketch in Lafenestre's Le Titien

THE CASA GRANDE IN THE BIRI GRANDE DISTRICT OF VENICE,
TITIAN'S LAST RESIDENCE, AS IT LOOKED ABOUT THE MIDDLE OF
THE EIGHTEENTH CENTURY

Book XII, of the *Monumenta Germaniae Historica,* Berlin, 1890.
Because of the still severely restricted supply of paper the Latin
text unfortunately has had to be omitted. The generous and ready
co-operation of the United States Gallery of Art made possible the
reproduction in full colors of the magnificent *Venus with a Mirror*
and the equally glorious and superbly painted *Venus and Adonis.*
The Gallery also permitted extended examination of its unrivalled
collection of photographs of Titian's paintings, thus greatly facili,
tating the otherwise exceedingly difficult selection of the illustra
tions used here. Particular thanks are also due the great Frick
Collection in New York for its kindly assistance and the loan of
certain photographs.

There has been a considerable question in my mind, since the
end of the war, with regard to the inclusion of an Appendix which
should contain as complete and authoritative a list as possible of
the authenticated Titians, with brief descriptions of their wanderings, present location and condition. This has been omitted for
the reason, which I believe will appeal to all conservative persons
as sound, that it is absolutely impossible at the moment to state
definitely where the Titians once in the various European continental museums and private collections are at present, or what
their condition may be. Many are undoubtedly held for the time
here in the United States in the custody of reputable institutions.
Some have disappeared completely. Looting, private sale in emergency, improper storage and other circumstances have unquestionably altered the location as well as the physical condition of
many others. The two Titians owned by Colonel R. M. Guggenheim, of Washington, D. C.—*Lavinia* and *The Falconer*—were
so damaged by heat and smoke in the fire that swept his mansion
on January 30, 1946, that they were completely destroyed. *Per
contra,* Colonel Guggenheim has since been offered two Titians, at
present in the possession of a private owner in Zurich, Switzerland,
to make good his loss. These two paintings are a beautiful por-

trait, the *Countess of Schönbrunn,* on canvas, authenticated by Bode and Gronau, and another fine portrait, supposed to be the likeness of the Jesuit *Andrea Spinola,* authenticated by Gronau and W. Suida. Both pictures seem fine examples, judged from photographs only, and both were painted during Titian's strongest impressionistic period, about 1550.

In the circumstances it seems obvious that any attempt at a truly comprehensive and accurate list would be so questionable as to be almost worthless. The visitor can always ascertain at any gallery or museum by a simple inquiry if the institution has any Titians, and if so whether they are fully certified originals or studio work. Private collections are seldom open to casual inspection in any event, and the omission of the Appendix is therefore felt not to be a serious loss. The text should be read with the understanding that all references to the location of paintings applies only—and especially as to condition—to the days before the holocaust of World War II.

A. S. R.

Cosmos Club,
Washington, D. C.
Easter Sunday,
April 21, 1946.

CHAPTER ONE

Asylum in Mud

A BACKGROUND, to be real and at the same time convincing, should be firmly in place before the unfolding of the plot is projected against it. Before we can readily grasp the character and personality of Titian and appreciate the details of his career, we must know the peculiarities of the surroundings which influenced the development of his pronounced and rugged nature.

So many ages ago we can think of the time only in terms of geological periods, vast masses of débris and alluvium were washed down from the Alps by eleven turgid rivers, from the Isonzo to the Po. As they sought the sea, these rivers on leaving the Alpine slopes turned eastward for the most part, the rich silt and alluvium they carried extending the mainland along their respective deltas at the rate of about a third of a mile in a century. The strong sea current setting north and west along the upper shores of the Adriatic caught up the material the rivers delivered to it, and laid it down in long bars or ridges called *lidi*. These banks, of mud on the landward side and sand on the seaward, roughly paralleled the shore in irregular groups separated by channels known as *porti* or "ports."

Eventually some of these oozy flats rose slightly above the water level. Behind and beside them open lagoons ruffled to the Adriatic

11

breezes, while the open sea forever pounded against their exposed flanks. Not only did the *lidi* thus form a perfect defense for the shore against the attrition of the restless sea, but between them and the mainland the open water of the tidal lagoon made a perfect moat. An enemy attacking the land from the sea must first penetrate the *lidi* through the narrow *porti* or openings between the flats. If he succeeded there, he must traverse the broad lagoon with its treacherous channels and hidden shoals before he could come to grips on solid ground with the natives awaiting his attack. Incidentally, no enemy ever managed to do both successfully.

Natural moles and natural fortifications that they were, the *lidi* were also something else, something entirely different. Far back in what we call the Dark Ages a handful of daring and adventurous fishermen moved from the mainland to the mud flats. What inspired them no one knows. Perhaps they went because from the flats it was a shorter distance to their usual fishing grounds. Perhaps some of them had suffered persecution at the hands of Roman nobles or soldiery. Perhaps they were so quarrelsome and opinionated they could not get along with their neighbors ashore. Whatever the reason, they took their boats, their families, their small possessions and settled in the slime. It must have been a ghastly existence for even them; yet they never returned to the land. Hardy, prehistoric monsters they must seem to us: uncouth, hairy, half-naked, unspeakably dirty creatures, squatting in the mud, breeding in the mud, dying in the mud; always wet, always begrimed with their environment, horribly odorous always of mingled rotten fish and stale muck. The lagoon had its first true inhabitants, but the aristocracy of the Venice that was yet to be had not discovered itself.

No one can prove anything, one way or another, but we have some reason to believe that these pioneers were probably Illyrians. Ancient Illyria is almost as elusive of outline as an income tax report. Roughly considered, it means the littoral of what is now

Dalmatia. Its people came from some equally vague region farther inland, spread along the shore, became fishermen, and eventually dwellers on the mud flats to the west and south. Seen from our twentieth-century standpoint they probably had not the faintest notion of why they were alive or why they persisted in working. The common instinct of all mammals to live was their motivating force. When conditions on the mainland no longer suited them, the courage to go out into the waters and exchange solid dry ground for quaggy wet ooze was by no means lacking. What they sought, they found. The untenanted flats were asylum, beyond the reach of the mainland, and, however uncomfortable, safe.

The natural consequence of this was the development of an amalgamation stranger than anything the world has ever seen before or since. It became as substantial and permanent as the union of soul with body in the individual. The spirit of those mud flats entered into their Illyrian fishermen, and men and mud became in a strangely commonplace way dependent upon each other until, with the passage of centuries, their identities merged to such an extent that either one typified and explained the other, neither could stand alone, and together they were able to crystallize into an independence so arrogant, so certain of itself, so self-sufficient that no monarch was great enough ever to lay claim to ruling them. Sturdily Catholic though they were, they did not truly acknowledge the lordship of any Pope, and their religion, where it was not intimately personal, was a civic ceremonial, an exceptionally satisfactory and gratifying appurtenance of the State, of which we shall see a good deal more as the Republic develops.

What a desolation these flats were for a city that was to flower as the fairest upon which the moon ever rose! Teetering in their frail boats across the mile or more of unstable lagoon between flats and shore when the tide was out, the temerarious amphibians saw waterlogged lines of black barely visible above the ripples. There was no heartening smell of life about them. The quaggy ooze was forbidding and insecure, treacherous in every black and slimy hummock. With the courage of desperation the newcomers laid down loosely woven osier mats, staked the jellylike mass about until some degree of solidity was obtained. Driftwood from the open sea, poles and boards and odds and ends of all sorts went into the crude shanties erected at infinite pains, while the hungry sea snarled at the edges of the mud only a few yards distant. None but the stout of heart could have risked living under such conditions. Digging out shallow trenches for their boats, the mudders also made each man his private miniature harbor in his dooryard.

On the highest of the *lidi,* such as the island of Torcello, birds had dropped seeds of various sorts, and reeds had emerged, strong fibred and pliant. Into the rough buildings and retaining walls and mats they went. Bit by laborious bit the settlements grew. In conditions that make such slums as those of today's unhappy San Juan, Puerto Rico, look paradisaical, the populace grew steadily. No infinitely fussy doctors stood by to prognosticate illness and evil, so the flame of life that sprang from the cold and yielding mud burned hot and clear. The unfit and the weak perished quickly, and the life that remained was fecund, rampant and brawny. We must not pity the women who went with their men to these horrible quagmires. Notwithstanding the usually slighter strength and physical resistance of the woman, she has proved times without number that she can survive and produce fresh, healthy life regardless of conditions. But it would be interesting to have a record of some of the domestic arguments and family squabbles of the first two or three hundred years when the wives disapproved of conditions. We should find, in all probability, the same wishes, the same waspish expressions, the same male attempts at rebuttal or growls of annoyance one could discover every day in any present town or city of electric lights, running water and private motorcars. Humanity does not change in essence, however much time and conditions do.

How long the slow process of development continued without meeting any serious obstacle we do not know. More and more fishermen came from the main, and more and more of the *lidi* were settled. There must have been a very considerable population by the middle of the fifth century, when the barbarian incursions made the whole of continental Europe unsafe. Until about the time of Attila and his ravaging Huns in 452, the dwellers in the mud presented no significance to the world. In that year, however, the "scourge hanging over sinners" *(imminentia peccatorum flagella)* captured and sacked Aquileia, the largest and nearest city on the mainland. Those of its inhabitants who could escape fled across the lagoon for asylum among the fishermen. The refugees were not especially welcome. None of the twelve settlements wanted them and the acute problems they brought with them. How, in communities entirely dependent for their food upon the outside world, could these *bocchi inutili,* these useless mouths, be fed? There was water everywhere, but it was salt. The little individual cisterns that caught the rain, added to by water brought toilsomely across the lagoon, would empty quickly under the thirst of the extra population. Except for the fish caught daily, every morsel of food had to be ferried over from the distant shore after being paid for, probably with fish and salt, which were about all the mudders of the period had to offer in barter for the other necessities of life. Then, as now, the logistic problem was the key to the situation.

But there was more. Few of the refugees had any intention of remaining. As soon as Attila withdrew they wanted to go back to whatever was left of their former homes. The history-making Huns vanished overnight, like the cobwebs they were. Attila himself, the dreaded "Scourge," died on his bridal night. It was not long until the lagoon dwellers once more had their islands largely to themselves. By this time, however, the once homogeneous groups had expanded into twelve communities upon twelve separate mudbanks. Their inhabitants, while all of the same sturdy and indomitable general character, had come from many different regions and of divergent racial stocks. Through the years widely varying ideas, prejudices, religious dogmas, ambitions, superstitions, jealousies and even local diseases had crept insidiously among the people. Fourteen years after Aquileia fell the condition had become so grave because of these dissidences that the wiser heads knew it could not continue if the community was to live.

As with everything else they attained, the islanders earned their unity the hard way. In 466, after discussions that must have racked the very soul of the islands, each community pledged itself to relinquish its sovereign rights and coalesce with its fellows in one central government. Eighteen years later, Christopher, Patriarch of the island of Grado, took the decisive step that eventually suppressed all rivalries and knitted the discordant elements immortally. At first the new government was as unstable as the mud from which it sprang. The jealousies and bickerings continued. Prospects for a strong, independent state were bleak. Nevertheless, orderly rule of a sort kept the islands in at least nominal control and maintained relations of dubious vassalage with the Ostrogothic monarchs. Cassiodorus, the prime minister of Theodoric, gives us an illuminating picture of Venice and Venetian affairs in the famous letter he wrote the Tribunes of the people, probably after September 1, 537. The title "Tribune," though originally military, was loosely employed for a long time in Venice, and the form Cassiodorus used does not in itself imply a military type of government. The Latin text, which may be found in Th. Mommsen's *Monumenta Germaniae Historica, Epistolae Theodoricianae Variae*, Book XII, Letter 24, is unfortunately too long for inclusion here, but the translation by Dr. David M. Robinson of Johns Hopkins University, who was years ago a student under Mommsen in Berlin, follows:

"To the Tribunes of the Maritime People, the Senator, Praetorian Prefect.

"Since the order has been previously given, we have decreed that Istria should direct with felicitations different kinds of wine, oil or wheat, of which she enjoys a special abundance in the present year, to the mansion at Ravenna. But do you, who possess numerous ships within its confines, provide them with equal devotion, so that you may be zealous swiftly to transport what she is prepared to supply. For surely there will be a similar gratitude of accomplishment to both, since one dissociated from these does not permit the performance to be completed. Therefore be most prompt toward your neighbors, who often cross infinite distances. In a certain way you are passing through your own lodgings, you who sail through your native territory. This is also added to your advantages, that to you another route is opened, which is tranquil and marked by perpetual security. For, when the sea is closed by raging winds, a way is opened to you through the most pleasant of rivers. [Reference is made to the Brento, Piave, Tagliamento.] Your keels do not fear the rough blasts: the earth with the greatest felicity they touch and do not know how to perish, though they frequently impinge upon it. From a distance they are thought, as it were, to be borne through the fields, when it happens that the channel is not seen. Drawn by ropes they move, ropes which have been used to keep them at rest, and by a changed condition with their feet men help their ships. They draw their transports without labor and instead of the favor of sails they use the more prosperous step of the sailors. It helps to recall in what manner we have seen that your habitations were situated. Venetiae [An allusion to the derivation from the Greek *Ainetoi,* "the praiseworthy"], the Praiseworthy, once full of nobles, stretches on the south to Ravenna and the Po; on the east it enjoys the delight of the Ionian shore, where the alternating tide going out now closes, now opens the face of the fields by reciprocal inundation. Here in the manner of aquatic birds is your home. For he who is now a mainlander, now is seen to be an islander, so that you might think that the Cyclades were there, where suddenly you see the faces of places changed. [The reference here is to Delos and Rhodes, once both floating islands.] In the similarity of them, over the far-reaching waters are seen your scattered domiciles, which nature did not produce but the care of men founded. For by twisted twigs bound together an earthy solidity is formed, and to the marine waves so fragile a buttress does not hesitate to be opposed, since forsooth the mass of waves is unable to carry away the shallow shore and without strength is borne along because it is not aided by the help of depth. Therefore the inhabitants have one idea of plenty, that they fill up on fish alone. Poverty there lives on an equality with the rich. One food refreshes all, a similar habitation shelters all. They are unable to envy their neighbor's penates, and living in this style they evade that vice to which all the world is exposed. In tending to the salt works, however, there is total attention and contention. For ploughs, for sickles, you roll cylinders. Thence is born to you your whole crop, when you possess in them what you do not make. There in a certain way is struck your victuals— money. To your art every wave is delivered like a servant. One can seek gold with less desire; no one is there who does not desire to find salt, and deservedly so, since all food owes to it the possibility of being most pleasing. Therefore with diligent care repair your ships which in the manner of animals you have bound to your walls, so that, when Laurentius, a most experienced man who has been directed to procure provisions, attempts to advise you, you may hasten to run out to greet him, and delay with no difficulties his necessary purchases since, because of the quality of the air, you are able to choose the shortest of routes."

It would be difficult indeed to improve upon the loquacious old Senator's picture of a city resting upon the waves like a flock of gulls, and of the spectacle of deep-laden boats floating serenely through broad fields, towed against the swift river current by gangs of sweating sailors. The letter is interesting, too, because of its reference to the salt pans as the mint from which the Venetians drew their wealth, and its emphasis upon the equality of food and housing, both the result of the ceaseless contest with the undependable mud. Yet even in the struggles of the sixth century the "Maritime People" quite evidently numbered some rich men among the populace. Half a century after Cassiodorus sent his message, in 568, Alboin and his Longobardi or Long Beards roared down from the mountains, and the cities of the mainland were depopulated for the last time. All their inhabitants had learned during preceding centuries suddenly took permanent effect.

Out into the lagoons swarmed the refugees. This time none returned. In overwhelming force they thrust among the old inhabitants and stayed. But even then there seemed no answer to the vexing problems. Not until, besieged on all sides, the island dwellers took refuge upon the *rivus altus* or Rialto, the inner and highest group of islands, and united firmly in defense, was any genuine cohesion attained. In 697 Venice of the Rialto elected her first Dux or Doge, Messer Paolo Lucio Anafesto. The asylum in the mud had come fully alive. After that kings or pirates, popes or Genoese or Turks accomplished nothing permanent against the Most Serene Republic so long as it continued to grow. All the mainland's attempts at siege, capture and rapine failed. Most of them today are mere themes in schoolbooks, fleabites to pester boys whose heads are full of wholesome sport.

For some eight hundred years and more Venice grew. Nowhere in history is there a more striking or brilliant example of a community that got everything it needed in the hardest possible way. Every particle of food, of water, of wine, of flour, of cloth for garments, of cordage and wood and metal for boats and nets, had to be laboriously brought from the mainland. All the timber and at first all the brick and stone for building had to be ferried over in the same slow way. By sheer undaunted courage, with strained muscles and copious sweat down through the centuries the Venetians built and rebuilt, fed and clothed and fueled themselves with complete disregard of hardship and the possibilities. As obstacles arose, they overcame them. Physical deterrents meant only more toil, slower progress. And all the time they were fighting Nature, compelling the elements and the material world to their service, they were growing more and more human. There was a subtle something in the mud from which they sprang that cemented them an inordinately proud and ambitious people to one another and to their State. Not Rome itself at the flood tide of its eminence boasted any loftier pride or carried the Roman name any higher. Venice, like her older sister, knew unerringly how to bind her children to herself, how to utilize their patriotism, their genius, their daring and skill for her own glory. City and inhabitants reacted upon each other always. As opposed to the Roman tradition, the Venetian aura was one of civic bounty and splendor instead of military grimness and force. Unique in time and unsurpassed in beauty, Venice was the one place in Europe where the Renaissance could put forth its flower in a lush color and warmth entirely foreign to austere Florence and pedantic Rome.

Like the mistily perceived pioneers of the mud flats centuries before him, Titian toiled ceaselessly for what he, like them, had the vision to see, the courage and power to grasp and hold. But it was because of the character bred into the city by centuries of daring and struggle that it became a fit matrix for the molding of one of the world's heroic figures and the greatest painter in most respects that Italian art ever produced.

CHAPTER TWO

Titian's Country

PARALLEL with the ardent life of the lagoons, another and equally hardy life distinguished the rugged mountain regions of the mainland that spread to the north and west until they mingled with the Tyrol. The area was wild and savage, peopled by inhabitants worthy of it. No invader, however thorough, was ever able entirely to crush out its life or even to hold it very long. Like fiddler crabs on a beach, the inhabitants scuttled silently into their holes at the approach of danger. When the wave had roared over their heads and wasted its fury, they silently came out into the open again. Homes had been looted and burned, livestock slaughtered, fields devastated. The "scorched earth" alone remained in the material sense. But these Alpine hillmen had indomitable courage and persistence. They took up life again calmly.

Lagoons and mountains acted and reacted upon each other powerfully from almost the beginning. Venice traded with the near-by hills through necessity; the hills practically lived to supply the demands of the islands. The welfare of each depended so largely upon the other that the natural result in time was the absorption by Venice of her neighbors in her first logical expansion by land. This occurred about the year 1420, and the name Cadore, already historic, became officially a part of the Venetian story as the Republic granted its proud citizenship and its mighty protection to the mountaineers.

21

The Cadore region spreads through the Dolomites, one of the most fantastic and needlelike of all the Alpine ranges. It reaches from the southeastern border of the Tyrol down the southern slopes of these sky-piercing limestone peaks which have a splintered grandeur peculiarly their own. Valleys matted with thick undergrowth and seamed with boiling torrents wind tortuous courses past the massive peaks of Antelao and Pelmo. The great torrent of the Piave, which rises in the Carnic Alps, cuts crookedly through the heart of the region to link mountains and lagoons and afford a turbulent highway down whose icy current flowed for more than a thousand years the precious freight of timber and supplies upon which Venice so eagerly relied. Set in the wildest part of this region, like a gem almost obscured by the elaborateness of its mounting, the principal town, Pieve di Cadore, lies squarely upon the road connecting Papal Italy and the former Carlovingian Empire. Down it came invading horde after horde, at times all the way to the coast, some eighty-six miles to the south. The disciplined armies of Emperor and King also made their way along its winding course between the turreted peaks; and the citizen militia of Cadore and Venice, the mercenaries and the usual rabble of camp followers and parasites sang and quarreled and plundered their way along its rough but certain length for centuries.

The vital crossroads of the entire region was and still is this town of Pieve di Cadore, dreaming to the unceasing obbligato of the Piave. North of the town the Carnic Alps lose themselves among the almost perpetual clouds. Southward their Venetian smaller brother peaks serrate the horizon in massive grandeur. It is to the west, however, that the Dolomites leap upward toward the heavens in such grim, grey, limestone needles as to give the landscape its most fantastic and unforgettable aspect. These are not mountains such as we know in America, vast mounds of rock partly covered with vegetation and tree-decorated. These are literally stone rockets shooting straight upward from the foothills, petrified in mid-flight, trenchant spires above the vast infernal cauldron from which they thrust.

Through this tumultuous landscape growls the Piave, sullen and always menacing in its rocky bed below the highroad that threads the hills together on its snarled and looping skeins. North and east, in what was Austria, the road enters Klagenfurt, from which most of the imperial armies and raids started into Italy. Westward from Pieve the road twists endlessly in meandering to Cortina d'Ampezzo in the Tyrol, nesting precariously among the ragged peaks. Southward, forming the upright of a huge *T*, the road winds down toward Venice and the Adriatic through Penarolo, Belluno, Vittoria and Treviso, eighty-six arduous miles in the days when transportation was afoot or mounted only. Today the railway desecrates the Alpine fastnesses and the roar of the stertorous locomotive dulls the grumbling of the restless torrent below. For sheer wild beauty and grandeur there are few regions to compare with this tangle of vales and hills, magnificent with trees in the full serenity of hoary age, livened in season by terrific thunderstorms whose cyclopean play with the lightning sends echo in reverberating crashes down winding valleys and rumbling in and out among the crags with the voices of the gods.

As the center and focus of all this, Pieve is as picturesque a part of the landscape as it is ancient. No one knows with certainty when it was established, but it was an organized community before Venice came into being. The passes east, west and south through the mountains undoubtedly determined the choice of the site, and the earliest trails developed into the highroad that made large-scale communication possible. The pioneers who surged back into the rocky sanctuaries of their peaks for asylum during invasion carried in their breasts the spirit of the eternal hills, exactly as their Venetian cousins held in their hearts the dogged persistence that enabled them to conquer the ooze. It was natural, therefore, for the hillmen when they descended to the sea-girt capital in the lagoons to view it and its people with eyes keenly attuned to the difference, and with minds apperceptive as well as objective. To a degree the same thing applies to all those outlanders of creative spirit who made Venice their workshop and home. They perceived the color, the beauty, the richness of the urban life flourishing so weedily about them, and were able, better than any native son of the city, to immortalize their impressions upon canvas and wooden tablet, in fresco and oils, in architecture and decoration. Gifted by nature, they were inspired by the genius of Titian as much as by the supranatural afflatus of the Most Serene.

Historically, this birthplace of Titian yields us its first reliable records back in the eleventh century. There we meet with the founder of the Caminese family, whose name was Guecello. He was the first Count of Cadore, and in the subsequent centuries his name, Guecello di Tommaso da Pozzale, descended eventually to the Podestà or Mayor of Pieve in 1321. It is not difficult to see, considering the ease with which names everywhere are corrupted, how simple was the change from Guecello as a family name to Vecelli. His granddaughter-in-law Bartolommea (if there be such a relation; she was Guecello's grandson's wife) had as a part of her dowry some of the revenues of the Chapel of St. Tiziano of Oderzo. Her husband, variously known as Vecelli or Guecello, died in 1451, and thus both the family name and the given name of Tiziano were established firmly a quarter of a century before Titian the painter was born.

The journey from Venice northward to Cadore runs the gamut of contrast. Crawling patiently up the Alpine slopes after crossing the plain that forms the Venetian hinterland, the road carved from the rugged mountainsides by human daring and skill hovers above the boiling river, darts midway along the faces of precipitous cliffs forming gulches strait as the eye of a needle, giving only a slitlike view of the sky, or winds through primeval forest where only the susurrus of the leaves dares speak. Now and again a shattered peak blossoms into a castle so unreal it seems literally a flowering of the natural rock. One marvels at the hardihood of its ancient defenders, at the indomitable spirit and endurance of their wives and families perched upon such inhospitable and constricted heights, dank, cold, isolated, swathed often in dripping mists. Ruined now, these defensive fortresses again and again held back the invader who lusted for the suave plains to the south and the riches of the cities fenced away from him by the chill Alpine barriers.

When the traveler reaches Monte Zucco, a bend in the road discloses just ahead the ruins of the partly dismantled Castle of Cadore, capping a precipitous height and reachable by a single narrow, winding path. About the base of the height snarls the angry Piave, and nestling close to the hillside at a respectful distance above the stream is the ancient village of Sotto Castello, clinging nervously to the skirts of its beetling fortress for protection. Pieve town lies straight ahead, and if one enters it from Sotto Castello, he turns into a winding lane which ascends steeply all the way from Perarolo and the gorge of the Piave. One of the farthest-out houses on this lane, and therefore one of the first the visitor sees, is the modest little cottage under whose eaves runs an inscription stating that Titian "began his celebrated life" within. Back in 1868, when Josiah Gilbert, the English mountaineer, landscape enthusiast and admirer of Titian, made his extensive study of Titian's Cadorine backgrounds, the ancient house had recently been converted into an *osteria* or inn. The author remarks drily that "as there is nothing to indicate the chamber where he was born, it is pleasanter to look at the place under the open sky . . . than to pry into the fusty interior of an artisan's house."

If it seems at first at all strange that so noted a man should derive from such humble surroundings when his descent was noble and his line distinguished, it need only be remembered that the entire Cadore region is a very thinly settled territory, that its foremost families were what we of today should call poor, and that character and achievement were infinitely more esteemed than material wealth. For generations Titian's ancestors had been stout soldiers and capable lawyers. Titian's grandfather, Conte Vecelli, was so highly respected by his fellow townsmen that once, when the councillors of Pieve were called upon to subscribe to a fund for replenishing the depleted food stores of the town, and the richer councillors gave hundreds of ducats, Ciani says Conte said bravely and simply that he would subscribe only ten because he could not afford to give any larger amount. Besides being a councillor, he was Captain of the Century of Pieve (Cadore was divided into ten centuries or districts, of which Pieve was one) from 1495 for perhaps fifteen years and held several other public offices of importance, including that of superintendent of the grain reserves.

Cadore had to import a large part of the grain for its flour since the nature of its limited terrain forbade agriculture on any scale. Most of the available land was laid out in orchards and pasture. Milk, butter and cheese and, in the fall, fruit, were plentiful enough. The flocks and herds provided a little meat, considerable wool and hair, and some hides. But the grain had to be dragged laboriously in and up from Germany or from the lowland farms near the Adriatic, over roads never safe from the depredations of both Nature and raiders. In such circumstances few could amass fortunes. Those who acquired any wealth were traders, and businessmen interested in the iron mines—long since exhausted—or in the cutting and rafting down of the timber with which Cadore met the needs in part of the growing Venetian naval and merchant shipbuilding industries. To this day one of the waterfront sections of Venice is called the Zattere, from the *zattere* or rafts of timber which banged their precarious way down the Piave, crossed the lagoon, and went to sea in new forms as parts of swift galleys and bulky merchant vessels of the Most Serene Republic.

The Vecelli house, standing at the edge of the Piazza dell' Arsenale, was remodeled about the middle of the eighteenth century but its main walls were not touched, so the general impression remains as it was originally. The cottage stands on an incline adjoining the Piazza, with a low-pitched tile roof extending well beyond the walls to shelter an outer stairway and balcony, which gives a very pleasing effect. The kitchen (apparently) takes the form of an additional lower wing tacked to the end of the structure somewhat like a lean-to or "summer-kitchen" in this country, its windows giving upon the Piazza and a little fountain of "fresh and limpid water." From the square a winding, narrow path leads to the castle on the hilltop. That doughty fortress has suffered far more at the hands of the Cadorines than from their enemies. Its walls are now shattered fragments, for the pious townsfolk pulled them partly down to utilize their stones in building the church and belfry which dominate the whole rugged setting and stand out with cameo distinctness against the craggy dolomite spires of the Marmarolo and the farther Alpine skyline.

Conte Vecelli, Titian's grandfather, owned a group of houses and small gardens where the present inn stands. Time has so altered the vicinity, and the existing records are so vague in details, that we cannot show definitely either which ones they were or even in which one Titian first opened his eyes. We do know that Conte willed his property to his two sons, Antonio, and Gregorio who was Titian's father. Since the records do not show that Gregorio lived anywhere but in this cottage, we may assume it was his talented son's cradle. At this point enters a legend which, were it only true, would explain why the son of a long line of soldiers and advocates was permitted to swerve from the courses of his fathers and carve fame from art instead of from the law or arms.

As Gilbert told it in 1830, Titian was a natural painter before he was twelve years old, the Englishman referring to Ticozzi, Rinaldis and Ciani, the Italian historians, as his authorities. One of the group of properties supposed to have been owned by Conte Vecelli was called in Gilbert's day the Sampieri house. Later it was known as the Casa Vallenzasco. It stands near the Titian cottage but is considerably more pretentious, and Gilbert saw upon one of the walls of an upper room a crude fresco of the Madonna and Child, to whom a lad (Crowe and Cavalcaselle call it an angel) is kneeling. Tradition had it that the fresco was painted with the juices of flowers when the eager boy was about eleven years old. Though the wall carrying it is now inside the house, Pieve believed it formed one of the exterior walls before additions to the edifice enclosed it. The picture, Gilbert declared, was about thirty-three inches high by some twenty-eight wide, and showed the Madonna seated. "Much of the background and drapery has been destroyed, but it does not seem to have been tampered with," the visitor remarked; "and there is a certain simplicity in the design and expression of the two sacred figures which commands respect, while the drawing and coloring are crude enough."

Whatever the facts, we cannot but regret our inability to accept such a tale. Crowe and Cavalcaselle dismiss it as mere fable gathered about the work of a sixteenth-century boyish amateur, possibly himself one of the Vecelli, who had already observed the radical change in art from the old Friulian style brought about by the pupils of the Bellini and Cima da Conegliano. It is easy, however, to understand from the nature of the town and the scenery surrounding the boy genius exactly why and how he must have disclosed to his parents such a strong tendency toward art as to make it clear he would never be successful or happy as either lawyer or soldier. Carrying indelible and affectionate memories of the scenes of his boyhood into his maturer years, he used familiar vistas repeatedly as the backgrounds or settings for some of his noblest canvases. Again and again we see the splintered peaks of the near-by mountains, the ruins of the town's old castle, the solemn magnificence of the forest, paths that glint among the trees. Nature was his mentor in much. Under the magic of his brush Cadore became

not only an international landscape but immortalized beauty, and
Titian stands easily where Ruskin placed him: at the head of romantic landscape.

Externally Pieve as Titian knew it in the last quarter of the fifteenth century and three-quarters of the sixteenth was probably
very much the same as it is today. Built upon very uneven ground,
it is typically a hill town of the Italian type, and except for the slow
growth the centuries brought the prospect is still ageless. Four
years after his father's death Pomponio, Titian's rascally priest-son,
sold the already famous house and all his other inheritance in Pieve,
outside the family. Other houses were sold, families died off, new
blood came in from both hill and plain, repairs and alterations
slightly changed the aspect in some ways. But in the main Pieve
dreamed on undisturbed. The moss that softly tints the thick old
tiles and walls struck its roots deep more than a millennium ago.
The rough paving of many of the narrower streets may easily date
in part from Roman days. Dominating every facet of the scene is
the distinctly forbidding brown, square tower or belfry close to the
Pretura or town hall. The Pretura itself is as odd and rugged as
the citizenry it served, and as reserved and sturdy. Its rough walls
and irregular design take one back to the ancestors of today's
townsmen, fiercely proud individualists who held their freedom
above wealth and preferment, deliberately choosing to fight for it
rather than die with it.

A massive outer stair leads to the principal floor within, where
one room of considerable size with a richly carved and decorated
ceiling tells of the town's prouder days, when it was a vital out-
post. In 1589 an unusually heavy snowfall crushed in the roof, and
the ceiling of what must have been the council chamber carries the
date of its restoration in 1590. The façade was almost entirely
carried away by the disaster, but it bears no date now. The time is
interesting because both catastrophe and restoration occurred after
Titian's death. That makes the external decoration of the belfry

exceedingly curious, for it shows what pretends to be a likeness of Titian. It was presented to the town about the middle of the last century by an unknown artist who had been retained to paint an altarpiece for the church. On the Piazza side of the tower Titian is shown as an old man in noble robes, outlined against a frightfully blue sky. Beside him stands a table covered with what Gilbert describes as a "gorgeous" cloth, upon which lie his palette and brushes. Whether or not his extended right hand is indicating the tools of his art or is pointing to his birthplace, only a few yards distant, no one can say, and the picture is so bad it merely brings out with greater glory the genius of its inspiration.

Few indeed visit Pieve di Cadore in these modern times of interest only in the obvious. For the thoughtful, for all who care for the underlying causes of works of genius, the region richly repays the visitor by giving him in full scale and quick with life not alone the scenery that forms so vital a part of Titian's work, but the inherent spirit of the mountains and their people. The mining industry has vanished. Trees are no longer felled to build either great merchant vessels or war galleys. Railroad trains and lumbering motor trucks carry the salt and wheat, wool and wine and other things advantageous to the district and to Venice. But the hills are still thinly populated, the winters are as severe, the storms of summer as sudden, capricious and violent, the general conditions of life sufficiently arduous, and the thought of the hillmen largely unspoiled. The conquerors have come, vanished, and left nothing behind to recall what they did. The accomplishments of a Titian, who brought to the city floating upon the water like a lotos the unflagging industry, the independence and clearness of mind, and the simplicity of life of his fellows as the bases for his towering genius, have made the world forever his debtor.

CHAPTER THREE

Prélude

As we study the real history behind the glittering superficialities of Venetian military achievement, it is easy to discern that the conquests in both military and commercial fields carried in their train little stimulus to that conquest of immortal beauty and significance which is the triumph of Thinking Man. In all the thousand years of Venetian history prior to the middle of the fifteenth century Venice held to the doctrine which made the first of the great trust magnates of America so significant in our progress: that production was the goal of the successful, who saw mankind as sharply divided into producers of wealth and those parasitic consumers of it which he, the success, more or less contemptuously carried inert as a part of the price of his conquests.

The so-called heroic period that carried Venice to the apex of her temporal power came to a full stop when Vasco da Gama sailed back to Portugal with his record of discovery, his charts of the new route to the Indies, and his consequent shifting of the geographical focus of distribution from the Adriatic to the muddy Tagus at Lisbon. Until then men had been too busy with sail and sword, with merchandise and intrigue, to bother much about things that brought no material wealth or fame. They were entirely satisfied to import them or the craftsmen and artists who could create them. At the same time the inky silhouette of Islam, pouring up dense and thick from the Levant, like the djinn from the bottle, was blotting out the Christian foothold in the Near East. Italian days of power and profit from the North Sea to the Euxine were gone forever. Venice as the *entrepôt* of world commerce was doomed to extinction.

Quite possibly the Senate understood the situation better than has generally been realized. Certainly the despairing merchants and bankers who carried on their business every noon on the Rialto could find little hope in the bulletins of recurring reverses that soured their discussions and left many of them tottering on the slippery edge of bankruptcy. Dramatize the scene, if you will, and see the yesterday wealthy owner of a dozen galleys, crammed to the hatches with rich merchandise, wrestling with an obdurate banker for a loan to enable him to equip and send out a new trading venture. Imagine the grim and desperate silence with which the news brought by a battered shipmaster just in port was received—seventeen vessels sunk and captured, all hands not killed in action or drowned sold as slaves to the dreadful Turk at Rhodes, all the glass and brocades, fabricated leather and Flemish woolens, cordage and canvas and everything else the spoil of the corsairs, and Nicosia and Famagusta permanently in Infidel hands. With a snarl the banker would turn on the shivering merchant and ridicule his pretensions, demand instant payment of his previous loan, threaten because his own venture in the lost cargoes would yield him not a single *scudo.*

Venice never had the slightest prejudice against merchandising. The hard life of the pioneers of the mud flats was made possible only by the shrewdness and industry with which they fished and traded. Dwelling on absolutely nonproductive mud, they had to struggle to obtain something worth offering their mainland neighbors in barter. The lesson was a trying one, and its effects endured for centuries. Development on the flats was, from our modern American viewpoint, exceedingly slow; but we must not overlook

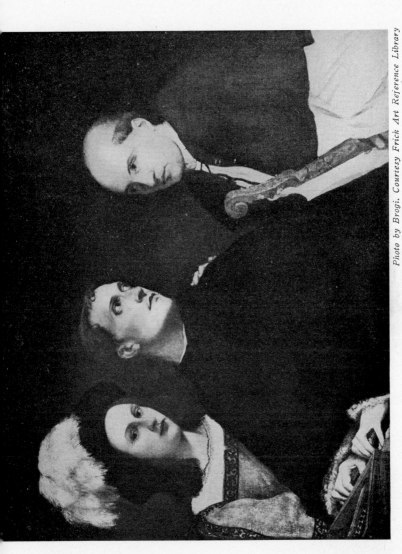

THE CONCERT, FORMERLY ASCRIBED TO GIORGIONE

ALLEGORY OF THE THREE AGES OF MAN

the fact that the Venetians learned while they earned. Both processes were arduous, and the earning was naturally of prime importance.

It goes almost without calling attention to it, incidentally, that men hard at work talk little. The late Senator Molmenti gives most graphic expression to the often misunderstood taciturnity of the Venetians in a memorable passage of his greatest book, the monumental three-volume *Vita Privata*, which should long ago have been sympathetically translated for American readers. (The one English translation, published years ago in London, is out of print and I have never seen a copy.) "The Venetians," the scholarly author declared, "were the least rhetorical people in the world: they paid far more attention to things than to words. They regarded literary culture as well enough in itself and worthy of study or even love, though it could never be the one aim in life." Reticence thus enforced by necessity is hard to shake off.

When after centuries of slow-motion progress Venice reached the status of maturity as a seaport and a capital throbbing with lustiness, her once completely democratic citizens assumed nobility. That, however, had not the slightest deterrent-effect upon their trading, and not even the Doges themselves were ashamed to be identified with any sort of reputable business or venture. The noble who sat during the morning hours in conference with his fellows in the Palace, went as a matter of course that required no explaining to his noonday haunts on the Rialto, where he transacted his business and financial affairs with the hard shrewdness which characterized all Venetian dealings. It was the mark of the good citizen that he produce, and since a State is no better than its people, the pride of Venice could be maintained only by an entire community giving its utmost in every sphere of activity. More than enough historians and critics have failed to grasp this essential point, and commented harshly upon Venetian ideals as, to phrase it mildly, "not the noblest." Such judgments would have us believe that here was an unbridled and thoroughly selfish community, wholly commercial-minded, shrewd to the point of dishonesty, daring, not at all troubled by scruples, intriguing, with the everlasting ducat always in mind if not actually in view.

Admitting that heredity, instinct and opportunity all pointed the Venetian way toward commercialism and that the things of the spirit were almost wholly incidentals, if we place modern progressive nations under the same magnifying glass can we find the record is much better? What of Britain, with her grasping of colonial empire; of Germany before 1914, with her scientific, industrial and financial skills, trading where she could and fighting when she preferred military conquests, insinuating herself into the core of the world as a worm bores into an apple? What, even, of supposedly altruistic America, dispensing largesse with one hand and dumping cheap exports everywhere with the other, while demanding open-door policies, spheres of influence and the like? From crude salt fish to predigested breakfast cereals or armor plate, all nations past and present have based their lives upon commerce. Only the Venetians were honest and frank enough to make a virtue of what in the beginning had been an acute necessity.

It was entirely natural, therefore, that when the Senate and Council saw the Republic's vast eastern markets and facilities for further growth in grave danger of being swept away, they should move with characteristic decision and force into a new field with the idea of continued expansion instead of accepting defeat. That spirit, incidentally, was another inheritance from the cold mud flats, one of the keynotes of Venetian power. Again and again shaken to her marrow by enemy activities or rivalries, even at times by internal dissension and conspiracy, the Republic never yielded to temporal force of whatever nature any longer than was necessary to stagger to her feet, clear the blood from her eyes, and reattack with old-time fury and more skillful strategy. So long as she refused to be drunk with her own power and glory, abstaining from expansion on the land where her destiny clearly indicated she did not belong, just so long did she remain a true nation, a distinct and highly respected people, both honoring and enjoying liberty in a Peninsula divided against itself, racked by feudal and political convulsions, and unable truly to unite for even the highest purposes. Small wonder then that Venice was able to absorb into her peculiar atmosphere every great creative spirit who came to her, turning his genius and industry to her own profit as well as his own. The robed and richly furred Senators and Councillors of the Most Serene Republic who were the breath and pulse of all this were true sons of the mud flats' fishermen and pioneers. Time, centuries of it, had changed for them only the methods, not the principles of successful living.

Until her eastern interests promised eventually to vanish, Venice had not meddled with the mainland to any extent. From very early times she had carried on a brisk trade with the Dalmatian coasts, several times cleaned up the pirates who sallied from cities like Zara to prey upon her shipping, and generally exercised a quasi-overlordship along that littoral. She had also sustained close relations with the Italian cities directly north of her islands, but the notion of expanding the Republic to include as much of North Italy as she could seize was so foreign to her maritime policies that it had never had serious consideration. Now, however, smarting under the waxing Turkish power she recognized as too strong for her, and soon to be smothered by losing her focal eminence as the distributing center of the civilized world, she turned north and west in a valiant but completely mad last effort to wring triumph from failure and disaster. Again the brilliance and power of Venetian strategy and tactics were demonstrated before an astonished world. Before the first quarter of the fifteenth century had elapsed her victorious arms and equally victorious traders had possessed her of all of northern Italy between the turbulent Isonzo and Mincio rivers, and her still farther-reaching commerce with the rich Lombard cities to the northwest ran into millions every year. Despite the subtler signs of decay, it looked for years as though this were her triumphant answer to losing the East, her defiance of every crown in Europe—and the preliminary to the development of her own peculiar and vivid art, which in its turn created a new world of the spirit which is still, after five centuries, more keenly alive than when it was born, since now its full meaning is realized. Whatever we think of Venetian principles and ambitions we are forced to admit a valor and a persistence of endeavor the world has never seen bettered.

The decisive fifteenth century was nearing its last phase when the boy Titian entered it as a student of the art he was to make so glorious. The city first beautified by the refugees from Padua had passed through two distinct stages of development, many of the wooden bridges and wooden houses had burned down and been replaced by more ambitious and better designed edifices, churches had grown in size and stateliness. Yet still the arts in Venice were supplemental. Painting was stiff and formalized, sculpture followed a debased classic tradition even more slavishly, music and poetry had not taken a single step forward, and only architecture, with its corollary of decoration, both within and without, showed anything like life. Notwithstanding this generally static condition, Venice was a city of freer and more diversified beauty than any of its contemporaries. All through the thirteenth century, while the classic forms and styles were gradually dying of inanition, Venice boasted artistic activity on a considerable scale which—so long as the artists continued to adhere closely to time-hallowed tradition—produced freely but was worth little. This went on, prolific but feeble, well toward the middle of the fourteenth century. Not until 1400 or thereabouts, when the decorations of the Ducal Palace and its chapel had to be completely renovated because they were in such bad condition, did Venice

SACRED AND PROFANE LOVE, ORIGINALLY CALLED TWO WOMEN AT A FOUNTAIN

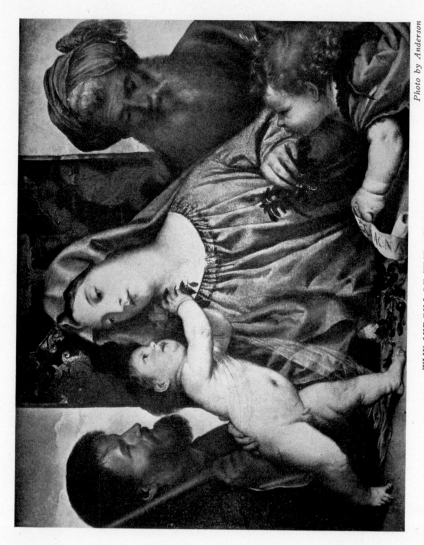

THE VIRGIN OF THE CHERRIES

realize that she had not one single painter gifted enough to be entrusted with even a part of the important task.

The commissioning of Vittorio Pisano and Gentile da Fabriano for the work makes the dividing line for all practical purposes. These two men might, indeed, be fitly called the fathers of Venetian modern art. Gentile particularly, as the teacher of Jacopo Bellino, father of the more famous Gentile and Giovanni, was a vital figure. Under the influence of the two younger Bellini, who settled in Venice after Jacopo died in Padua, the crude Byzantine forms, softened and made somewhat more human by contact with the schools of Umbria and Verona, rapidly passed away. Until the Bellini established themselves there had been practically no general grasp of composition and perspective, no appreciation of either nature or action. The brothers brought with them clear principles of true linear perspective and the fundamentals of naturalistic landscape; they also displayed a substantial familiarity with the nude and with ancient sculpture. Their naturalism went too far in its meticulous detail of every wrinkle in the flesh, every harsh line of tense muscle or protruding bone. But they swept the moribund Byzantine and its weaker Muranesque successor out of existence as the sun dissipates a thin morning fog. Their impact was terrific, dissolving. The old Byzantine culture, notwithstanding Venice always kept her spiritual eyes to the East rather than to Rome and the Peninsula, left only symbols of its pristine glory, such as St. Mark's. To replace it there sprang up a strong native culture which fell naturally into the successive periods of the Italian Gothic, Renaissance and Baroque. The fourteenth century accordingly saw a new architecture and decoration, predominantly Gothic, and spiritually ready to flower with all the lush magnificence of the High Renaissance.

This, then, was the foundry into which the lad Titian came to be taught, smelted, poured, cast, hammered and chiseled into perfection. His eager and exultant eyes seized avidly upon scenes remote from anything the silent forests and mountains of his boyhood had given him. The child of the Alps, as they manifested themselves in the rasping malignities of the Dolomites, held his breath before the resplendent silken shimmer of silvery domes floating at opal sunset, vast fairy balloons loosed against a lustrous, burnished sky. The very air he breathed into dazed, uncomprehending lungs was no dry, sharp, bracing mountain ozone, poignant with the heady fragrance of pine and oak and beech, but languid and voluptuous. The modest stone houses and primitive churches he knew in this totally strange ambient of the lagoons proved palaces rising lofty story upon story out of the sluggish green that never changed with the seasons or vanished under the white breath of a ferocious blizzard.

One of the elements soon to modify the entire subsequent history of art, and immediately to change the thinking and practice of Italian painters, was the discovery by the Fleming van Eyck of the use of oils and varnishes as vehicles for color. Antonello da Messina heard the strange tale, promptly grasped its significance in relegating tempera and fresco to minor importance, and made a special journey up to Flanders. Van Eyck was old and tired, and we may believe that he parted with his secret more or less easily. In any event, Antonello acquired it, left Flanders and came straight to Venice, where he introduced the process and was hailed by many as its discoverer.

Francesco Sansovino, the author of that amazing guidebook, *Venetia Città Nobilissima*, published first in 1580 and added to by Don Giustiniano Martinioni, priest of the Santi Apostoli, in 1663, is probably as much responsible as anyone for Antonello's reputation as the discoverer. Sansovino and Martinioni between them were responsible for the statement that many pictures by Titian and Tintoretto were so popular that cheap copies of them were freely printed and circulated—including *"Giona vomitato dalla ballena"* (Jonah spewed out by the whale). Probably correct enough in this, they hardly troubled much about verifying a popular legend of the previous century. Sansovino wrote, in describing the church of San Giuliano: *"Nella Chiesa Vecchia Gian Bellino dipinse . . . Lazaro Sebastiani . . . Boccaccino Cremonesi vi lasciò di sua una Nostra Donna con quattro Santi. Et Antonello da Messina che fu il primo inventore di Pittura olio, fece il San Christoforo,"* etc. This is the passage referred to by so many writers, none of whom make it clear how the statement originated or what its words were. They are simple enough: "In the Old Church Gian Bellino painted . . . Lazaro Sebastiani [also painted] . . . Boccaccino Cremonesi left his Our Lady with Four Saints. And Antonello da Messina, who was the first inventor of oil painting, did the St. Christopher." Bellino's first oil, according to Sansovino, was in the Church of St. Job: ". . . on the near-by altar one sees an Our Lady with St. Sebastian at the right and St. Job at the left, painted by Gian Bellino; and it was the first picture in oil that he showed."

It must certainly have been painted after Antonello's *St. Christopher,* because the new method of mixing and applying colors was so different from the old that some time was required before the Venetian painters comprehended its intricacies of behavior, and could employ it with discretion. When they did their palettes suddenly awoke to a life so brilliant and rich and varied, so susceptible of delicate nuances and subtleties, that art took on an entirely new significance. Instead of the flat, almost muddy qualities of tempera, their canvases and panels disclosed a sparkling rendition of the entire spectrum. Sansovino adds, about the Bellino: ". . . and as it was then much esteemed by excellent masters, so now at the present [The passage was written before 1580] it is held at a great price because of its excellence." By the time Titian was born, some five years after the process came into general acceptance, oil was the established vehicle. The medium best adapted to his genius was ready, waiting for him to show the world what could be accomplished for beauty by exercising its full possibilities.

Besides this, Venetian expansion on the Italian mainland was swiftly erecting a new and different sort of empire, making the Republic—perhaps no longer quite so Serene but spiritually mightier than ever in the past—a powerful magnet which attracted keen and virile culture in every field of creative activity. Painters from far flocked in, bringing with them the sweet freshness of unfamiliar landscapes and habits, the strength and contrasts of color schemes the lagoons had not previously known, and what might perhaps with some justification be designated as a more human approach to their problems. This, in bald outline, was the basis on which Titian within half a century created the supreme expressions of an art which will continue to move both the hearts and the sensibilities of men the world over so long as color lives.

We have only occasional flashes of revelation during the formative years when the lad Titian was gradually coming into his own. Curiously enough, considering the voluminous correspondence available touching his maturer years, we know nothing of much intimate concern regarding the period between about 1488, when he was brought to Venice from Cadore, and his emergence as a powerful if still incompletely trained aspirant. Not many Venetians of that day left behind them such biographies as this twentieth century has spawned by worthless shoals. Senator Molmenti's remark about Venetian personal silences applies with especial emphasis to Titian's student days and earlier craftsmanship.

If, as assumed, the boy was eleven years old when his father let him come to Venice, the date is fixed as 1488. The youngster was entering his world which, in its turn, was entering its Golden Age of Discovery. The mists of the Unknown were shifting, thinning, dissolving on every hand. Ferment was the essence of all life. Men stirred and expanded to the yeast of achievement that every year grew more potent. The Piazza di Rialto, where the life of the Most Serene focussed sharply, swarmed and buzzed with politics, business, colonial affairs, shipping, finance in the clatter of a score of tongues. The vague but vivid charm of the ancient on every side, so far from being vitiated by the rattle of current affairs, made a special, lucent setting for them that distinguished both them and itself. Acquisitive, eager boy nature, drinking in every unaccustomed sight and sound, must have felt itself transported; the innate genius awaiting development could not have been less than permanently fired.

In 1488 the Piazza was very different in aspect from the one of today, and the business and political life centering in it and in the contiguous streets was far more vital to Italy and to the world than any such gathering in the same district is now. Sansovino, our authority for so much in the Venice of his time, tells us that the merchants and Senators congregated beside the old church of San Iacopo at midday to discuss events and trade of the moment. Directly across the way the foreign merchants gathered. A long portico or colonnade sheltered both groups from bad weather. Under it a great relief map of the world as it was then understood showed everyone what we of today would call the track-charts or routes taken by the ships of Venice on their far wanderings. Bankers, brokers, manufacturers' agents and factors had their counters in and above the portico. In sharp contrast with all this yet in entire harmony with it were the art schools or studios of the master painters, housed in the same structure, and, interestingly enough, schools of music as well. The strains of lute and viol mingled with the quotations of Flemish and Italian weaves, the bickering over exchange rates and credit, and the bargaining for favorable freight rates to distant ports. We can understand, also, how such painters as Luciani and Giorgione acquired a smattering of music while they mastered painting, and understood the chaffering of the marketplace almost as well as the secrets of their profession.

Not far away, and still in the Rialto, lived Gentile Bellino, in whose studio Titian studied for some time. It was a considerable mansion, one to be pointed out by Venetians to visitors because not only had Bellino embellished it with mosaics and paintings by his own hand, but for an unusually fine collection of classical antiques which included a head of Plato and a statue of Aphrodite said to have been executed by Praxiteles himself. Bellino's will, dated February 18, 1506, and the mention of the statues by Valeriano effectively dispose of Vasari's statement that the Venetians, having no museums of antiquities, had to confine their studies to what Crowe and Cavalcaselle call the "dry and timid manner of the day" with their models. Since Titian studied in this house and beyond any question was thoroughly familiar with all it contained, there is not the slightest reason to assert that he was ignorant of Greek art and so paid no attention to the beauty and value of classic sculpture.

Much as Titian learned from Gentile and his compeers, he learned even more from his surroundings. His acutely sensitive mind quickly grasped the fact that painting was the great universal medium for imparting information as well as beauty to the world. Whether or not he so phrased it to himself is unimportant. The vital thing is that he knew his art and that of his fellows was the only vehicle besides the printing press and personal speech for conveying those ideas and aspirations which differentiate men of culture from savages. Since reading was the arduous privilege of the few only, and speech entirely unreliable where accuracy was required or desirable, masterful painting was supremely essential to the masses. For a thousand years the Church had recognized and enjoyed its utility; and now that Italy was stirring strongly in its sleep, the tremendous curiosity that produced a Gutenberg and a Columbus and their discoveries, turned the popular mind irresistibly to painting as the key to vast, almost entirely forgotten storehouses of knowledge that captured the spirit and fired the imagination. Titian felt this, breathed it in his daily contacts with his fellow townsmen. His work was his recognition of its vitality and of his responsibility to mankind.

Those daily contacts were interesting. The tangle of streets leading from the Rialto to the Piazza di San Marco, forming the principal concentration of city activity and known as the Merceria—more or less literally, the goods section, hence, the market place—bore much the same relation to the ambitions and strivings of the age in Venice that Times Square and the streets for a block to east and west of it, with their shops and monstrous electric signs, their gawking, idle, thrusting thousands bear to the same things in the New York of today. Show window space in Renaissance Venice was at a premium everywhere. The unceasing stream of traffic gave tremendous advertising value to the space rented for the display of goods and merchandise of whatever sort. "Window shopping" then as now was a highly popular pastime. Titian no doubt bathed in that very dirty and restless human ocean daily, listening as it splashed its comments about, feeling intuitively its reactions to everything it saw.

It was natural, therefore, that the Venetian artists should vie with their frankly commercial brethren in seeking to display their productions in the effort to find buyers. Painting, like medicine and letters, was the business of a handful of master practitioners and hordes of pretenders, most of the latter hopelessly incapable. Public taste, moreover, was as lamentable then as now, and if anything less instructed and conscious. So many a young artist had to confine himself to doing crude decorations for coffers and other furniture. The bolder spirits painted ornamental panels and exposed them for sale in the windows of shops in the Merceria hoping to attract patrons. The demand for such things was, however, relatively very small. Ridolfi tells us in his *Marvels* that the only steady demand was for religious subjects, "devout, finished and carefully executed." But it must be remembered that these religious themes disclosed none of the dry austerity of the Florentines. It is Berenson, I believe, who says that the moment people stopped heaven-gazing, they began to recognize themselves, and found what they saw far more tangible and interesting than any of the doctors of the Church had led them to suppose. So, though the paintings were decorously enough of madonnas, saints, entombments, descents from the cross and so on, the people in them were comfortable, mostly well fed, handsome, normal human creatures easily recognizable, and wearing luxurious robes with an ease and dignity which betokened Venetian satisfaction in the substantial fact of living as citizens of the only free and liberal State in the world. Naturally the paintings that disclosed this youthful attitude were much in demand. A few of the painters, who had the eye for large-scale work and the courage to toil dangerously, perched on scaffolds high above the stony pave or the sluggish green of the canals, and executed agreements with building contractors calling for the frescoing of the exteriors of the more pretentious mansions. One such successful job might bring a young man several wealthy patrons. What generally occurred, though, was that the contractor, who was a good businessman, hired the painter for little and charged the patron much, the artist himself deriving little or no benefit beyond a bare pittance.

Titian himself engaged in this precarious work for a time. Sansovino says, in describing what he declares to have been the four most magnificent palaces along the Grand Canal in his time—the Loredano at San Marcuolo, the Grimano at San Luca, the Delfino at San Salvadore and the Cornaro at San Mauritio—that "today over the main door on the landward side [of the Cornaro Palace] is painted a fresco in the likeness of Hercules, and it is said to be one of the first works of Titian." This fresco, long since vanished, is the one mentioned by Crowe and Cavalcaselle as being over the door of the Morosini palace. Incidentally, their version in English of the original text is not quite accurate in some respects.

The cost of these great palaces, and indeed the rentals for which the poorest shopwindows or counters on the Rialto or in the Merceria were held, make one thoughtful in view of the recurrence at intervals throughout the world of this same type of over-valuation and rent-inflation as results of more than ordinary congestion. The gold ducat of Venice, the standard coin, was worth something like three dollars and a half in American money. Such a relatively poor man as the Doge Francesco Foscari, whose fortune was certainly not more than an hundred and fifty thousand ducats, owned a palace on the Grand Canal that cost him a round twenty thousand. Scores of other mansions either abutting on or near the Rialto cost varying sums ranging from ten to fifteen thousand each, and the ordinary residence of five or six thousand was a commonplace.

Rentals for space in the shops were on a par with building costs. No one could rent the tiniest counter in a Rialto shop for less than an hundred ducats a year, according to Romanin. The Bell Hotel, owned by the Sanudo family and occupying a favorable site on the Pescheria, with its front tenanted by small shopkeepers, brought the owners a yearly revenue of eight hundred ducats. As for tenants in the poorer sections of the city, where the laboring class lived, their rentals rose from the fifteen or twenty ducats a year charged during the fourteenth century to as much as from six to a dozen times as much, according to the location and the proximity of the house to the Ducal Palace. Many a private dwelling during the middle years of the fifteenth century contained a principal apartment on the gilding, mirrors and decoration of which the owner had spent from eight hundred to two thousand ducats. Sansovino caps Sanudo's story by stating that "as for the furniture and incredible riches of these houses,

it is impossible to think of, to say nothing of writing it in full";
and Senator Molmenti adds the significant remark to his quotation
from Sansovino: "As the public life in monuments, so private
customs are written all about the houses, in the household goods
and furnishings. The various manifestations of art favored lordly
caprice and enlivened the genteel sense of good taste not alone in
the external aspects of life but in the intimacy of the home." The
grandiose exteriors and their decorative frescoes inspired the interior decoration, and it again made further emulation in festive
exteriors a necessity for the ambitious, until palaces rose from the
dull green waters as by enchantment, blossomed in colors and
gold, and made of the Grand Canal and many another lesser
waterway winding rainbows veining the city with streams of
beauty that fed its full and opulent life.

CHAPTER FOUR

The Curtain Rises

IT IS hard for the American mind, with its traditional coddling of children, save among the very poor, to conceive of taking a boy of eleven from his home and planting him with relatives in a distant city as an apprentice. We think of a child of eleven as being anything but able to begin carving his own life from the rough. When occasionally some poor and fortunate lad has the intelligence, courage and persistence to do that we hail him as a prodigy, one to be envied and admired, but not necessarily imitated. To the Venetians of the late fifteenth century it was entirely natural to give their boys an early start in life. Life, indeed, was in most cases short enough, for the vast majority of both men and women died at what today is considered an early age.

Titian was brought down in 1488 to the house of his uncle and put to work in the studio of Sebastiano Zuccato. So much we know with apparent certainty. From that point until about 1507, when he appears as a painter strong and well enough known to be given one of the principal frescoes on the exterior of the Fondaco de' Tedeschi, or German Warehouse, we have little more than hints and suggestions. The boy's first master, Zuccato, was a mosaicist who was also a painter of considerable standing, and from him the new apprentice derived his first practical lessons. Tizianello, the distant relative who wrote the anonymous "Life" about half a century after Titian's death in 1576, believed the boy had already had lessons, and came to Venice to carry on his work. Both Dolce and Vasari indicate that his first instruction came from Zuccato. Whatever the facts may be, we know that Zuccato finally relinquished his student to Gentile Bellino who, according to tradition, soon frowned upon his pupil's graphic speed, warning him that he could not progress through haste. With this very dubious legend entering the story to cloud the record, all we actually know is that Titian left the studio of the greatest painter of the day and entered that of his brother Giovanni.

Who shall say, after the facts, how genius learns and works? The mass of correspondence and other records Titian left behind him reveals a man of remarkable sagacity, shrewd in money matters, according to most of his chroniclers, to the point of avarice, gifted beyond his compeers in building up both fame and fortune, and respecting himself as he respected the dignitaries and monarchs for whom he did much of his work. It is a fair assumption, then, that Zuccato, who was able enough as an artist to have been chosen at one time as the syndic of his guild, probably realized early the possibilities of the bright-eyed and aspiring apprentice, who must very soon have displayed something of his quality, and released him for his own advantage to the greater man they both knew could teach him more and develop in him to the uttermost the imagination, skill, power and ease the budding art of the day so greatly needed.

In this supreme city, "rich in gold," as Petrarch said of it, "but richer still in reputation . . . safeguarded by the salt encircling sea, but safeguarded still more by the salt of good counsel," Titian began his studies at the very moment of the birth-pangs of an art which was to differ radically from the art of every other locality and to affect all subsequent painting because besides its inherent beauty it carried truth in the most legitimate expression possible of every subject it portrayed. Until the Bellini began painting in oils all the truly great art in Venice was the work of the Tuscan and Sienese masters of the thirteenth and fourteenth centuries, who determined, by their religious fervor and individual genius, the whole future of Tuscan art, passing their influence down irresistibly by mortmain to even such giants as Leonardo, Raphael and Michael Angelo himself.

No such men as Duccio and Giotto could have sprung from Venice. As Hutton has pointed out in his study of the matter, the work of these men was to a great extent religious in character and produced for the Church, forming an interesting and important "part of the furniture of religion." A single glance at any of their works reveals conclusively their thematic character and complete disregard of everything not coherent with their purpose. Aside from their ecclesiastical significance and their value in the technical sense, they could not exercise human and public appeal any more than a tract put out by a modern organization can catch and hold the general public interest.

The Venetian School, on the contrary, as has already been indicated, had no concern directly with religion or the Church, but was State-inspired. It was humanistic above everything else. In other words, it was secular through and through. Besides that, in its technical aspects it was not, as were the Sienese and Florentine works, chiefly concerned with the "nobility and integrity of its drawing, nor the beauty and delight of its decoration, but the splendor of its color, its occupation with the gestures and joy of life." Put perhaps more simply, it was not Siena which fathered the Sienese School, but Duccio; not Florence which decided the character of the Florentine or Tuscan, but Giotto. Those two cities, because they had never been able to learn what Venice knew and had practiced from the beginning, could not draw to their hearts and use for their own glory the genius of their most spiritual children. It was inevitable that no master, not even Gentile Bellino, could either create, inspire or control the character of the Venetian

School, but Venice herself, truly the Most Serene. More than a city, more, indeed, than a Republic, she was a nation, unique in Italy and in the world, and the School she established was equally unique, besides being the first national school in modern times.

Perhaps it were wiser to say instead of secular, that the Venetian School was civic. Its works included numberless paintings with religious themes, many of them masterpieces. But if we expect to find most of them in the churches where such works might normally be expected, we shall be disappointed. They are at their best, their brilliant, revealing glory of magnificence, in the Ducal Palace. In the churches there is nothing today to stand beside the superb frescoes of the austere Sienese and Florentine masters. These gave unmatched expression not to their native cities, not to humanity even, but to the narrow north Italian concept of religion. Their detachment from the normalities of urban life and the beauties of landscape harked straight back to the perfectionism of the Greeks of the Golden Age, with their statues of the gods whose remoteness from human affairs was the accepted ideal until the slow warming of artistic experience in the Hellenistic period turned the gods and goddesses away from Olympus and made them recognizable as super-human beings. No one, therefore, could possibly experience the tang and savor of either Siena or Florence from the works of their respective schools.

If on the contrary we examine the Venetian works in detail, we have not only innumerable phases of the pageantry of the city's life and affairs, but landscape so exquisite that not until long afterward, with the appearance of the Frenchman Claude Lorraine, could any painter even approximate its beauty and truthfulness. Again and again the Bellini, Carpaccio, Giorgione, Titian, Tintoretto, Veronese and their pupils and followers in canvases, altarpieces, decorations, ceiling and wall panels strike the same ringing note. If we knew nothing about the architectural development of the city, it would be almost possible to reconstruct much of it in outline from these paintings, exactly as it would be possible to identify many of those majestic or slumbrous landscapes against which the painters set their glowing figures. At least three times were the paintings of the Ducal Palace burned and replaced, eventually by the transcendent work we of today can enjoy. Fortunately the flames that so often swept Venice spared most of the masterpieces not in the Palace. To find them one must go to the Academy, not the Frari, to the guild houses or "union headquarters" of the various craft and labor organizations, to the Schools of the Carità and of St. Rocco, not to the great churches in general. In almost every other city in the world man's greatest genius and most lavish outlay have been for the temples of Deity, from Memphis, Thebes, Babylon and Athens to the present. But Venice stands alone, arrogant in her beauty still, unashamed as Phryne that her beauty should be a glorification of the tangible rather than of the spiritual.

In another and quite as important a characteristic the Venetians differed from their western predecessors. Study of the Sienese and Florentine Schools down through the centuries reveals clearly how implicit the work of even such a giant as Michael Angelo is in that of Giotto, two hundred years earlier. Raphael is with even greater clearness the pupil always of Perugino, even when he transcends himself. The greatness of the master becomes more fluid, brighter, possibly somewhat more individual in the pupil, but it is discernible always as the original greatness of the master. In other words, creative originality is lacking in both systems.

The same attention given to the Venetians makes it apparent with striking force that not one of the lagoon painters was, so to speak, a transfiguration of his teacher. Not one of the greater men reveals anywhere his debt to any individual to the exclusion of others. As one English critic has put it, these men were not prophesied by their forerunners, but themselves are prophets in their own right and time. Bellino himself, founder of the

school, struck a fresh note and gave its initial impulse to a new
and consummate art. After him Giorgione, Titian and the other
peers of that glowing realm, while they owed a great deal to
Gentile, were themselves creators, originators, not mere gifted
followers with imagination, and the work they have left us is due
not to any great master who taught them, but to Venice herself,
to the Most Serene Republic. It is legitimate to say that the
greater breadth of interest, the wider range of subject matter, the
civic motivation of the Venetians and the fact that while devout
enough they regarded religion not as their *raison d'être,* but as one
of many functions, kept them from the desiccation and circum-
scription which cramped the imagination and humanity of the
Tuscan and Umbrian Schools. In the case of Titian, the style and
power of the man not only were not the direct artistic descendants
of any previous master, but of the combined art of all, rein-
forced and elevated to greater beauty by the outstanding personal
characteristics of the painter. He came as close as one man could
to epitomizing his city of wonder for all time. And his artistic
legacy carried down to all the later European painters of consequence with the vital exception of Rembrandt. Velázquez, Rubens,
van Dyke, Reynolds, Claude Lorraine owed him a debt each
acknowledged in his own fashion in canvases sharply individual
yet touched with their inspirational heritage. Even El Greco as
a portraitist, though never in landscape, showed the Venetian influence in his lucidity of conception and use of eloquent color.

With the fable of the wall fresco at Pieve disposed of, and
nothing surviving of Titian's work of student days so far as we
now know, we can form our opinions of his growth in mastery only
after 1507, when he was already well known in Venice and had
undoubtedly had a hand in many of the works supervised and
touched up by his teachers and colleagues. In that year Titian had
reached the age of thirty, and was in the full physical prime of a
remarkably vigorous manhood which had more than sixty years to

run, still strong and capable, before the plague ended his work. The period between the six or eight closing years of the fifteenth and the first decade of the sixteenth centuries was a stormy one for Venice. Losing ground steadily in the Levant, harassed by threats from both north and south, realizing with the shrewd sense of age and experience that they must rely upon strategy and diplomacy rather than upon the brute force of previous ages, the Venetians matched guile with guile, contracted alliances for the opportunity of the moment and quickly made counteralliances against their quondam allies as soon as material considerations prompted the new course. Whether, as Cicogna intimates in notes on a manuscript of Tizianello's anonymous "Life" in the Seminario at Venice, Titian was known during this period at the court of Lodovico Sforza of Milan we cannot be certain, for there is no corroborating evidence. We do, however, know he was close to the powerful and wealthy family of the Pesari, who were close to the Borgias, and whose fortunes were deeply involved in Constantinople.

Regardless for the moment of the Pesari, who will appear again, their presence in Titian's career points a vital issue. Biography, however constricted, cannot possibly give a true picture of its subject if he be isolated. No man has ever been great enough to be considered unmodified by his times and his acquaintances. The greater the individual, the more clearly do his characteristics appear when seen in the light of the events and persons associated with him. It is therefore entirely out of the question to weigh so outstanding a figure as Titian apart from his background. Without all the color, movement and disposition of Venice and the Venetians as the master-key to his nature we should have nothing more than a flat etching of the man, perhaps little but a critical appreciation of the artist long dead. To see him alive and in the round, a plastic figure molded by and appreciative of all the innumerable influences of his long and varied career, yet standing out sharply as an individual quite apart from his fellows throughout the world of culture, we must seek the essential details of the life he lived, himself serene among friends, enemies and a world public anything but serene. No other man so well and so completely has ever manifested in himself the major virtues of his school of art, no other so masterfully typified the great Republic of which he remains an immortal citizen. His personal dignity, his tremendous vitality and incredible productivity, his business sagacity, his human qualities and friendships, even if we make no account of his towering genius, reveal him the individual complete in himself who stood for Venice and spoke for her in the language of all mankind untroubled before pope or king or commoner. With amazing strength yet flexibility he yielded to the currents of events and the practical business of life without sacrificing his personal or artistic integrity. In his shrewd brain all this combined to give him effective guides for material success, and today yields to us of four centuries later an insight into the cultural life of the time as no other source could. Titian's genius resided not merely in his painting. He charted accurately the swirling lagoons of political and military as well as artistic and religious opinion, and rode them all with unruffled certainty. Separate such a man from such a background and the result is a dull monochrome. Fused with everything that made up his world, he shows instantly with glowing intensity as a part of the universal character, yet as distinct from the rest as the white face of an exquisite cameo is both part of and distinct from its onyx or agate-hued background.

While all his compeers had some degree of mastery in the refinements of a contemplative art, Titian stood head and shoulders above them because of his triple equipment of comprehensive genius, temperament and solid character. All the Venetian painters who followed the Bellini's leadership, and who were truly Venice-conscious as opposed to their fellows of other schools who trusted in religious or purely philsophical formulae, grasped, each in his own way, the delicacy of nuances of color, the value of expressing everything lovely in the natural life all about them. They recognized, and depicted as beautifully as they could, the lyric of life, whether it chanced to be in the sheen of the passionless lagoon in the afterglow that Shelley called "the inmost purple spirit of light," the opulence of a ceremonial State pageant, the delicate charm of a golden-haired Venetian beauty, or the majesty of a sweeping landscape. One of these men, Paul Veronese, equalled Titian as a colorist; others matched him in composition, others in imaginative force and fertility, others in drawing. None, however, was master of so complete and inexhaustible a total of the essentials of supreme art. Titian's was the great, resonant organ-tone of leadership followed by the entire orchestra. They knew, these men of the brush and palette, and knew even better than their brethren of the pen in most cases, the need to express in terms all humanity could apprehend, and comprehend as an end entirely sufficient unto itself, everything in both nature and man of a poignant and sensitive character. They were able at high moments to evoke on their canvases even the instant which slips irretrievably into the vague and shadowy limbo of the past; to bring to men the "music of the spheres" and the pathos of dying; to teach, in color and stroke that needed no footnotes in any tongue, the exquisite appreciation of all a busy world usually overlooks in its straining after wealth and power.

There were other and further influences at work in the world of the fifteenth and sixteenth centuries. Unique and in a sense isolated as Venice was, the Republic not only could not remain ignorant of the profound changes transpiring in every quarter of the compass, but she could not escape the impact of the men who wrought these changes upon her intellectual and artistic as well as her commercial and political life. Most of both are immaterial here as merely scarce visible threads in the weft of the interminable web of history. Men and events alike emerged startlingly in every human activity, and even when both exercised their direct effects only upon remote countries, Venetian thought and life responded to their indirect repercussions. A partial list of the more recognizable men of Titian's century with their achievements would easily fill a volume by itself. Such a list would disclose the outlines of a period of tremendous forces at work in a world no more prepared for them than the world of today was ready spiritually for the breaking up of the atom, its frightful use as a destructor, and its promise as an eventually docile tool. Only a fool could live in either era and disregard events powerful enough to change the entire course of history and the destiny of man.

This golden era of achievement and discovery was, like the present, an age of youth. Like youth, it did not and could not endure. Life all over the known world began to take on the sterner visage of experience and age as men of every race gradually learned there is more to life than any passion for glory or knowledge or individual prestige and power. But as the spirit of the Renaissance had been tardy in manifesting itself among the lagoons, so it was slow to fade out, and Venetian painting in the sixteenth century rendered a glorious display of that chastened and riper spirit which followed on the heels of the earlier glory and irresponsibility. We see it clearly manifested in the quieter joys Titian depicted so masterfully; canvases that revealed the minds of men turning away from trivia to the more substantial and permanent satisfactions conveyed by the deeper human relations and the things of the spirit.

Berenson has ably pointed out in his essay on the *Venetian Painters of the Renaissance* that the difference between the young Titian and the old was precisely the same as the difference between the Shakespeare of *A Midsummer Night's Dream* and *The Tempest*. Both men were creative artists produced by the Renaissance. Both passed through the same cyclical changes. Each in his own field was the loftiest and most thorough utterance of the age. Titian is of especial interest to us because he is the one painter who made permanent in beauty practically everything in the Renaissance that was possible to form and color. One needs only to read the brutally frank confessional letters of Aretino to understand why, for in them appears a cool, detached figure of a man of supreme character who never wasted either his intellect or his physical powers. Lafenestre calls him and any other Cadorine "a mountaineer robust and laborious, patient and frugal, economical and stubborn, attached to his family and to his habits as to his mountains."

CHAPTER FIVE

The Molding Influences
and Success

To REALIZE as fully as possible the ambient in
which the young Titian formed his opinions and general impressions of his world, and ourselves to visualize the scenes and people
to whom his brush gave immortality, we must paint an international as well as a local canvas of the widest scope. Wherever the
young man looked he saw plainly the evidence of his city's importance and reputation, above all in its amazingly conglomerate population.

Between 1487 and 1505 the city grew weedily. Across the wide
Tyrrhenian Sea in Spain the four-hundred-year campaign against
the desperate Moors was drawing to a close under the able leadership of the "Third King," Cardinal González de Mendoza, and the
Catholic Kings, Ferdinand and Isabella. Little by little the relent-
less attrition begun centuries before at Covadonga by grim old
Pelayo and his handful of Asturians had drained the Moorish
power and driven it from city after city until Boabdil and his court
alone remained nominally strong, the Alhambra of Granada the
one first-class fortress-palace in alien hands. On that memorable
New Year's Day, 1492, the Spaniards entered the city and Boabdil

fled weeping like a woman for what he could not defend like a man.

No sooner was her triumph complete than Spain began to make the tragic mistakes for which her governments have been forever famous. Every Jew must leave Spain, every Moor. Only good Catholics might remain, and the doctrine of racial purity got away to a strong start under the malign urge of the Inquisition and its despicable Familiars. Africa naturally received back its own by thousands. But both Moors and Jews also fled to Venice in such large numbers that the old Ghetto had to be enlarged.

Sansovino, the guidebook scribe, gives a vivid account of this quarter of the city in the midst of his description of its more attractive features. "This country," he says tersely, "being a place frequented by many men of every speech and land, the Hebrews also came here. At first they settled in the Long Thorn, which then changed its name and became known as their Giudecca [Ghetto]. The year 1349 it was ordered that they should not remain in Venice more than fifteen days, and that they might not give themselves to usury, and that they should carry upon the chest an *O* of the size of a [loaf of] bread. And the year 1423 they were forbidden to own houses in the city. [The punctuation and capitalization are Sansovino's] and the year 1425 wearing black berets, and employing various frauds and deceptions, there was confirmed the order to wear the *O.* and the year 1426 there was added that they should carry the *O* hung on the collar on a yellow cord, and that they should not have a synagogue.

"Since the year 1416, when they were confined in a separate place so that they should not mix freely with the Christians, and so that they should be more easily recognized, it was ordained that they wear yellow berets. And under the severest penalties they might not issue from the place assigned them after 2400 hours, and they were collected inside at San Hieronimo in a little island into which they entered by two gates, called the Ghetto. In the middle of it is an open square with the houses about it, and in the evening the gates are locked with a key by the guardians. And in the middle of that piazza is an inn under the care of a Citizen salaried by the public, which person had charge of seeing to it that the pawn tickets were just or not as regards payment of usury and principal, so that poor persons and women be not cheated by the money lenders.

"These fellows by their business became most opulent and rich, and lived more freely in Venice than in any other part of Italy. Because they were not used with the violence and tyranny employed in other parts, and are secure in any occurrence within their faculty, and can obtain justice against whomsoever. for reposing in most singular peace, they enjoy this country as if it were a veritable land of promise. By the arrival of many Hebrew families from Granada and other parts of Spain, the Ghetto has been added to, new houses being assigned to it, and a new gate made, so that at present there are three."

Almost four hundred years have passed since Sansovino wrote his dry indictment. It is of interest to us not in comparison with the turmoil in the world today regarding Palestine and the relocation of displaced Jews, but as showing the turgid life of the city in which Titian lived and worked. The young painter found it a beautiful and stimulating place. Not the city we of today know, of course. The Bridge of Sighs over the Rio del Palazzo and the marble prison linked to the Ducal Palace by the bridge had not been erected. The curious humpbacked Rialto Bridge every American knows was not begun until years after the great painter's death. But the city was rapidly increasing in beauty and wealth of an intellectual as well as a commercial nature. The rigidity of the Gothic houses and palaces was giving way to the more ornate and delicate structures of the Renaissance style. The change in the hundred years since Doge Francesco Foscari's time was so great, Ruskin points out, that had he in Titian's day been called back from his grave and set upon his galley at the mouth of the Grand Canal close beside the steps of the great church of Santa Maria della Salute, he could not have recognized where he stood or called by name a single mansion in the long line curving away toward the Rialto before him. What was left of the city he knew was even then hidden behind Ruskin's "cumbrous masses which were the delight of the nation in its dotage; hidden in many a grass-grown court, and silent pathway, and lightless canal."

In the city Titian and his friends enjoyed, notwithstanding the constrictions of its location, innumerable palaces rose from the water on one side and from exquisite gardens of the most elaborate and fanciful arrangement on the others. All the wealth and imagination of Venice had gone into these astonishing closes. Courts and porticoes, many of them vividly frescoed by young painters, of whom Titian and Giorgione were the leaders, vied with their adjoining palaces in beauty and dignity. Rare trees and flowers brought alive from as far away as Cathay itself bloomed luxuriantly beside tinkling fountains. Adroitly conceived and executed subterranean channels wound about like a labyrinth, and miniature mountains of spongy ashes freighted over from the island of Murano, in some cases covered with multicolored pebbles, contributed everything that lavish expenditure of wealth and the imagination and skill of expert craftsmen could produce to make these fragrant breathing-spots places of delight.

One such residence and garden, owned by a Signior Cataneo, who lived on the Giudecca and who was therefore probably a Jew, moved Sansovino to rhapsody. "Above all this a Garden on the Lagoon with a most beautiful loggia, elegantly painted, with corridors, rooms and other commodious places, and delightful. In sum, one may say that in this Habitation may be seen the Earth, the Sea, Mountains, Plains, the City, the Villa, the Grove, the Forest, the Garden, and finally, everything that can delight and recreate the mind and spirit: Where, if the above-named Signior Cataneo had thought in this his place, something restricted, to create marvels when he could have had larger grounds, by his Magnanimity and the grandeur of his soul he wrought such visible beauty as to ravish everyone with admiration." It would be absorbingly interesting to know what Titian thought of such an extravaganza as this. His genius was so sound, his temperament so sane and cool, it must have appealed to him as anything but the marvel it appeared to the less cultivated taste of the guidebook author.

Fortunately all such miracles of efflorescence are gone today. The gardens were only the external evidence, partly open to the world, of the treasures within the mansions themselves. Many a Venetian gentleman owned a library which covered history both universal and local, languages, poetry, mathematics, travel, the classic drama in both Greek and Latin, medicine, philosophy, astrology, politics. Maps and charts of the world constituted an important part of every such large collection, for the interest in geography was as keen politically as it was commercially. Many of the books, especially those issued by the Aldine Press, were magnificently bound in gold-stamped covers of the finest and most beautifully colored leather and parchments—the superb Grimani Breviary remains an exquisite proof of the taste and craftsmanship of those Venetian book-makers. Not a few of the volumes, in the growing predilection for French style, were bound *alla francese,* that is, contained in slip-cases as lavishly decorated as the books themselves.

Painters are not usually also very bookish men. We know very little of what Titian's successive residences contained besides paintings and *objets d'art* which he himself had executed and collected. It seems quite likely that, not being an educated man in the usual sense of the term—Ridolfi, always one of Titian's most ardent admirers, admits *"benchè non fosse di molta letteratura:* though he had not much book learning"—but especially as a creator of the rarest beauty and value himself, he should be largely satisfied with his own form and color, leaving the dull black and white of the printed page to those scholars incapable of doing more than enjoying the creative work of others. Nevertheless, his membership in the Aldine Academy, the clear source of the composition and figures in his glorious *Bacchanal* and the evidence presented by the *Venus Anadyomene* of Bridgewater House, indicate either Titian's possession of and ability to read the Greek and Latin classics or his careful attention to them as rendered for him by associates. The mere fact of his supremacy in one branch of the arts presupposes his ability to grasp with speed and ease enough of the others to give him that charm of manner and happy facility in intercourse which made him so esteemed by every noted man of his times. Dolce wrote to Aretino that Titian is "a first-class speaker, has much cleverness, and excellent judgment on all subjects." It could not have been otherwise, as he proved again and again by the adroit use he made of classical themes in some of his paintings, the language he used in rebuking, for instance, the city fathers of Brescia, and the eagerness with which he was sought out by scholars and prelates, emperors and commoners.

Collectors of antiques and their brethren the numismatists did not at all appeal to the practical Sansovino, for he dismisses in one long paragraph these owners of mere *anticaglie,* which means worthless old curiosities. His annotator, Martinioni, however, devoted seven full pages to a detailed catalogue and eulogistic references to the statuary, coins, bronzes, medals, glass and whatnot possessed by those of the city's notables who preferred them to collecting musical instruments and arms and armor. "Music," observes Sansovino drily, "has its proper faith in this city," adding that Catarin Zeno owned the organ once belonging to King Matthias of Hungary and considered so valuable it was bequeathed in entail to prevent its ever being willed outside the family. The same Zeno had a remarkable collection of weapons and armor, both ancient and "modern," and he was only one of many who hung historic arms on the walls of their offices and living rooms. It seems more than likely that Titian had an ear for music and at least some skill as a musician himself. In that he resembled three other famous Venetian painters: Giorgione, his boyhood friend of student days, Sebastiano del Piombo, and the fiery young Tintoretto, just rising above the horizon. All three of these men were proficient musicians. Besides, Paul Veronese painted Titian in his *Marriage in Cana* as playing the violoncello in a quartet, and Aretino, in a letter dated April 7, 1540, tells with gusto of arranging a trade whereby Titian painted a portrait for Alessandro degli Organi in exchange for a specially built organ the expert constructed for him. It may be the small instrument shown in the Prado (Madrid) *Venus*.

To the astonishment of the visitor, the most incredible thing in Venice was the fact that every window was paned with glass. Unbelievable richness, where even the poor could enjoy glass windows instead of those covered with the waxed cloth or paper used elsewhere! All the bedrooms had fireplaces and chimneys, but curiously enough the salons did not. It was these chimneys that until a fairly late period in Venetian architecture were frequently the cause of disastrous fires. Constructed often of wood, daubed with clay mortar or loosely held together with a sort of cement, they quickly developed cracks in which the sparks lodged, or the covering flaked off and exposed the bare timbers to the heat and flame. As stone and brick gradually succeeded wood, the chimneys came into better repute, but the skill that labored so assiduously to build beautifully and well in other respects apparently regarded them but little.

In this city of gracious unity, wealth, genuine culture and the love of things finer than mere money-grubbing, it is strange that Vasari should have been so blind or so careless as to believe Titian knew nothing of classic sculpture or general antiquities. The will of Gentile Bellino, filed in 1506, is definite evidence to the contrary, since it itemizes the estate, including the two marbles already mentioned. That an art apprentice in such a private museum should not have been thoroughly familiar with every object in it is obviously impossible. Moreover, examination of practically all Titian's earlier work shows that he invariably painted bas-reliefs of ancient subjects somewhere in each picture, disclosing a thorough understanding not only of the general topic but of the technical means to make it evident and appealing. What happened in 1507, when Titian was given one side of the Fondaco de' Tedeschi to fresco, while Giorgione did the Canal façade, was the natural thing and to be expected. The more noted man adhered to the traditions; the lesser modified them considerably, proving himself as modernistic in temperament as he was able in execution.

Vasari, unreliable as he is in some respects, nevertheless gives us the key to the profound difference in method between the schools of Venice and of Central Italy, which so strikingly appeared in these frescoes on a grand scale. The Bellini based their work and their teaching upon a thorough understanding of living nature so prodigally displayed all about them. Elsewhere, and especially at Florence, portraiture played no preponderant role. Michael Angelo's classic retort to the critic who said his statues above the tombs of the Dukes Giuliano and Lorenzo de' Medici were not likenesses, was typical of the Florentine attitude. "Who," disdainfully growled the rough-tongued sculptor, "in a thousand years will care whether these features resemble theirs?" In a word, the departure the Bellini began from the accepted style, and which under Titian reached its greatest glory, was the substitution of personality and natural life in all forms for abstract figures representing ideas or traditions. Vasari, in his monograph on Titian, goes into detail, naturally from the standpoint of a Florentine, about the way in which this change was wrought through the careful study of living nature, the offhand painting with colors rather than a meticulous sketching out of minutiae later given color, and, in the case of the human figure, draped or nude, of such ceaseless observation and sketching practice that "little by little one reaches accomplishment with greater ease in design as in painting, practice thus mixing with art, gradually perfecting hand and judgment until the fatigue and effort which reveal themselves in the pictures spoken of are overcome." He adds significantly of Titian that he who can draw does not "need to labor to hide his want of design beneath the attractions of coloring, as many of the Venetian painters, Giorgione, Il Palma, Il Pordenone and others who never saw the treasures of art in Rome, or works of the highest perfection in any other place, have been compelled to do."

It is most unfortunate that of the two men most closely allied in the artistic sense in these early stages of the Venetian School, Giorgione and Titian, we know practically nothing so far as their student days are concerned. Giorgione is generally supposed to have been born in 1478, a year after Titian. When the former came to Venice from Castelfranco, how a boy of humble origins managed to get into the studio of Bellino, what his contacts with Titian were, we can only imagine. Titian suddenly bursts upon us as a full-fledged painter on the walls of the Fondaco de' Tedeschi in 1507. Giorgione, however, three years before that had been retained to paint the portrait of the *condottiere* Gonsalvo Ferrante. That same year he did an altarpiece for the church in his native Castelfranco. All this argues that he had not only by the age of twenty-five thoroughly formed his style, but that he was publicly recognized as a master.

Titian is usually supposed to have been first the apprentice to Gentile and then to his brother Giovanni Bellino. Dolce says that, dissatisfied there, he formed a partnership with Giorgione. From that point on the critics have a field day at guesswork, and following Vasari's statement, mainly agree that Titian imitated his younger fellow artist. Is it not possible that there may have been either mutual development or that Giorgione profited by Titian's example or skill? What peculiarities of style Giorgione might have developed had he survived the plague of 1510 no one can even imagine. We know that whatever of tightness there was to Titian's style in his earlier works disappeared in the later ones, and that he departed more and more from the old Florentine doctrine of subordinating color to form. Instead of making his pictures what Byll has called "the woven raiment of the painter's thought," he deliberately chose to pour out lavishly in sensuous color and luminous impression all the poetry of Nature. In doing so he proved his understanding, for Nature is lavish with color always, not always precise as to form.

What a cradle of immortality those Bellini studios must have been! The boy from Cadore did not of course know it any more than the Bellini brothers themselves did, but the laughing, chattering, prankish student groups were all marked for fame. Rarely has such a championship field been gathered in any school. There Titian quickly came to know Giovanni Mansueto, Marco Marziale and Lazzaro Bastiani, all in Gentile's workshop, and in the house of his brother Giovanni, Andrea Previtale (whose *Annunciation* in the church of the Nunziata at Ceneda he was to admire all his younger days), Vincenzo Catena, Marco Belli, Girolamo da Treviso, Pier' Maria Penacchi, Lorenzo Lotto, Cima da Conegliano, Marco Basaiti, Jacopo Palma of the sweet and tender nature, Giorgione his future partner, and a host of others. It was this youthful group, all of them about the same age, and all bubbling with life, enthusiasm and health, who played the active role in the freeing of Venetian painting from its ancient shackles. In their strong young hands liberty of conception crossed by a fecund imagination manifested itself in the warm harmonies of clear color, the development of poetic sentiment which was the opposite of the old austerities, a delicate but profound enthusiasm for the voluptuous seductions of the feminine—for all, in fact, of the revelations of real life, the luminous phenomena of nature. "Tradition," declared Lafenestre, "is most affirmative in this regard.

The honor of having invented the 'new manner' goes clearly to Giorgione. Vasari, on this point, is the mere echo of his contemporaries."

Whatever the relations between the two young men may have been, and regardless of the influence of either one upon the other, we find Giorgione because of his previous experience in such matters given the contract in 1507 to fresco the two façades of the Fondaco de' Tedeschi, or German Exchange. Vasari says Titian had also done exterior frescoes "which cannot be named here individually, having been dispersed in various places." The visit of Leonardo da Vinci to Venice in 1500 unquestionably exercised a profound influence on all these young men, especially in the technical sense. The world was then, as it still is, a world largely for youth. It is hardly astonishing, therefore, that at the ripe age of twenty-two Giorgione was already favorably known for his poetic fancy and the fertility of his imagination on an heroic scale. Palma was another rising star promising the first magnitude. Lafenestre asks—and begs—the question of the effects these men had upon one another. "To what extent," the cautious French critic inquires, "did Titian submit to the influence of these two rivals, of whom one was barely his senior, the other his junior? Is it true, as MM. Crowe and Cavalcaselle think, that he owed to Palma as much as to Giorgione, taking from the one the easy grace of his figures and the *éclat* of his accessories, and from the other the suavity of his expressions and the tenderness of his coloration? With our present knowledge, it is difficult to say."

Titian began, perhaps early in this formative period, "with a decision perhaps less striking but with an ambition not the less vast, and an intelligence not less open, fortified by an extraordinary self-sufficiency and marvelous prudence, slowly to disengage the originality of his genius. The impossibility of establishing with certainty the chronology of their paintings during this short period will never permit us to attribute to each of the

Photo by Bruckmann

THE CHRIST OF THE TRIBUTE MONEY

Photo by Alinari

THE ASSUMPTION OF THE VIRGIN

members of this glorious triad the exact part each rightfully bore in the formation of the new style. Their own contemporaries frequently tricked themselves and confounded their works. Nevertheless, certain persistent traits of both Giorgione and Palma make us feel they were the inventors and Titian the receiver until he appropriated the ideas. To balance the scale may we not believe that at the same time certain special qualities which Titian speedily developed, belonged exclusively to him from the beginning?"

The distinguished life of Titian in German by Georg Gronau, conceived and carried out on a basis entirely different from the work of either the English or the French scholars, takes somewhat this view of Titian's formative period, but points out the slow maturing of his originality. "At a time when Titian's powers still lay dormant," Gronau remarks, "the quiet, often fascinating beauty of Palma's works and their healthy contact with nature made a deep impression upon him." In the same way, powerfully moved by Giorgione's "spiritual conception of portraiture," Titian adopted his method as well as his view. Yet in even such a work as *The Concert* there are clearly discernible touches that bespeak a hand and an intelligence stronger and more delicate than Giorgione's. Later Gronau adds the significant observation which gives validity to his entire criticism when he says: "After the manner of true genius he did not hesitate to take from others what was lacking in himself, to refashion it and give it the impress of his own individuality." We find also, all the way through his astonishingly long productive career, that the truest and fullest rendering of his genius glows only in those works wherein he felt his spirit free from the shackles of religious dogma, priestly custom, tradition, the frequently impossible demands of donors or patrons, and the like. Gronau feels this expression most illuminatingly presented in the *Sacred and Profane Love* and *The Three Ages,* the "two works wherein he was free to realize his ideal of beauty."

The fresco of *Hercules* on the Morosini palace façade, one of

Titian's very earliest works, vanished long ago. All trace has been lost of his portraits of his father and mother, Gregorio and Lucia Vecelli. Though the distemper painting of the *Virgin with Saints Rocco and Sebastiano* in the church of Pieve di Cadore is still in existence, it is a work done perhaps as much by his brother Francesco as by himself, and therefore is impossible to evaluate correctly. Gronau does not so much as mention it. The judgment of Lafenestre on the *Passage of the Red Sea* in the Ducal Palace, and the *Visitation* in the Academy of Fine Arts—which Venetian guides proclaim as examples of Titian's first manner—is that both not only date from a subsequent period but that they have been so retouched and transformed that even their origin cannot be conclusively determined. Crowe and Cavalcaselle aver that the *Red Sea* is a Pellegrino da San Daniele, and the *Visitation* a poor specimen in the manner of Sebastiano del Piombo. In any event, Titian clearly never touched either one.

We are therefore more or less reduced to a meagre five pictures as the base on which to rest our judgment of Titian between 1499 and 1505, all striking works. They are the *Virgin and Child,* in the Belvedere Museum of Vienna; *Ecce Homo,* in the Scuola di San Rocco, and *Christ Bearing the Cross,* in the church of San Rocco, both in Venice; *Bishop Pesaro Kneeling before St. Peter,* in the Antwerp Museum; and the world-famous *Sacred and Profane Love,* in the Borghese Gallery, Rome.

In these five canvases the critics find "constant affinities" with Palma, Giorgione and the Bellini, all mutely testifying to the young painter's conscientious eclecticism. The difference between the imitator who boldly plagiarizes and the genius who uses the best his predecessors or contemporaries could produce is that however excellent a copy may be, it remains only a reproduction in weaker form of the original, with all the original's defects, while the work of genius is so infused with the spirit and skill and originality of its creator that it is itself original in both conception and form.

It is impossible to believe that a man of Titian's power could ever consciously imitate anyone. His blending in his own work of all the best he was able to study in the works of others, in what I have called eclecticism, is the only proof we need of his supremacy and his personal recognition that by using all the finest his fellows had done as the base upon which to rear his unapproachable fabrics of color and life, he was the follower and pupil of no man but the exponent of his own power and boundless vision.

The *Virgin and Child,* also called the *Virgin of the Parapet* because of the low wall behind and to her right, is a remarkable work for more than the usual technical reasons appealing to the critic. Here are sound painting, admirable composition, luminous color and adequate pattern. The brushwork already betrays the hand of mastery. Then what remains to be said beyond the customary sniping at the allegedly Giorgionesque type of model, the pose suggesting the women of the Bellini, and so on? Such comment is a mere scratch on the gleaming paint. A deeper scrutiny reveals the spirit rather than the technique. Both Virgin and Child tell us clearly what was in the painter's soul when he set them before us on his canvas.

How, we may ask ourselves, should one paint the Virgin so that she may appeal to all mankind; more, so that she convince all men? Should she remain the wooden, expressionless doll of the Florentine austerities, a mere painted symbol without life or mind? Should her face, her hands, her expression, her pose reveal the lady of position, or the adult mother fully conscious of and comprehending her immortality as the mother of God? Titian did not think so. With the profound intellectual discernment of his extraordinary faculty for creation, he understood and translated for us the utter mystery of the simple story. Fully appreciative, he painted for us a naïve young woman of the peasant type, fit wife for a humble carpenter in a small town, thick-necked, heavy-featured, with large hands and all the normal characteristics of her physical group.

But then, regardless of the facial expression of his actual model, he gave us a face so lovely and appealing, so convincing in its shy, almost dreamy acceptance of destiny, that we recognize her instantly for what she was as well as for a singularly beautiful human creature.

The Child—prototype of all those myriad exquisite children and amoretti Titian so loved and so joyously painted year after triumphant year—is equally remarkable. This is no ordinary male baby of peasant parents, no infant with nothing beyond vague emotions and hungers as his guide to life. He is in some respects even more striking than His mother. The large, proudly carried head, the bold and finely chiseled features, with character and endurance already indelibly stamped upon them, the broad brow and, above all, the subtle expression of sadness overcasting the entire face, are a brilliant concept of infant Divinity far removed from any similar attempt in the previous art of any school. The whole picture is the embodiment in singing color of the insight of a master whose originality, thus early proclaimed, is always apparent.

In the Scuola di San Rocco the *Ecce Homo,* second of the five we are considering, is a radiant example of the greater intelligence and spiritual vision of the Venetians as compared with their neighbors of Padua and Flanders: such "dramatic naturalists" for instance as Mantegna and Squarcione with their groups. Where the earlier men had invariably accentuated the external evidence of physical suffering rather than spiritual grief, often emphasizing the former in writhings and facial contortions which approached grimaces, Giovanni Bellino led a reaction in favor of a profounder conception. Without suppressing the material evidence of mortal pain, he rounded it out and ennobled its evidence by giving the face of the murdered Saviour an unforgettable expression of spiritual agony. Titian, going still deeper, and painting with a technical skill which understood every device for utilizing light and shade, color and impasto, rubbing and brushwork, has left us a brawny Christ, sav-

THE BACCHANAL IN THE PRADO GALLERY

THE WORSHIP OF VENUS

agely wounded but with body relaxed in death. It is the bearded face that arrests the eye: a face from which all has been drained but the ability to whisper in His last agony: "Father, forgive them, for they know not what they do."

The necessary but unfortunately parrotlike guides of Venice frequently ascribe this and the *Christ Bearing the Cross* in the church of San Rocco to Giorgione. Even Crowe and Cavalcaselle, reading their confusing Vasari perhaps too closely, admit themselves doubtful. Gronau declares flatly it is the work of Giorgione. Sansovino had no doubts that Titian was its author, and the anonymous biography of Tizianello is equally decisive. Vasari came to Venice, saw the picture, ascribed it to Titian in his first edition and later changed his mind and credited it to Giorgione. He overlooked one rather vital consideration. Giorgione apparently matured more rapidly than Titian, and the disproportionately large head of the Christ, as He turns His tortured face to the beholders, is far more likely to have been the work of an eager but not yet fully formed genius than that of a finished master of scale. The canvas is on an altar in a side chapel of the church, where it was first widely admired for its striking beauty and drama, and then worshipped because of the miracles it was believed to work. Whatever the faith of its worshippers, the alms given to it enabled the fraternity of San Rocco to rebuild their edifice. Sansovino said: "Working divers miracles, this painting attracted the most considerable alms and gifts not alone from all Venice but from the villages all about."

Today the canvas is all but lost. Blackened and retouched by unskilled hands, it nevertheless slowly discloses the imposing qualities which made it originally so powerful. The suffering figure of the Christ, bent beneath the weight of the massive cross, and dragged with a cord about the neck by a ruthless executioner, detaches itself vigorously from the dark background's gloom. Two other figures, spectators both, tell the very human story of vulgar curiosity or morbid interest. The strongest light falls upon the face of the victim, and except for the exaggerated size of the head, we have matchless form and lofty expression. All the critics agree that the disproportionate size of that serene and noble head is due to the inexperience of the painter. May it not, however, be legitimate to inquire if perhaps Titian, with the poetic license of the artist, did not purposely emphasize it to bring into all the stronger relief his conception of suffering Divinity? We must not make the mistake in viewing paintings, of seeing the forest to exclusion of single trees; in a word, must not permit our critical and philosophical faculties to be clouded by technicalities and a reasoning that at best may be but specious. However concrete our opinions may be of the artist's achievements as a painter, if we miss his purpose as an idealist and philosopher we have accepted the husk only for the full grain.

Bishop Pesaro Kneeling before St. Peter, in the Antwerp Museum, tells a still different story of the powers of its painter, and again we must go behind the canvas we see to realize the forces at play out of which the picture developed. The truism that art has no concern with morals was never more strikingly illustrated. Titian knew, quite as well as every other Italian, the execrable nature of Pope Alexander VI. He knew also that a mitred bishop of the Church had no business to act as a military leader of a combat fleet, no matter what the obvious excuses. But "Baffo" the Bishop was the painter's friend; the subject stimulated Titian's imagination. The fact that "Baffo" was going to clean up Constantinople where his and his family's fortunes were heavily involved, with the sanction and commission of the head of the Church, was unimportant to Titian. He saw his opportunity to represent the Pope, clad in his most magnificent robes, on June 28, 1502, presenting to the Prince of the Apostles the kneeling Pesaro in the habit of a Dominican monk but with a richly chased helmet beside him and carrying a standard charged with his armorial bearings. The subject was dramatic, romantic even. Any onslaught against the hated Turk carried its own special magic, and the little squadron of twenty galleys of war gave the touch of verisimilitude the Venetians loved in all their ceremonial pictures.

It has been said before that Titian successfully rode the surging tides of self-interest that swayed the various factions in the Republic. What he himself thought of the matter we do not know; but that is of no importance. The vital thing is that he grasped the opportunity, executed a commission full of drama, and let his brush tell the story for others to consider and rationalize afterward. The man was therefore as much the historian as the master painter, and as we grasp this fact the canvas itself assumes even greater importance than as an evidence of his increasing capabilities.

Another point of interest is that we can date it almost exactly. Messer Jacopo Pesaro, Bishop of Paphos in Cyprus, or Baffo as it was colloquially known, was commissioned by the Pope in April 1501 to lead a fleet of twenty Venetian ships against the Turk. Alexander VI Borgia, detested and feared by all decent Italians, died on the 18th of August, 1503. It stands to reason that so thoroughly abominated a personage would not have been painted for public exhibition after he had died, even to gratify a wealthy noble like Pesaro. The picture's date, accordingly, falls within those two years. From the technical standpoint it is a magnificent achievement marred by certain defects due to immaturity and haste. Placing St. Peter on a throne on which the painter wrought incidents sacred to Eros proves his love of and familiarity with the classical while it also reveals the careless youth of his thought. The Saint himself is not so vigorously masculine as Titian would have made him a few years later, but the portraits are unusually significant: Pesaro from life, Alexander idealized as a saint, perhaps from a portrait painted by someone else, yet so masterfully accomplished it is difficult to believe the Pope did not sit for his likeness. "Seizingly truthful" is Lafenestre's characterization of the two heads, by a young painter who must still study and work before he attains perfection, while Crowe remarks that by now Titian has shown a clear advance over the accomplishments of his former work, is "all but free from every archaism of the previous age," and gives richer promise than any other painter then living.

Of all five pictures the so-called *Sacred and Profane Love,* in the Borghese Galley in Rome, is easily the best known and the greatest. This canvas in Titian's own day was known simply as *Two Women Seated by a Fountain.* Crowe and Cavalcaselle dislike its usual title and call it *Artless and Sated Love.* Lafenestre prefers simple *Allegory,* Gronau accepts the familiar name, and the erudite Burckhardt astonishingly calls it *Love and Prudery.* Certainly the painting is charged with subtle intentions we wish we could penetrate. It is probable the acute Lafenestre resolves the perplexities as to its enigmatic meaning better than any other because, with Gallic clarity of vision, he has seen the perfectly obvious and therefore unsuspected. Perhaps, he says in so many words, it is not really necessary to ask too precise a meaning for such poetic compositions as these, then the accepted vogue in the Most Serene Republic. These gifted creators, enchanted for the most part by the seductive beauties of form and color, not infrequently gave themselves little concern to make such creations logical. In other words, they set down beauty as an end sufficient unto itself without troubling to consider what the critic and the logician might imagine they had attempted. Giorgione had developed this tendency to "plastic reveries" among his students; and for a limited period in his youth Titian seems to have let himself go unchecked in a vague but ardent lyricism of virility intoxicated with life, love and beauty. "If one does not understand this well enough to comprehend it, at least one understands to the point of admiration," the French critic comments. "Nothing in Titian's work exhales the perfume of love more fresh and more exquisite than this springtime flowering of his genius. . . . The emotion is irresistible. Never have beauty nude and beauty clothed been, before or since, presented side by side with an equal charm of living and discreet seductiveness. . . . It is a beautiful dream of a summer evening in a southern landscape, recounted with enthusiasm by a true poet who found himself subsequently to be the greatest of painters."

CHAPTER SIX

The World Beyond the Lagoons

Titian was full twenty-eight years old and a successful painter in his own right before we can begin tracing with any degree of either accuracy or certainty the details of his prolific career. Our knowledge begins with one of those disastrous periodic conflagrations which in the course of centuries necessitated the rebuilding with more durable materials of a large part of the city, including many of its most important bridges. The particular fire which gives us our start completely destroyed on January 28, 1505, the centuries-old structure to the east of the Rialto bridge on the edge of the Grand Canal, known as the Fondaco de' Tedeschi, or German Headquarters (literally, Drapery, or Cloth-Shop, of the Germans). It was a combination of warehouse, customs depot, salesroom, dormitory, mess-hall and exchange for all the importers and agents of Teutonic affiliations, including besides the Germans themselves men from Hungary, Bohemia, Poland and Savoy. In this huge building these difficult but highly essential visitors were almost prisoners, and every native Venetian about the place spied upon the slightest word and act of the turbulent aliens day and night. Venice recognized so thoroughly how wild and dangerous a crew she was harboring that a law was rigidly enforced prohibiting all blasphemies, quarrels, the carrying of any arms, the playing of all games of chance, and so on. Administration of the establishment was entrusted to three public officials called Vice-Domini, who exercised freely the combined functions of economic superintendents and ranking police officers. The weighers, brokers, notaries, auctioneers and others were all of them also State employes. The office of broker was one of paramount importance, and since Titian held one of the sinecure appointments in this group for a long time, it is of special interest to us.

The brokers' staff of the Fondaco numbered thirty, all at the disposal of the foreigner. But no Teuton was permitted to choose his broker. Instead, doubtless with the idea of preventing venality on both sides, the brokers' numbers were mixed in a hat or other receptacle, and drawn for honestly. This was important, because the relation between merchant and broker was constant and inclusive. The former was compelled by law to transact his business through the broker, who controlled as well as registered all sales. He always accompanied his client when the merchant wished to make purchases, and would not let him buy from any but native-born Venetians. Toward the end of the fifteenth century, if we may judge by the references to the brokers in the *Capitolare* (Regulations) of the Fondaco, only about half the holders of the office actually exercised it personally. The others apparently farmed out the right to real brokers, who did the work and paid the original holders for the privilege. Such a sinecure was customarily held by the official painter of the Doge. Giovanni Bellino and Titian each held such office, but neither one ever did any of the routine work connected with it. In fact, it was recognized as a sort of pension or recompense for artistic work.

Vasari says that Giovanni Bellino's death left a great panel in the Hall of the Great Council unfinished. The picture was to show the Emperor Frederick Barbarossa kneeling in submission to Pope Alexander III in the most thrilling ceremony Venice ever witnessed. The Senate ordered Titian to complete the work. He did so with distinction and, following the custom that gives practically all his work freshness and historical importance, introduced many contemporary portraits, "of his friends and others," says the Florentine. One can imagine the opportunities such a theme would give a great master to immortalize enemies in the group about the two main personages, as well as the satisfaction of giving his friends distinction and satisfaction as figures of grave charm and nobility. "For this," the record goes on, "he received from the Senate an office in the Exchange of the Germans called the Senseria, which brought him in three hundred crowns yearly, and which the Signori usually give to the most eminent painter of their city, on condition that from time to time he shall take the portrait of their Doge or Prince when such shall be created, at the price of eight crowns, which the Doge himself pays, the portrait being then preserved in the Palace of San Marco as a memorial of that Doge."

All that concerns us here in the interesting history of the Fondaco is that the law decreeing its reconstruction after the fire provided that not a single piece of marble and neither carved nor fretwork be used anywhere about the building. To give it the effect of ornateness necessary to harmonize it with its companion edifices along the Grand Canal, the authorities could only order its façades frescoed. Giorgione, then in his twenty-eighth year, and well known for his work on other façades, was given the contract, frescoed the Canal front himself and gave Titian the subcontract for the wall facing the Merceria.

By May of 1507 the roof was in place, and exactly a year later the huge structure was dedicated with a solemn mass celebrated in the inner courtyard. This was followed within a year according to Sanuto's diaries in the Lazzari manuscripts, by a typically delicate German festivity whose chief attraction was a riotous affair in which blind men chased greased pigs. The frescoes of the exterior walls were no doubt finished before that, because a quaint memorandum of December 11, 1508, tells exactly the amount Venice paid to Giorgione, who undoubtedly divided with his assistant Titian. The record says: "Ser Lazaro Bastian, Ser Vettor Scarpaza [the famous pupil of Bellino, Victor Carpaccio], Ser Vettor de Mathio, named by Ser Zuan Bellin [Giovanni Bellino], painter, are gathered in the presence of the magnificent signiors Mess. Zuan Zentani, Mess. Maria Gritti, Mess. Alviso Sanudo, Overseers of the Salt Office, in the quality of deputy painters to examine into what may be the value of the painting made upon the façade of the Fondaco de' Todeschi and made by master Zorzi [Giorgio] da Castelfranco; and, having come to agreement, they have said that in their judgment the said master merits for the said painting one hundred and fifty ducats in all." Apparently Venice was as shrewd a bargainer in matters of arts as of commerce and statecraft, having had the work done without fixing the price. The memorandum adds drily: "The same day, with the consent of the said master Zorzi, he was given 130 ducats."

Thus far such bald facts as we can clearly disentangle from the confused web spun by the Italian historians and snarled up by translators, copyists and commentators until we can only approximate the realities. At one place we must follow the unreliable Vasari, at another desert him for Tizianello in order to present an apparently reasonable sequence for Titian. Before the fresco contract was arranged, Titian had had striking success with a number of portraits for wealthy families, many of the pictures being copies of older partly effaced or unsatisfactory works. In his brilliant hands the old chromos became the inspiration for vivid family likenesses glowing with all the sensuous color the city loved. Among his patrons was the Barbarigo family, one of whose members he painted from life. "And this," Vasari says, "was considered very beautiful, the coloring being true and natural, and the hair so distinctly painted that each one could be counted, as might also the points in a satin doublet, painted in the same work; in a word, it was so well and carefully done that it would have been taken for a picture by Giorgione if Titian had not written his name on the dark ground." Signior Barbarigo was so pleased that he is alleged to have used his influence to have Titian given the Merceria façade to decorate.

There we leave Vasari for the moment and turn to the *Anonimo* of Titian's distant relative Tizianello, who says clearly that Giorgione voluntarily shared his commission with Titian, at that time his assistant. This on the whole seems more credible despite the malicious story first circulated by Vasari: "Now it chanced that certain gentlemen, not knowing that Giorgione no longer worked at this façade and that Titian was doing it (nay, had already given that part over the Merceria to public view), met the former and began as friends to rejoice with him, declaring that he was acquitting himself better on the side of the Merceria than he had done on the Grand Canal; which remark caused Giorgione so much vexation that he would scarcely permit himself to be seen until the whole work was completed, and Titian had become generally known as the painter; nor did he thenceforward hold any intercourse with the latter and they were no longer friends." Since it was Titian who finished Giorgione's incomplete nude *Venus Asleep in a Landscape* and the *Dead Christ Borne Up by an Angel* it is hard to believe the two men parted over a stupid mistake made apparently in all innocence. At any rate, Titian's name appears in none of the official records of the frescoing, Giorgione alone being named as the master of the work.

The frescoes themselves long since evaporated under the salty kiss of the Adriatic winds. Their subject matter, of which we have a fair general impression, is interesting because Vasari's sour comment of 1542 upon it reveals with the clearness of a lightning flash how far ahead the two Venetians, and particularly Titian, were of the school-bound Florentine. He failed completely to grasp the purpose of Titian and understand why what he had painted was so marked an advance in decorative pictorial art.

We know the project for embellishing the exterior consisted for the most part of architectural and ornamental motives or designs, some with figures, and some framing minor compositions. These figures and compositions, sprung from the quick imagination of Giorgione and variously worked out by himself and Titian in their respective tasks, were a Venetian liberty with art which shocked the stodgy Vasari, accustomed to the dry reflectiveness and logical progressions of the school of which he was so typical an exemplar. Bitterly he assailed Giorgione for having created fanciful figures merely to display his virtuosity. The Florentine could not find in any of the frescoes any sequence of action or any personages behaving in the accepted manner of either ancients or moderns. "For myself," he scoffs, "I have never understood anything about it and have never found anyone else who did. Here is a man, there a woman in different attitudes; one has a lion beside him, the other an angel in the guise of Love. Nobody knows what it all is. There is, indeed, over the principal entrance on the Merceria side a seated woman, her feet upon the head of a dead giant, as it were a Judith, having a sword, holding the head and addressing a word to a German at her feet; but I could not imagine what he wanted to do, unless perhaps make an allegory of Germany."

Whether Vasari's disgust prevented him from seeing the frescoes correctly or his pedantic spirit made him unable to admit as a cardinal point in decoration of this type the harmonious combination of well-chosen ornaments in pleasant colors, we cannot now tell. We do know that Giorgione's work carried far more of logic than Vasari would admit. On the Merceria side of the building Titian carried out the same general idea in harmony with Giorgione's master plan, leaving as his own chief contribution a noble female figure sitting upon a stone plinth behind which rose a considerable edifice. To the left a heavy wall cut off part of the sky. The woman's left leg, bared to the knee, was raised, and her foot was in position to trample on the lifeless head dangled before her by a crouching soldier, the head in one hand, a dagger held behind his back in the other. The woman herself held high a naked sword, bloodstained. Tradition has given the picture the title of Judith, and certainly it suggests the tragic end of Holophernes. Nevertheless, as Crowe and Cavalcaselle remark, the same figures and emblems occur in Ambrogio Lorenzetti's wall painting at Siena, done before his death in 1348, and called there *Justice.*

Above this main group Titian painted a nude female between an Eve at the Rialto angle and two male figures at the opposite corner, one a member of the gay society Fraternity of the Calza, the other a Levantine. Along the wall ran a broad frieze in dull color, embellished with fanciful animals and arabesques. The *Judith* was engraved by Piccino in 1658 and later by Zanetti, so that we have an excellent idea of Titian's purpose if not of the splendor of his work. A comparison of what he did with Giorgione's decoration of the western façade of the structure illustrates perfectly Giorgione's adherence to the spirit of classical sculpture, and Titian's fresher, more humanistic conception in breaking away from the Greek for the sake of contemporary nature and picturesqueness.

The Fondaco fresco promptly established the young painter's repute as a master among the great families of Venice, who immediately began his vogue with orders for portraits and easel pictures of poetic fancy. The Calergi had him fresco the façade of their palace, and at the same time do a *Holy Family in Egypt* which attracted wide attention. The Marcelli ordered a portrait of the Doge Niccolò Marcello, who died three years before Titian was born, and the Barbarigo family one of Doge Marco Barbarigo, whose death occurred in 1485, when the painter was but eight years of age. Had it not been that 1508 was a very bad year for

Venice there is no doubt Titian would have had many other significant commissions.

The Emperor Maximilian, eager to prevent Louis XII of France
from encroaching upon the rights of the Empire by invading the
Duchy of Milan, demanded of the Venetian Senate the right to
pass an imperial army across Venetian territory. The cautious
Venetians refused passage, except to the Emperor, and to him only
if he were unarmed. Maximilian responded to this lack of confidence by gathering an army in the Trentino, invaded Cadore in
midwinter, and by a brilliant night attack executed in a snowstorm,
took the strong fortress of Bottestagno. Gregorio Vecelli, Titian's
father, was there with his Cadorine militia. What followed makes
one of the most thrilling tales of war and intrigue in which a
painter's family was ever concerned. Maximilian was eventually
defeated, and in one of those astounding political upsets of the
times, linked his fortunes for the moment with those of the Spanish
King of Naples, Pope Julius II and the King of France in the
League of Cambrai which was to work such disaster to Venice. On
May 14, 1508, the Venetian General d'Alviano was defeated badly
at Chiaradadda, as a result of which Venice lost Cremona, Ber-
gamo and Brescia to the French, and Padua, Verona and Vicenza
to the Germans. Francesco Vecelli, Titian's brother, who had
dropped his art studies to take up arms in this campaign, was
severely wounded in the retaking of Vicenza some months later,
and at Titian's earnest plea gave up soldiering and again began
to study painting with his brother.

While all this hurly-burly was going on Titian shut himself in
his studio and gave unceasingly laborious days and nights to perfecting his art. What was in his soul we do not know. He left no
records of that. But he was the creative artist, and we can imagine
that in his absorption with his task the anxieties and cares that
would have driven a man of lesser quality into the line of battle,

troubled him but a small part of the time. The theatre of operations was in part his native Cadore; the fellow countrymen involved included his own family. But the human element is short, while art is unceasing. Deprived of his usual activities and unable to revisit his native hills, Titian worked with fierce eagerness, especially since the visits of two distinguished foreign painters shortly before—Albert Dürer of Nürnberg in 1506 and Fra Bartolommeo della Porta of Florence in 1508—had shown all the Venetian painters methods they hailed with enthusiasm. The precise and energetic expressions of Dürer and the broad, simple magnificence of Fra Bartolommeo exercised an effect in Titian's development which must not be overlooked. Eager to increase his knowledge by familiarizing himself with the work of all schools, and alert to every progressive movement, during this period he surrounded himself with Flemish landscapists who assisted him. Titian's assimilation of their contribution is evident in the many paintings dating from this time, most of them religious in theme.

Between the signature of the League in December of 1508 and the truce with the Emperor Maximilian in April 1512 was a very dry time for Titian. Crowe and Cavalcaselle state with emphasis that "we fail to discover that Titian obtained any order in Venice worthy of his talent or his fame. But the paralysis caused by war—though it might affect the quantity and sale—could not diminish the quality of the work which Titian got through; and it is characteristic of this period that it yielded not only Madonnas of the highest finish, but the splendid portrait of a Doge in the Vatican Museum and that marvelous example of polished fashioning, the Christ of *The Tribute Money* at Dresden."

The period was one of flux. Art, if it be alive at all, is as fluid as quicksilver, and its exponents in whatever field must change with its spirit or be lost, for the truly worth-while art of any period definitely reflects the soul of the time and the thinking of the majority. So flexible and acute was the genius of Titian that he changed easily with the swift changes all about him, if anything keeping ahead of the popular attitude. As he studied and experimented in his studio while he had the relative leisure to do so, he gradually evolved the method that made his greatness so appealing to us of today: a technique in which color and modelling with it took the place of sharper contours and draftsmanship alone, plus a worship of living nature which made everything he did of permanent interest and value. That he owed something to the dry precision of Dürer's finish may be admitted, but it is hard not to be a trifle impatient with the verbose and polysyllabic commentators and critics who fill pages to prove the point. The fact is that we know Titian did not sketch out cartoons for his works in the accepted manner, but joyously, swiftly outlined his themes with a brush, changing design and detail while he worked and thought, and at last lavishing the most extraordinary care to give the finished work the "delicate smoothness and gloss" so notably his and so inseparably a characteristic of Venetian art at its glorious best.

Again five canvases give us an idea of the progress Titian made during these studio years when, despite the bloody battles and the ravaging of his native province, he kept his mind upon his art and achieved in all five Madonnas, as well as in other paintings, an "allure" as easy and stimulating as it was peculiarly his own. The *Virgin of the Cherries,* the *Virgin with Three Saints,* the *Virgin of the Roses,* the *Virgin with St. Bridget,* and the *Virgin on the Wall* reveal to us the type toward whose perfection Titian was steadily working: a young Madonna gradually disengaging herself, as Lafenestre shows, from the previous types of Bellino, Giorgione and Palma, and becoming steadily more human and naturalistic. The canvas in the Madrid gallery, the *Virgin with St. Bridget,* is one of the five that most clearly indicates its origin, so much so, indeed, that for a long time it was popularly supposed to have been painted by Giorgione. Gronau assigns it probably to "about 1505," in other words to a period earlier than the war years, but the other critics do not agree with him. The picture harks back to the *Virgin of the Parapet* in the Belvedere, and by its combination of familiar settings and graceful portraits suggests the work of Palma the Elder, while at the same time manifesting a harmony and grandeur the older painter was never quite able to attain in even his most successful work.

In all these notable productions Titian's main effort, highly successful and illuminating, was to give us his realization, in the most penetrating and splendid manner possible, of the truth of his subjects. In his hands color, brilliant and convincing, was no longer the mere vesture of addition of the Florentines, but the throbbing, vital essence giving life and force to figures and setting alike. Claude Phillips has called this "the very body and soul of painting" in which Titian "never condescended to vaunt all he knows, or to select his subjects as a groundwork for bravura . . . but above all to give the fullest and most legitimate expression to the subjects he presents, and through them to himself."

In the Uffizi canvas, the *Virgin of the Roses,* we have the same gracious conception and brilliant execution as in the *St. Bridget,* with the Madonna showing a more alert and sagacious head, which possibly may be accounted for by a different and more suitable model. The two children, the infants Jesus and John, their hands full of the flowers, with St. John gazing up at his little friend and offering more roses than the other's chubby hands can hold, make delightful contrast with the sweet calm of the Madonna, who watches her Son as He squirms against her breast, while St. Anthony Hermit looks on admiringly at the pretty family scene. Crowe and Cavalcaselle say of this that "nothing as yet approaching this work in sweetness of tone, freedom of modelling or clever appeal to nature has yet come from Titian's hand."

Somewhat of the same composition characterizes the *Virgin of the Cherries,* in the Belvedere. Of the five this is beyond question the finest expression of the painter's gifts. In the technical sense it discloses the work of the experienced master of his craft who, not-withstanding his experience, retained the fresh eagerness of youth, characterized by what the French have charmingly called *"accents d'une fraicheur matinale"*—"accents of dewy freshness." Categori-cally, the Virgin stands or sits behind a stone ledge, between St. Joseph on her right and St. Zacharias on her left. The infant Jesus stands on the ledge, in a running position, holding up to His mother both hands full of cherries, while the older St. John leans on the stone, looking up at the Virgin, and holding a small scroll in his left hand. One of the Madonna's hands is on her Son's waist, the other holding a sprig of cherry leaves. Her face is turned to-ward the Child in a tender regard. At her right Joseph looks on with interest, and his opposite, the heavily bearded Zacharias, bal-ances the composition and gazes thoughtfully down at the young St. John. What the Englishman Crowe calls the "polish of the modelling," probably meaning its anatomical correctness and ease, is the answer to those jealous critics and painters of other schools than Titian's who assailed his draftsmanship and anatomy. The color, too, is superb, the jewel-like reds and blues of the Virgin's garb, the gauze of her veil, the thin bit of drapery about the Child, are delicate, exquisite. Thanks to modern skill in restoration, when this canvas was rebacked years ago the experts discovered that Titian originally painted the Madonna with her head turned to her left, gazing down at the figure now seen as the boy St. John. Evi-dently Titian, as he proceeded with the work, decided that his first idea was not the best and reversed his composition, his amazing technical mastery enabling him to ennoble and give greater sig-nificance to the result. The two other pictures in this group, the *Virgin on the Wall,* in London, and the *Virgin with Three Saints* (Stephen, Jerome and George), do not measure up to the stand-ards set by the three already discussed.

Apparently toward the end of this period in which studio work was paramount, Titian commenced those contacts with the great which were to have such emphasis through the rest of his career. The Christ of *The Tribute Money,* which may have been painted for Alfonso d'Este, Duke of Ferrara, was the first of a long series of commissions from ruling princes and emperors, and a composition of such outstanding importance and beauty that it was not only the master's *chef-d'oeuvre* but still, after the lapse of centuries, compels our unstinted admiration in any company. It is illustrative of the familiar words: "Render unto Caesar the things that are Caesar's, and unto God the things that are God's." Unfortunately, we have no way of knowing now the date of the picture or the circumstances under which it was produced, any more than we can tell when Titian and the Duke came first into contact. Both Crowe and Cavalcaselle and Lafenestre refer to the story told by Francesco Scanelli in his *Microcosmo della Pittura,* published in Cesena in 1657, eighty years after Titian's death. Scanelli, an ardent admirer of Titian, related an interview when he was a young man with an old friend of Titian in Venice. The old gentleman told him that Titian was visited upon one occasion by a group of cultivated Germans whom he invited into his studio to look at his paintings. When asked what they thought, they replied that only one master was capable of finishing paintings as they should be finished. In comparison with their own Dürer, the Venetians always failed to justify the promise they had given when they began. Titian's retort was that if he had felt extremes of finish the object of art, he would have made the same major point of them that Dürer had. Since he did not, he proved the vitality of his belief by painting in such a manner as to show his guests that it was wholly possible to unite the force of expression resulting from a sternly simplified whole to a scrupulously truthful impression of living reality. *The Tribute* Money, according to this story, was the result, a marvelous achievement of sheer power, with a finish never before approached by any Venetian painter, and as subtle a delineation of character as any brush ever put forth.

The painting, which measures some two feet eight inches in height by two feet across, was painted on wood and was framed in the door of a clothes-press or closet in the private study of the Duke of Ferrara. Vasari reports of it not that "it was considered by all the artists of his time as the most perfect and best handled of any that Titian ever produced," as stated by Crowe and Cavalcaselle, but that it was "a most beautiful and admirable work . . . other pictures, executed in the same place, are declared by our artists to be among the best ever produced by Titian, and are indeed singularly fine." Whatever the judgment of time, the judgment of history is definite. The two figures, practically life-size, are cut by the frame, and the entire action is concentrated in the two hands and two faces. In the center the Christ, majestically calm, detached, benevolent, authenticates the pointing fingers of His hand as they indicate the coin held out by the coarse and perfidious Pharisee. The head and face of the Christ are young, vigorous, exquisitely chiseled, with the distinction due to His divinity, which brings into sharp contrast the brawny Pharisee's crafty and evil visage. The same antithesis between the respective hands adds to the summative effect remarkably, that of the Christ being as strong in its slender grace as the gnarled, work-stiffened fingers of the older, heavier, workman type of his provoker. The graceful folds of the robes, the delicate treatment of the hair, the perfect rendering of the different textures in the robes and shirt, and, above all, the exquisitely delicate and truthful modelling of the bodies and limbs of the contrasting figures make a whole that Titian himself never improved upon, and no other Venetian ever approached. From the spiritual standpoint, this is the ideal beauty for the Christ, and of its kind the most perfect painting that close study and knowledge of the best that Palma, Giorgione and Dürer had done was capable of producing: a painting, as Vasari admitted, "marvelous and stupefying."

The young painter of thirty-one had become the great Master.

CHAPTER SEVEN

The Great Decision

THE wars, in which occurred the already mentioned battle of Chiaradadda, with the defeat of General d'Alviano and his Venetians on May 14, 1508, had effects upon Titian which went further than keeping him grinding away in his studio. In fact, the campaigns consequent upon the signing of the League of Cambrai exercised almost as disastrous an effect upon all Venetian artists as the sack of Rome in 1527 had upon the masters in all the arts who served that great patron of the Renaissance, Giovanni de' Medici, who sat the papal throne from 1513 to 1521 as Leo X, and his successor, Giulio de' Medici, Clement VII, who reigned until 1534. Since the imperial armies were running wild over much of northern Italy, many of the artists fled to the safety of Venice. The effect of this panicky overcrowding was immediately felt by all of them as both artists and expert craftsmen cut their prices to compete successfully in the struggle for a bare existence. In such circumstances it was not a great while until the master painters began shifting about uneasily, seeking conditions and patronage under which they could live in some comfort and less mortifying anxiety. So far as we are here concerned, the effect was to mark the beginning of Titian's contacts with the outer world by sending him to Padua and afterward to Vicenza.

Exactly when he started for Padua we do not know, but it

was probably some time during 1509, not long after both cities had been recaptured by Venice. Regardless of Titian's feelings at the moment, it was fortunate for us today that he went. The results of his visit to the mainland city give us a clear and accurate understanding of the difference between his forceful designs and the completed work after it had been painted out full-scale on the walls. We are thus clear as to its date, know the name of his assistant, and understand various payments made and received. Since the frescoes on the Fondaco in Venice vanished long before the era of modern criticism these Paduan frescoes are of the first importance in judging style and technique.

Padua, renowned as the birthplace of Francesco Squarcione (1394-1474) and Andrea Mantegna (1431-1506), the seat of a great university founded in 1222 and a city of culture and fine living, fell upon evil days when the imperial forces captured it. The University went on strike and the citizens split into sharply partisan groups. Exactly the same situation obtained then that we found so unhappily prominent in World War II, with quislings and lesser traitors co-operating with the enemy to the dire confusion and punishment of loyalists. When the city was retaken by Venice vengeance was naturally exacted from the long list of nobles and prominent citizens who had thrown in their fortunes with those of the Emperor Maximilian. Tremendous fines, torture, imprisonment, executions fell upon the unhappy town like a wet pall, and years had to pass before the horrors of the period could be remembered without a shiver, and eventually forgotten. In such circumstances, with all her own artistic activity dead and no one quite sure where next a lethal blow might fall, it is evidence of astonishing vitality in Paduan culture that any attempt was made on behalf of beauty; more so, indeed, than that she should have invited artists she knew only by name, and from a distance.

One of the foremost citizens of Padua in 1509 was Ser Alvise

Cornaro. He, like St. Francis, had been a gay, wild blade in his youth, a patrician by birth, and, having discovered the mischief of his ways, reformed so successfully that he established lasting fame by a solemn monograph or *Treatise on the Sober Life* which was quickly translated into all the European languages and proved the Continent's "best seller," if we may use a modernism, until the eighteenth century. Two hundred years of sales for a moral essay of this sort is something of an achievement. Besides being thus a convert-moralist, he was quite a vocalist, a noted sportsman, playwright, farmer of sorts, engineer, amateur poet, friend of actors and, to back up his enthusiasms substantially, was possessed of a huge fortune which he shrewdly increased. Such a Maecenas was well qualified to become the friend and intimate as well as the generous patron of a genius like Titian, and it would have been curious indeed if he had not employed him, especially since Titian had for a long time known the Cornaro family to his advantage.

Ser Alvise received the painter with his accustomed benevolence and generous hospitality, and had him fresco the façade of his mansion. Unfortunately, the great house was reconstructed in 1524 by Cornaro's architect friend Falconetto, and the façade thus changed was decorated by Jerome of Padua. Titian is also supposed to have done a remarkable series of decorations, perhaps for the walls of his own room, drawing the designs on wood blocks himself, from which proofs were published in ten sheets under the name of the *Triumph of Faith.* Again unfortunately, these decorations were destroyed, if they ever existed. There appears to be considerable doubt that they were ever executed. Nevertheless, Ridolfi is our authority for supposing they were either the originals or copies of drawings Titian made in 1508 before coming to Padua. Whatever the facts in the case, we have a series of reproductions which show the artist's mastery when left to himself, and as in the case of *The*

Tribute Money, his ability to accept the challenge of another master—in this case Mantegna—and outdo him in his own sphere.

The ten sheets, engraved by Andreani on wood, are as rough and rugged as anything that can be imagined, full of such life-like energy and beautiful, spirited drawing and finish that they hark back to Dürer almost more than to Mantegna. If they were carried out full-scale on the walls, and proved to have anything like the thought and fire of the designs, they rose above everything Titian left in the religious edifices of Padua. The story told is an allegory. The Christ, sceptre in hand, is seated in a ceremonial car drawn by the symbolic angel, bull, lion and eagle. A tiaraed pope, a cardinal, two bishops tug at the wheels to help the car along. Preceded by Adam and Eve and the Doctors of the Church, angels trumpeting, and cherubs cavorting gaily about the stalwart who carries a tremendous cross, the car is followed by a long procession of patriarchs, prophets, judges, the Old Testament kings, saints, martyrs and citizens. The background for this heroic conception is a familiar Titianesque landscape, varied and mountainous. Lafenestre laments that the Paduans were so careless as to permit the disappearance of such an epic composition, and A. F. Rio declared some eighty years ago that they were masterpieces worthy of a Christian painter. Gronau praises both drawing and composition as "rich in life-like, noble and beautiful forms." He says nothing of Andreani as the engraver, but asserts the ten sheets were "cut in wood from Titian's drawings by an unknown artist, supposed to be Master Jacob of Strasburg. This work is the more important in the history of Italian wood-cut in that here for the first time one of the great Masters worked with a view to reproduction, and contributed to the success of a branch of technical execution already beginning to make its way. In place of the simple wood-cutting in outline, now was introduced that rich treatment by cross-hatching in the shadows, which alone was capable of rendering the characteristics of the original work of an artist who like Titian, strove after pictorial effect."

With the Paduan religious frescoes we encounter the name of Domenico Campagnola as Titian's assistant and associate. Very bad draughtsman, weak on composition, but seemingly a good copyist and lively imitator far more than an original painter, he was the steady collaborator of Titian in all his Paduan work, and after the Master returned to Venice carried on by himself in both the Carmine and Santo Schools. Crowe and Cavalcaselle say his origin was never determined, and they did not know whether he was Venetian or Paduan; nor did they know when he was born or died. He simply appeared in Padua and later in Venice for a brief period and vanished. Lafenestre, without stating his authority—the Englishmen also gave none— declares Campagnola a Venetian, adding that he so cleverly imitated Titian's manner that contemporary observers could not always distinguish between the work of master and that of assistant where the two had worked together on the same subject. As the frescoes are still visible *in situ,* though so damaged as to be almost worthless, this is not only a serious loss but a record which does Titian no good. In the Scuola del Carmine it seems perfectly evident that while Titian may have sketched the designs, he left the rest of the work almost entirely to Campagnola. This is comprehensible when we remember that the Venetians regarded fresco as temporary decoration only; and apparently Titian, thinking of it as such, and not being truly interested in or inspired by a job of some size for relatively very low pay, let the lesser man ruin with hasty accomplishment and inferior color and handling what might in other circumstances have been excellent.

The Scuola del Carmine, where this work was done, during the Austrian occupation of Italy was used as a barracks on the

ALLEGORY (Alfonso d'Este and Laura Dianti?)

THE MADONNA DI CASA PESARO

upper floor. Leaks developed in the roof, and it was not long before seepage washed away a great deal of the color, which had been hastily applied, leaving most of the figures spotted and bleached or seriously discolored. Campagnola left many of his own compositions on the walls, and there is only one fresco sufficiently notable to be assigned to Titian with some degree of justice, despite its bad condition and the perfectly apparent negligence of its execution. This is a representation of the meeting of St. Joachim and Anna at the Golden Gate, treated in the same conventional manner that Giotto, two centuries before, had used in handling the theme. At this late date, with the painting in such lamentable condition, it is impossible to judge correctly of the original color. The landscape background is Titianesque in character and outline, and the kneeling shepherd or servant is fine, while the head of St. Joachim is grave and full of expression. Anna, on the contrary, is a fat, muffled-up Venetian beauty of a distinctly coarse type without much character in her smiling features. The other figures are negligible, and even the best parts of the fresco are such evidently impetuous work as to be unworthy of Titian's genius notwithstanding the broad, swift execution. The stiff and meaningless drapery betrays the inferior skill of Campagnola, as do his squatty figures and harsh tones.

Titian is represented by three frescoes, the first, eleventh and twelfth of the series depicting the miracles of St. Anthony which decorate the walls of the main hall of the Scuola del Santo. These, though they were also negligently done, apparently did not lean so heavily on Campagnola. Consequently they bear a much better reputation. The first scene, to the right of the door on entering the Scuola, shows the Saint giving speech to a recently born infant to permit it to clear its mother of the charge of adultery. A friar raises the baby on outstretched hands. Leaning forward, the child takes the Saint's hand in both of his, facing his astonished and resisting father and his calmly confident, innocent mother. The masterly serenity characterizing the scene adds remarkably to its dramatic intensity. In the original design upon paper no one but a superb draftsman could have solved the problems presented by the subject with such economy of line. On the wall, though the figures have been transferred literally except for some changes of headdress, the fire is gone, the work was hasty and often slurred, and the coloring was on the whole flat. The effects of light and shadow, natural landscape and sunshine to be expected are objectionably missing.

Lafenestre is much more enthusiastic regarding this work than are his English predecessors. He calls the confident wife awaiting vindication a "superb patrician . . . magnificently garbed in her splendid red robe embroidered in gold, one of the most attractive figures any artist of the sixteenth century placed upon a wall. She is living beauty, palpable and real, standing in the majestic tranquility of certain triumph. Her three followers, in their more modest attitudes, are also natural, younger, and charming. By this powerful simplicity of expression Titian proves that he is in full possession of his genius." To the extreme left a young gallant in the parti-colored hose of the Calza —perhaps, according to Lafenestre, the youth supposed to have been the lady's seducer—leans forward gripping the edges of his long white mantle in a magnificent poise of tension, ready to spring.

The second fresco, eleventh in the series, shows St. Anthony restoring to life a young man who, because in a rage he kicked his mother, afterwards in remorse cut off the offending foot. This picture is freer and bolder in sweep, more masterly than its predecessors. The dead youth lies on the ground, his severed foot awkwardly placed where it should grow. Behind, a young woman supports his shoulders, in much the attitude we see in various Pietà canvases. Beside her the grey-haired mother appeals to St. Anthony, who steps forward, holding up his robe with his left and comforting the mother with his extended right hand. Farther behind, another young woman tells three men friends, two of them old and bearded, her excited version of what happened. Standing to the rear of the Saint, a knight in armor has removed his helmet and rests his shield on the ground. He gazes at two other men, one hatless and almost hidden, the one at the extreme right evidently a patrician or noble, if we may judge from the coronet embroidered upon the breast of his robe. The composition of the figures is compact and yet fluid; they play their parts in the dramatic scene without effort, and their widely different expressions afford a brilliant study in psychology. The rugged, hill country background of landscape is typically from Titian's brush, a dolomite mountain piercing the sky with its shattered slabs, a castle with a lofty donjon keep, a fisherman seated by a stream at the foot of the castle hill, and in the meadows rolling away to the horizon a shepherd with his flock near three poplar trees. It is this part of the picture which enables us to see clearly how, merely suggested by lines and lustreless color in the fresco, the landscape would have radiated light and vibrated with color in oils.

The third Titian in the Scuola is that of a *Gentleman Killing His Innocent Wife* in the foreground, while St. Anthony in the rear pardons him, assuring the peevish gallant that his perfectly faithful wife has been restored to life. The fresco has been seriously damaged during the course of centuries by both accident and restoration, and it is a pity it has not completely disappeared. Crowe and Cavalcaselle rightly proclaim it theatrical in grouping, mannered in action and conventional as a whole. The Frenchman Lafenestre goes to the antipode of this, declaring: "The attitudes are of poignant reality, without scholarly reminiscence, without theatrical declamation; the execution is of such surety and vigor as cannot be surpassed, and the brutally vivacious play of color between the red-and-white tabard of the husband and the yellow robe of his victim marvelously complete the seizing effect of the violent scene." It is hard to feel, from the standpoint of today, that a mind as keen as Titian's could have experienced any genuine inspiration from such a subject, and that when, obliged by the monks to execute the miracle-record to their order, he should have done his merely human best, and therefore failed to produce a miracle.

He must have sighed his relief when he wrote, on December 2, 1511, the receipt for four ducats of gold paid him by the monks of St. Anthony of Padua for the *"tre quadri jo ho depicta sudita scuola"*—"three pictures I painted in the said school." Lafenestre reports a memorandum by Campagnola on a sketch in the Crozat collection indicating that after having collaborated with Titian in the Carmine, the two began their work together in the Santa on September 24, 1511. "The three paintings, accordingly, were completed within the space of two months." Such haste accounts in part for the carelessness of design in transferring the sketches to the walls, and the bad coloring. Campagnola, whatever his shortcomings, was able in a bold, rough, freehand manner, and entirely capable of painting landscapes as art worthy to stand unaided. The best thing he ever did was such a series in distemper on the façade of a Paduan mansion belonging to Marco Mantova. There must, therefore, have been some reason greater than appears for the poor work in the two Schools.

On leaving Padua Titian did not return immediately to Venice but went to Vicenza, Crowe says, accompanied by Campagnola. Gronau, however, gives the date of Titian's receipt for the four gold ducats as December 4, 1511, and says positively of the Vicenza trip that Titian returned to Venice either early in or sometime during 1512. Not until ten years later—1521—did he

FLORA

VENUS ANADYOMENE, OR VENUS OF THE SHELL
(Bridgewater Collection)

go to paint in the loggia of the Vicenza town hall. The conflict between these two statements by Gronau, who gives no direct authority for them, and the data cited by Crowe and Cavalcaselle is completely unimportant in itself. It does, nevertheless, perfectly illustrate the impossibility today of final exactness when access to the original documents is disabled because we do not know what they were or of what standing.

Regardless of the chronology, while Titian was in Vicenza he executed a *Judgment of Solomon* in the loggia of the Palace of Justice (the town hall) so effectively that Ridolfi declared the painting must forever serve as an example to judges in learning how to render judgment. Fate overtook this fresco swiftly, for when Palladio reconstructed the Palace it vanished, and all we know of its worth is Malvasia's brief reference to the scandal its disappearance caused. One wonders a little if there is any essential difference between past and present in such matters, especially where government property is concerned.

The Vicenza episode concluded, Titian returned to Venice where, Vasari says, his first task was to fresco the façade of a Grimani palace. Perhaps; but Vasari fails to say which branch of that great family was concerned, and where the palace was. Whether or not he executed such a commission, there is not a palace in Venice today with any frescoing on its exterior, and as he did not like wall-painting, either exterior or interior, he abandoned it entirely to work only on canvas and panels in the more lustrous oils. During the approximately two years he had been away from Venice a profound change had affected both art and politics. Giorgione had died of the plague in 1510, the wars had seriously impaired Venetian arms and financial resources, absolutely ruined Cadore temporarily and driven the citizens of Pieve into caves and the ruins of the castle, and now old Giovanni Bellino, determined not to yield leadership to any of the younger generation he had helped to train, was making a desperate effort to maintain his place in the breach, but with the greatest difficulty because of his failing powers.

Titian must have been very thoughtful on his homecoming, probably in April of 1512. Looking to the northern mainland he could visualize as a bystander the senseless carnage and the futility of the temporary conquests being made and unmade by Frenchman and Spaniard, Swiss and German, and lament the devastation of the loveliest parts of Italy. But gazing about him in Venice he could also perceive that the Republic had reason still to remain Serene. Her suzerainty of the waters was unchallenged seriously, her inexhaustible salt pans were as always the base of her revenues, and she could remain aloof and thankful for her segregation, busying herself about her overseas ventures and rebuilding her finances while her enemies wasted theirs. It was no doubt the better times that seemed dawning in the near future that led Doge Loredano and his Council to institute the splendid thanksgiving ceremonial procession of the Andata on July 17. After worship in the Cathedral, Doge, Senators, dignitaries, guilds and citizens made their way in full state to Santa Marina to thank Heaven for the recovery of Padua. As the procession was repeated annually for several centuries we see clearly the importance the city attached to its mainland supremacy. Also, as the Venetians became convinced that to the intervention of St. Mark, their always militant patron, they owed the Republic's survival of the dangers of the League of Cambrai, we find again politics and popular sentiment directly reflected in art. It was undoubtedly at least in part because of this feeling that Titian was commissioned to paint for the canons of San Spirito in Isola his great *St. Mark Enthroned among Saints.*

This period of a few swift and eventful years immediately following 1512 marked the swelling of the tide of achievement and recognition which eventually carried Titian to the pinnacle from which he has never been pulled down. It was a time of tumultuous happenings. War, truce, the death of one great master which immediately preceded it and the growing incapacity of the aged Giovanni Bellino, the gathering in Venice of distinguished men of the arts and letters, the publishing and other activities of Aldus Manutius and his formation of the Aldine Academy, the wandering away of several noted painters, and not least in moment, Titian's personal efforts to wrest the leadership of the Venetian School from Giovanni's faltering hands, with eventual success, made a scene of such activity, intrigue and struggle as few artists could survive.

In addition to his professional and political ambitions, Titian also found time to marry and settle down to a sober, well regulated life with a prudent regard for the future which Lafenestre sharply decries as "cupidity, if not avarice." In this he joins Senator Molmenti and a majority of the art historians. Yet Titian can with justice be considered hardly more than decently regardful of his natural interests. His insistence upon being paid the sums promised him is not cupidity or avarice but common sense, comparing to its own advantage with the grasping tactics of the businessman of today. The pleading letters the painter wrote about his affairs disclose repeatedly that his pensions, allowances, fees and whatnot had been delayed or diverted by venal officials and he had not received them. Why should he not protest, and ask kings and ruling princes for what was his clear due? Also, to anyone who knows the Italian temperament, the charges that he neglected official work for which he was being paid are nothing extraordinary. He did neglect certain work; he was rebuked and threatened about it; and he completed the work as commanded when the pressure upon him became severe enough. It must not be thought, however, that Titian's neglectfulness was due to laziness or indifference. Quite the contrary was true. We have but to note the amazing total of his paintings during the more than eighty years of his artistic career to realize that he produced during that entire period at the rate of one picture every month, year after year. No other creative artist has ever established a comparable record, as no other colorist has ever approached his finest work for depth, richness and finish. To talk of avarice in such circumstances is an unjustified reproach which smells of malice in view of the fact that at Titian's death his fortune, so far as we know, was modest. It did not take his rakehelly son Pomponio long to dissipate all his laborious father had left.

Exactly when Titian married we do not know. Ticozzi erred so evidently as to the name of his bride and the dates of the births of his children that Lafenestre's supposition may be taken as approximating the truth. The lady was a certain Donna Cecilia, a Venetian, and not Lucia (who was his mother), and the marriage probably occurred at some time between 1512 and 1520. Again without documenting his statement Gronau declares Titian married in November of 1525, "thus legalizing a connection by which he already had two sons. His wife Cecilia was the daughter of a barber from the district of Cadore. At the time of the marriage she was ill in bed, and Titian was induced to have their union blessed by the church through fear that the stain of illegitimacy would cling to his children. A priest, Paolo, performed the ceremony. The witnesses were Francesco Vecellio, his brother, Niccolò, goldsmith, Silvestro, a stone mason, and Girolamo, the priest's brother. . . . The death of his wife, who was buried on August 15, 1530, affected him deeply."

The Abate Cadorin, who performed such a notable work in exhuming documents regarding Titian, declares this Cecilia to have been a superb woman, so beautiful and charming that she become widely known as Violante, and was supposed to have been the painter's mistress when as a matter of hard fact she was his wife. By comparison of dates we also know that she began to appear in his pictures either just before or immediately after the presumable dates of their marriage. After having suffered the loss of one daughter, they had in rapid succession two boys, Pomponio and Orazio, and a daughter, Lavinia. The two younger children were a great comfort to their father all their lives, but Pomponio proved a devil-may-care playboy so dissipated and worthless that Titian intervened against him on one occasion when a bishop's mitre was proffered, as we shall see later.

Notwithstanding Vasari's statement about the frescoing of a Grimani palace façade as Titian's first work on his return from Vicenza, it seems much more likely that he turned to the completing of the canvases his quondam friend and master Giorgione had left unfinished when the plague of 1510 carried him off. Who gave him the commission and who paid the bills we do not know, but the fact is certain for the inimitable touch of the master is clear in at least two notable works, a *Venus Asleep in a Landscape* with Cupid, equally nude and sleepy, and a *Dead Christ,* sustained upon His tomb by an agonized angel. In the *Venus* it is easily Titian who painted both the landscape and the chubby Cupid; in the other he is declared to have rearranged the composition.

His first major commission was the *St. Mark Triumphant* for the monks of San Spirito in Isola, now, with the whole series Titian did for the same church between 1512 and 1541, in the great church of the Salute in Venice, whither it and the others were taken when the smaller church was closed in 1656 on the suppression of its monks. Gronau proclaims this first of all Titian's altarpieces to have been commissioned in 1504. This is somewhat misleading, since he says nothing as to the date of its execution. We know from the technical data left by Vasari, Palma and others that Titian often took years to complete paintings. His studio was lined at all times with canvases on which he had sketched his ideas and color schemes with such assurance and firmness that he could return to them after long intervals and recapture the mood and purpose of each at will. With a painter of less genius or of a mechanical turn of mind and hand, such a protracted method might easily have resulted in performance marred by discrepancies in the impasto, the richness and depth of color, the handling of lights and shadows, even in the drawing. Titian, however, possessed such correlation of mind, eye and hand that nowhere in any work after say 1512 is there the slightest evidence that the painting, like the subject's conception, was not executed as a whole.

It is difficult for anyone of realistic tendencies, in studying the *St. Mark* in the Salute, to coincide with either the fulsome praise of Lafenestre or the almost apologetic description of Crowe and Cavalcaselle. Color, rich, warm, luscious color, is here in full, and we can revel in it. The play of light and shade and refraction is superb; the portraits are masterly, and the contrasts between the characters of the five saints are graphic in the extreme. But the principal figure, had Titian never left us anything else, would not have earned him much mention in any serious history of art. With the memory of the disastrous plague of 1510 which the Saint was supposed to have stopped with the aid of Sts. Cosmo and Damian, patrons of medicine, and Roch and Sebastian, martyrs, one would naturally assume St. Mark's expression to be one of humility and gratitude. Instead of giving us that, Titian made him defiant and grim, much more ready to dictate from his book of laws than to intervene between the demons of the plague and helpless humanity. The whole central section of the picture is artificial in the extreme: St. Mark in a great chair like a throne, upon an antique column, glaring at the heavens, his body tortured into an unbalanced posture, his head so stiffly set it seems as though it were on a pole, and the whole figure squeezed and misshapen. Lafenestre admits that while "almost all the figures are portraits executed with the conscience and following the principles of Giovanni Bellino, it is still the traditional disposition, the precise, closed work of the fifteenth century, though with what new research in ensemble and harmony through the expressive distribution of shadows and lights, with what desire for movement and what feeling for life in the attitudes!" We must not forget in passing judgment upon this as upon any work of art of whatever period, that there are always two ways of considering it. Whether it be painting or sculpture, music or poetry, we may judge the work on the ground of its direct appeal to our sense of sheer beauty, its power to afford us emotional gratification and pleasure. The other way might be called the intellectual, in which the work of art must be regarded as the passionate expression of a creative artist whose soul burned within him to give tangible form to the thought and spirit of his epoch. Considered from both these viewpoints, Titian's St. Mark partly satisfies the first, triumphs in the second category, and thus stirs us to correlative thoughtfulness.

Whatever we as individuals may think of this celebrated painting, and whether or not we agree in finding parts of it reminiscent of Palma, Giorgione and Giovanni Bellino himself, it brought Titian instant acclaim and additional honors. It also brought him into direct contact with scholars and philosophers who, under the impulse of the Hellenist Aldus Manutius, had formed the astonishing Aldine Academy. Lovers of the fine arts, men of letters, eminent prelates, historians, wealthy Greek refugees, public speakers, diplomats—in a word, the élite of the cultured world—made up this association, whose language was Greek, and whose meetings must have been a rare intellectual delight. To this erudite Academy Titian was invited. It seems a little difficult to believe that the painter, who by no stretch of imagination could be called a scholar or man of letters, would have exposed himself in such surroundings very often, revealing his ignorance of most of the subjects under discussion, especially when the talk was in a language he probably did not speak. Nevertheless, from the time of his admission most of the members of the Academy constituted themselves his firm friends and protectors.

One of these men was the famous Cardinal Pietro Bembo, collector, poet, critic, editor, prelate and politician. Aldus had published Bembo's *Aetna* and *Asolani,* and Bembo edited some of the classics which flowed in an unceasing stream from the Aldine Press. During the winter of 1512-1513 Bembo was in Rome, busily intriguing for favor with the powerful Medici family. Pope Julius II died suddenly, Giovanni de' Medici was elected Pope as Leo X in March, and Bembo's political activities bore fruit when he was made secretary to the man who for the eight years between 1513 and 1521 was the foremost patron of Renaissance art.

One of the Cardinal Bembo's first thoughts, apparently, was to invite Titian to come to the Eternal City. Michael Angelo had already immortalized the Sistine Chapel, and Raphael was engaged in doing the same for the Vatican. What a temptation for an acknowledged master in the full prime of his physical and artistic vigor to pit his genius against the glory of two such men as Michael Angelo and Raphael! Sebastiano Luciani, the Venetian painter who had gone to Rome and done not at all badly for himself there, probably added his urgence to that of Bembo that Titian should come.

Full well the Master knew what that invitation meant in recognition, power, wealth. To work under the direct protection of the head of the Roman Church would give him unassailable position, to say nothing of inducing demands from all over the world for his finest work. To any but a truly great man the temptation would have been met in Wilde's epigrammatic manner: overcome by yielding to it. But Titian had no delusions about the life in Rome. He understood perfectly what it would mean to him to exchange his free and independent existence, his position, now unchallenged except by the fading Bellino, as the leader of the Venetian School, for the sordid intrigues, shallow morality and wearisome ceremonial of the papal court. He knew, too, the flatness of the Roman Campagna, with never a dolomite peak or a great, mysterious, aromatic forest of oak and beech and pine to freshen his weary spirits, no luminous prospects and far horizons with lightning playing through them to foster his imagination. With the sound common sense of the mountaineer turned urbanite, he preferred to be of the first magnitude in Venice rather than of the second in Rome. So he said no.

The wise man never stops trying, for action is life, inaction death. Having decided not to go to Rome, Titian did not stop thinking. On the contrary, he went into immediate and definite action. Crowe declares, on the authority of Vasari and Dolce, that the Paduan poet, Andrea Navagero, an old friend, was the one who dissuaded him from going, probably by pointing out that if he went, when Giovanni Bellino died there would be no one left in Venice capable of working in the Ducal Palace and of painting the portraits of successive Doges. Crowe supports this opinion by Titian's petition to the Council of Ten, dated May 31, 1513. It was a master-stroke of business acumen, and no modern advertising or publicity expert could have phrased and timed such an appeal with greater effectiveness. As I have not seen the original Venetian text in Lorenzi's *Monumenti,* with its curious misspellings, I translate the French version given by Lafenestre.

"1513. Last day of May. In Council.
"Most Illustrious Council:
"Having from my infancy, Most Serene Prince and Most Excellent Signiors, devoted myself to learning the art of painting, I, Titian of Cadore, being not so desirous of gain as to acquire a little renown and to be counted among those who presently make art their profession; and furthermore since I have been and also am at the present sought with

insistence by His Holiness the Pontiff and by other Lords who wish me to serve them; also, desiring as a faithful subject of Your Sublimity to leave some memory [*souvenir*] in this glorious city, I have resolved, if it pleases you so to charge me, to come to paint in the [Hall of] Great Council; and to place all my talent and spirit so long as I shall live, in commencing, if it please Your Sublimity, with the canvas which is the Battle, on the side of the Place [the Piazetta], which is the most difficult, since until today no one has wished to attempt such an enterprise. As for myself, Most Excellent Signiors, I shall be well content to receive as satisfaction for this work such recompense at may be judged appropriate, and even less. But, as I have said above, as I esteem only my honor and wish only a means to live while pleasing Your Signiory, deign to concede to me for life the first Senseria in the Flontego di Todeschi which becomes vacant, notwithstanding all previous expectations regarding it, with the modes, conditions, obligations, exemptions which Missier Zuan Belin [Giovanni Bellino] now enjoys; also that two youths [be appointed] whom I wish to take with me to aid me, [they] to be paid by the Salt Office; and at the same time, the colors and all the necessary things, exactly as has been done these past months by the Most Illustrious Council for the said Missier Zuan. And I promise Your Most Excellent Signiory to accomplish this work with such promptness and excellence that you will be content. And I commend myself humbly to you."

The Signory did not at all resent the painter's frank demands. Approval of the petition showed clearly that instead of regarding Titian as the grasping or avaricious self-seeker most of his biographers would have us believe him, the hard-headed businessmen and politicians who ruled the Most Serene saw in him a highly important creative spirit who thoroughly understood his own value. Venice could not risk losing such a man. For once a prophet was not without appreciation among his own. The great decision was confirmed. Titian remained Venetian.

CHAPTER EIGHT

Symphony of Spirit and Flesh

Titian, in common with other geniuses in the fine arts, was not from the layman's standpoint a normal human being. Genius never is what we understand as normal, meaning usual. Since the law of averages is inexorable in humanity as well as it is in the natural and physical realms, it follows obviously that a predominating quality must be balanced by the entire lack or the necessarily smaller force and quantity of other qualities in the individual if we are not to have that condition of mind known as evident abnormality or insanity, where equilibrium has been completely destroyed or lost. Today, for example, we do not expect the magnate who is self-made by having smashed or toiled a laborious way to the top and independence by sheer force and determination, to be possessed of the graces and culture of the born gentleman. On the other hand, we look in pity at the soft-handed gentleman suddenly reduced by circumstances to the pick-and-shovel type of existence. We know accurately his entire unfitness, spiritual as well as physical, for hard manual labor and persistence of effort when every shrieking, weary nerve and muscle cry protest.

Such considerations are the merest superficies of our attempt to evaluate correctly Titian's character. When the layman has finished

111

his estimate the physician and the psychologist begin theirs, endeavoring to probe down delicately to the utter subliminal, to ascertain if they can what may be those generally unrecognized and obscure forces that subconsciously motivate the individual's contacts with the world. In the case of genius we are helped to comprehension of its works by understanding what actually produced them, and why at times they differ so radically one from another.

About forty years ago the biologist Élie Metchnikoff, in his *Prolongation of Life,* wrote in that part of his work particularly considering the German poet Goethe: "The truth is that artistic genius, and perhaps all kinds of genius, are closely associated with sexual activity. I agree with the proposition formulated by Dr. Moebius that 'artistic proclivities are probably to be regarded as secondary sexual characters' . . . a man of genius loses much of his quality with the sexual function." In other words, the man of genius produces his loftiest expressions under the influence of the biological urge toward woman, whether gratified or frustrated. In Goethe's case, his noblest lines were invariably so produced. Here is no case of a dogmatic conventional morality. Metchnikoff points out clearly from the scientist's angle of approach in another place: "From the point of view of a naturalist I cannot agree with the moralists who have blamed Goethe for his sexuality, nor do I share the views of those defenders of him who have wished to deny the facts or explain them away by the suggestion that they did not relate to sexual love."

It may be objected that the deductions of Moebius and Metchnikoff are so old as to be completely superseded by the results of modern research, and that in any event what may have been thought of a Teutonic poet already severely handicapped by his racial peculiarities can scarcely apply with any cogency to a man of entirely different race and genius. But what shall we say in rebuttal of a study made this very year by the world's foremost neurologist of one of the great masters of Italian painting contemporary, for a part of his creative career, with Titian? Dr. Sigmund Freud, the famous Austrian physician and psychologist, in his just-published monograph on *Leonardo da Vinci,* that confounding genius— twenty-five years Titian's senior [born 1452; died 1519] but contemporary with him until his death—traces in the modern manner the growth of Leonardo's "libido" and parallels it with his creative work. Freud says in part: "We are justified, however, to look also in him for those emotional streams which imperatively force others to the sexual act, for we cannot imagine a human psychic life in whose development the sexual desire in the broadest sense, the libido, has not had its share, whether the latter has withdrawn itself far from the original aim or whether it was detained from being put into execution." Toward the end of his thesis Freud remarks further: "We would gladly report in what way the artistic activity depends on the psychic primitive forces were it not that our material is inadequate just here. We content ourselves by emphasizing the fact, concerning which hardly any doubt still exists, that the productions of the artist give outlet also to his sexual desire, and in the case of Leonardo we can refer to the information imparted by Vasari." Late in life, when the great Florentine had grown *impacientissimo al pennello* (most impatient with the brush), and turned away from it and all art to his pseudo-scientific inquiries, Dr. Freud observes: "The investigation, however, which now took the place of his artistic production, seems to have borne certain traits which betrayed the activity of unconscious impulses; this was seen in his insatiability, his regardless obstinacy, and in his lack of ability to adjust himself to actual conditions." The same careful observation and study applied to almost any artist in any field, but particularly to present-day painters whom we may all watch attentively at first hand, will reveal to us, at times shockingly, the true reasons for much of the distorted and vulgar commonplace masquerading under the name of progressive art. With that psychic condition as its base, it is evident immediately that the painters producing such works, in the full realization that their craftsmanship can never equal that of the masters of the past, give their more animal instincts free rein. The "art" they produce is a sick art; the producers are to be pitied as sick men.

To return for the moment to Leonardo, we find him an enormously curious investigator and dreamer, about whose unusual personality a cloud of fable and anecdote hangs so thick as almost to conceal the real man. He left hundreds of ideas incomplete. His impulsive nature led always to excess, and he loved the mysterious, the dramatic, whether or not it bore any relation to fact. Titian had what Symonds calls "exquisite humanity." "His large and sane nature gives proper values to the imaginative and the scenic elements of the Venetian style, without exaggerating either. In his masterpieces thought, colour, sentiment and composition—the spiritual and technical elements of art—exist in perfect balance; one harmonious tone is given to all the parts of his production, nor can it be said that any quality asserts itself to the injury of the rest. Titian, the Sophocles of painting, has infused into his pictures the spirit of music, the Dorian mood of flutes and soft recorders, making power incarnate in a form of grace."

Leaving Leonardo out of the argument because he was even more the scientist and inventor than the creative artist for a good part of his life, we find two geniuses could hardly be more antipodal than Titian and Goethe. The German poet's imagination was morbid to a considerable degree, his morality based upon sentiment and therefore, as Schopenhauer caustically remarks, a mere caricature of true morality. Titian on the contrary had the wholesome extrovert type of imagination, as has just been pointed out, that regarded beauty, especially when given its fullest possible expression in form and color, as a sound reason for being. Goethe loved fiercely and often, with complete recovery between attacks of the malady. Titian married once, was devoted to his wife and family, and left not one scrap of evidence behind him to show even by implication that he joined at all in the conventionally amoral life of his times. Each man produced beauty. Marguerite is a classic figure. So is Faust. They are completely earthy creatures, rent by spiritual forces; but for most of us they are more vague incarnations of generic ideas than they are clearly cut personalities. With the whole spectrum flowing easily from his swift brushes, Titian gave the world, in jewel-toned language that needs no translation for anyone, literally hundreds of concrete examples of life with never a touch of sentimentality or morbidness in any of them. Both men, if Metchnikoff and Freud are correct in their estimates of artistic activity, did their creative work as the secondary evidence of their superabundant masculinity. Both carried their vitality and their fiery productiveness into advanced old age. Goethe's poetry reached its noblest heights spasmodically, at times as a result of erotic frustration. Titian's genius burned with a steady flame, and no smoke. All the imagination and vigor he might easily have wasted upon a woman he poured with increasing mastery into his canvases, sublimating his technique, raising with practically every successive picture his already high standards by a constantly increasing suavity which tempered the significant truths of nature. Every canvas by Titian will always exert its characteristic message and be remembered as an individual creation, while poor Marguerite and Faust remain what they are, pitiable types. The secondary traits that gave the world a Goethe, in Titian's case seem to have become primary outlets for all the fire and vigor which in smaller men divided their attack and effects.

At first there may seem no logical connection between Titian's petition to the Council of Ten, his refusal of Cardinal Bembo's invitation to become papal court painter beside Raphael, and the analysis just made of his character. The relation exists, nevertheless, and it is a strong one. Rome at that time was a honeycomb of rottenness from top to bottom. Every walk and phase of life was affected, and the whole world knew it. Titian, with the clean sim-

plicity and strength of his mountain ancestry and childhood surroundings, instinctively turned away from the festering congestion
bestriding the Tiber. More than that, he had a fresh young wife
and small children to whom—as the years ahead were to prove—he
was devoted. Like all other Italians he knew perfectly the sort of
moral cesspool he should be immersed in if he went south. Strong
as his sex life was apparently, he had it in control, he preferred to
live with his family instead of squandering energy in unjustifiable
excursuses, and he knew that as an independent leader in Venice
he could pour out his vast surplus of energy with greater joy and
with far more benefit to himself, possibly also to the world, than
he ever could among the jealousies and compulsions of the City of
the Seven Hills. He did not, of course, in reaching this conclusion,
psychoanalyze himself consciously; but as we study the times, the
conditions and his actions, his motivations become perfectly clear.

In such circumstances the natural, indeed, the obvious, thing to
do was to become an official painter to the Signiory, with a stipend
he could depend upon as a foundation for all his other work. If he
could not conscientiously go to Rome, at least he could make Rome
serve him well in Venice. As a man of action he wasted no time,
and the mud was hardly dry on the horse of the courier who brought
Bembo's invitation before Titian had presented the petition translated in the preceding chapter. As has been already said, Titian's
timing of it was as perfect as the appeal itself. The Ten were in
session the day the petition was handed in. *Incipit bellum novum!*
The Council adopted the memorial by ten votes to six, and the war
was on. A week later, on June 8, the Council ordered the Proveditors of the Salt Office to "prepare for the said Titian all the
necessary things, as he demands in his petition, and as you have
provided them for Zuan Bellin in previous disbursements, and pay
from month to month the two young men who will be presented
to you by Titian himself, at the rate of four ducats each a month,
also as he has insisted, because they are necessary and capable in

this art of painting. Nevertheless, it is not intended that their salaries shall commence until they have begun to work. And so do ye."

There was reason for the war. For more than a third of a century Giovanni Bellino had been the official painter of the State. For years he had held a *senseria* in the Fondaco de' Tedeschi. No one had so much as challenged his priority since Luigi Vivarini passed out of the picture. Now, at eighty-six years of age, with but three years of life remaining to him, he was forced to become conscious of failing powers at the very moment a young, formidable rival seemed to have acquired the favor of the authorities and a position equal to his own with the easily recognized threat of soon thrusting him out entirely. Old as he was, Bellino had fighting spirit, and Titian knew his former teacher would not yield without a vigorous struggle. Taking advantage of his temporary triumph, Titian immediately secured permission to establish a studio in a large house in San Samuele, formerly the property of the Duke of Milan, but afterward the property of the Republic, about halfway between the Rialto bridge and the Piazza di San Marco. Persons in the service of the State lived there free, the city architect among them. Titian moved in presumably with his family, and lived there for fifteen years. The building was in bad condition at the time. The roof leaked, and other repairs were needed, so the Council ordered the Proveditors to expend "not more than six ducats at most" so that the work in the Hall of Great Council should not be delayed "by the lack of anything."

Titian must have felt an enormous personal satisfaction at the convincing evidence of his personal importance thus publicly given. We can imagine the noisy merrymaking and celebrations he and his friends held in the old house near the Canal. But dour old Giovanni was not defeated yet. Silently mustering his friends, laying his plans with characteristic Italian guile, he seemed to do nothing for months. Titian started his sketches for the dark and awkward corner of the Palace Hall he had requested, his assistants were being paid by the Salt Office, and everything was proceeding in orderly fashion. Then the blow fell with startling suddenness. Less than a year after granting Titian his privileges, the Council on March 20, 1514, recalled its decree of May 31, 1513, ordered that Titian must take his turn on the list of applicants for a *senseria*, and that the Salt Office stop paying his assistants forthwith. The Bellino partisans had triumphed in part for the moment. Perhaps Giovanni was satisfied with that; but he had not succeeded in depriving Titian of his right to the broker's patent eventually, nor was the young man dispossessed of either his studio in San Samuele or of his right to paint the picture for the corner of the Great Hall too difficult for anyone else to dare.

On November 28 Titian filed a new petition, and again the Council was thrown into lively debate. Quite frankly the painter attributed his misfortune to his jealous rivals who feared him as a successful competitor and had woven tangled webs of intrigue to harass him. If he had not been interfered with he would already have finished his difficult commission, but this had been prevented by the withdrawal of his right to the first vacated broker's patent; and he would starve to death had he to wait his turn with the unpreferred candidates. The story reads with a very modern suggestiveness of World War II priorities and the shortages of manufactured goods and foods. In this fresh petition the artist asked that as he could not of course expect the first open patent, he be given the one that would become vacant on the death of old Giovanni Bellino, and that the Salt Office should, as before, pay his assistants and provide the colors, canvas and other materials for the work.

There must have been a very hot session of the Council that day, for each painter undoubtedly had his supporters among the lawmakers. Before the discussions and wrangling were over, the previous deprivative order was cancelled by a majority of one lonely vote, and by nine to four Titian's new offer was accepted. Instructions were also sent to the Vice-Domini of the Fondaco that a new grant had been made to Titian. One of the members of the Council that day was the same Francesco de' Garzoni who had been charged with the rebuilding of the Fondaco in 1506. It would be wearisome to go into the details of this *opera bouffe* quarrel between two high-strung painters and their political promoters were it not for the significant fact that we have the records showing exactly how it delayed the decoration of the Hall of Great Council and how ruinous was its cost to the Republic. No twentieth-century bureaucratic red-tape mess could be more typical.

Quite evidently neither master troubled himself much about doing any work to justify his trust. At last the Council wearied of such flagrant disregard of its patience, and ordered Francesco Valier of the Salt Office to investigate and report. With the vigilance of a true auditor, he nosed into the accounts, examined what had been done, estimated what remained to do, and finally presented a picture so black it well may have terrified the shrewd and thrifty Council.

Lorenzi tells us, with the dry factualness of a chronicler, what occurred at the sittings of December 29 and 30, 1515. Valier showed that the Republic had spent enough money on the canvases in the Hall of Great Council to finish the entire palace. This, he declared, was the same as saying three times as many paintings might have been bought as had actually been put in place, besides which the painters had had grants and offices, perquisites, etc., whose accounts had never been inspected. Two canvases, thus far nothing more than sketch outlines, had already cost more than seven hundred ducats. This was clearly indefensible, since there were able masters in Venice willing to paint each picture for two hundred fifty ducats. With one sweep, by twenty-eight votes to two, the Council dismissed all the artists, authorized the head of the Salt Office to hire the best man available, make a bargain with him at a fixed price for each canvas, and named the three "Sages of the Kingdom of Cyprus" as auditors charged with overseeing the accounting. The Senate, to whose final authority the case was submitted, acted even more vigorously, approving the Valier report by 150 votes against six, with only one blank ballot.

Crowe and Cavalcaselle assert that "the prime mover in all this was clearly Titian, but it is doubtful that he gave authority to any-one to limit the price of a canvas to 250 ducats." Lafenestre is not at all sure, but thinks the appearances warrant the supposition that it was at least Titian's adherents who were responsible. In any event, since all the painters were summarily dismissed, Titian was free, though he cannily retained his residence and work-shop or studio in San Samuele. Shortly after the upheaval, on January 18, 1516, Titian wrote the Doge offering to paint one pic-ture for 400 ducats—Perugino had had the same sort of contract at twice that sum—the monthly pay of four ducats for one assist-ant, three ounces of blue, ten ducats' worth of other colors, and succession to Giovanni Bellino's patent to the *senseria*. Whoever was responsible for the shift in events and policy, Bellino was in no condition to fight back successfully. He died on November 28, 1516. Titian's star was never in eclipse from that January day when the College of the Pregadi accepted his suggestions as he made them except for the price of the finished canvas, which was reduced to 300 ducats. That in itself was considerably less im-portant than the grant of the *senseria*.

As we have already seen, though the broker's commission was a sinecure really meant more as a recognition of quality and as a retainer than for any work it involved, it was nevertheless inti-mately connected with the personal dignity of the Doge himself, of which it was considered as an external part. With each acces-sion to the throne, the official painter had to execute a portrait of the new prince for inclusion in the series adorning the Palace. The Doge himself paid for this. Besides, the painter had to execute another one representing the new Doge surrounded by saints, kneeling before the Madonna in Heaven. This was an official duty, and the finished work was installed in the College of the Pregadi. Considering the very shrewd way in which Venetian ducal choices were made, and the political bargaining that went on behind the scenes, a good many of the completely cynical nobles and patricians must have smiled in their beards as they pondered certain of their rulers in such lofty celestial company. Finally, the painter had to decorate a shield with the ducal arms for placement aboard the Bucintoro, the official State barge of ceremony.

Though the *senseria* or stipend for all this was an honor keenly sought after and good for life, it was also revocable at the will of the authorities. Besides its income, it remitted to its holder taxes to the amount of eighteen to twenty ducats annually, so it was important to keep in the good graces of the Council of Ten. At least one would suppose that any artist with ordinary common sense would perform his tasks with enough of effort and speed to satisfy the very moderate demands of his paymasters. Titian, however, once secured in his honors and privileges, with Bellino dead and out of his path, went serenely along with personal private commissions. He did paint the different Doges who took office one by one with fair promptness, but the pictures in the Hall of Great Council were neglected year after year. Again and again he was rebuked, at times sharply. In 1513 we had his written wish to paint the battle scene. He began sketching it out, abandoned it, and in 1516, as we have just seen, again promised to attend to it. In 1518 little or nothing had been done on the canvas, and he was warned. Four years later, in 1522, another warning, sterner than the first, was given him, but still nothing was accomplished. The Council of Ten told him flatly that if he did not finish the battle canvas they would take his *senseria* away from him.

Instead of bowing to such an ominous threat, Titian apparently

mollified the indignant Council by doing a splendid piece of work
in completing a great picture Giovanni Bellino's death had left
unfinished. This was the intensely dramatic scene showing Pope
Alexander III placing his foot on the Emperor Barbarossa's neck
in the famous interview in Venice when Church and Empire were
nominally reconciled. Titian made several changes in Bellino's
original scheme, and included the portraits of no less than a dozen
close friends he knew through their membership in the Aldine
Academy, and two others, Marco Grimani and Domenico Trevi-
sani, who were chosen procurators in 1522. Among Titian's fellow
clubmen were the scholar Pietro Bembo and the poet Ariosto, the
outstanding individuals of the brilliant galaxy of notables gathered
about the Pope on that day of thrills. Contemporaneously this
canvas was generally considered the finest in the Ducal Palace.
The Senate, knowing that the dark, badly illuminated section of
wall Titian had promised to cover with his battle scene was the
least felicitous location in the Hall for an important picture, and
quite probably feeling that if Titian were harshly dealt with Venice
might lose him forever, did nothing until 1537. Then exhausted
patience curtly informed him that if the work was not done immediately, he would have to make restitution of all the revenues he
had enjoyed for the past twenty-one years. Lafenestre refers to
"the Battle, become as legendary as the interminable weaving of
Penelope."

It is a curious commentary on human nature that if a creative
artist exhibits common sense and business sagacity, fills his engagements promptly, and in other ways behaves like an ordinary
businessman, he is regarded with some suspicion. If on the other
hand he flouts engagements, disappoints everyone, works spasmodically, indulges in outbursts of temperament and is generally
an impossible creature, he assumes the proportions and stature of
sheer genius. We have all known such pretenders. But when a
man of Titian's established powers shows himself now the one
sort, now the other, we can but marvel at such a duplex mind,

especially since at the close of his career he left such an amazing number of masterpieces to record the earnestness of his labor despite his apparent neglectfulness.

Exactly how or when Titian established close relations with the ruling Este family at Ferrara we do not know. Probably chance had much to do with it. We do know that while the battle picture remained unfinished in the Ducal Palace, the reigning princes of several bordering mainland states were cultivating and as far as possible gratifying a strong taste for the arts. The Este family at Ferrara, the Gonzagas at Mantua and others were the leaders in this. Titian's now undisputed leadership in Venice naturally made him much sought after. Duke Alfonso d'Este, who married Lucrezia Borgia in 1503 and succeeded to the throne of his father, Ercole I, in 1505, was a strong and colorful character. He almost lost his throne shortly after ascending it because his people thought he had dishonored his rank by working as a blacksmith, a carpenter, an armorer, a potter not afraid to mold the clay with his own hands, an engineer of sorts and a successful founder of cannon. Besides all this he had a keen eye for art, and when, in 1506, he began rebuilding his gloomy castle, he besought, one after the other, the foremost artists whose works he had seen during his travels, to decorate the interior for him. Giovanni Bellino accepted, Raphael made promises, and Pellegrino da San Daniele shared for a while the honors and work with Bellino and Dossi.

Bellino was the first to accept though, as already indicated, the Titian panel of *The Tribute Money* was finished and in place in the Duke's study between 1508 and 1510. In this room the Duke intended to gather the finest work of the finest artists of his time. He succeeded better than was to be anticipated. Bellino painted a glowing *Bacchanal* for him, which was either left unfinished or was soon damaged, to be eventually repaired or completed by Titian. Raphael never came to Ferrara, and after vainly coaxing and blustering by turns in his usual impetuous manner, the Duke finally turned from him to Titian. The real relations between the two began about 1516, as an extensive series of documents in the Ferrarese archives demonstrates. From February 13 of that year to the end of March he and two others, either assistants or servants, were lodged in the Ducal Palace, and provided by the Duke's orders with "salad, salt meats, oil, chestnuts, oranges, waxen candles, cheese and five measures of wine each week." Once installed there comfortably Titian began the work which completed Bellino's famous *Bacchanal,* now at Alnwick, England.

Crowe does not believe it possible that Bellino, bitterly jealous of his young rival and former pupil, could possibly have left so important a canvas unfinished. He, in common with all masters, designed his paintings for the exact places they were meant to fill. Laying out the groundwork, and doing all he could privately in his studio on this great picture, Bellino finally took it to the castle and spent several days there working on it. The Duke's account books note on November 14, 1514, that Bellino had been paid eighty-five ducats for work completed *instante domino nostro,* that is, in the Duke's presence. Crowe points out that this statement, which he quotes from the Marchese di Campori's *Tiziano e gli Estensi,* does not prove that the picture referred to was the *Bacchanal.* Vasari, however, says Bellino was incapacitated. "This picture the great age of the master had prevented him from completing; and Titian, as being more eminent than any other artist, was sent for to finish it." Blashfield, in his notes on Vasari, does not express any opinion, but Lafenestre observes that "the great age and infirmities of Giovanni Bellino prevented him without doubt from making the trip to Ferrara to complete his work, though he was still in full possession of his faculties. . . . It would be odious to assume, as has been done, without the strongest proofs, that this labor of achievement, complicated by some restoration, would have been undertaken by Titian without his [Bellino's] assent."

All the contemporary authorities seem to have agreed that the figures were all completed, but the background was not. This offered Titian an opportunity he was not slow to grasp. The theme of the picture was a huge vat of red wine surrounded by "Bacchantes, Satyrs, and other figures, male and female, all inebriated, with Silenus entirely nude mounted upon his ass, a very beautiful figure," according to Vasari. "Around this group are crowds of figures with grapes and other fruits in their hands, and this work is so carefully coloured that it may be called one of the finest ever executed by Gian Bellino, although there is a certain harshness and stiffness in the draperies, he having imitated a picture by Albert Dürer, which had just then been brought to Venice. . . . Within the vat above-mentioned Gian Bellino wrote the following words:

JOANNES BELLINUS VENETUS, P. 1514.

"This picture the great age of the master had prevented him from completing . . . desirous of progress and wishing to make himself known, he [Titian] depicted two stories [incidents in the wall series] which were still wanting to that apartment: the first is a River of red wine, beside which are singers and players on instruments, half inebriated, females as well as men. There is one nude figure of a sleeping woman which is very beautiful, and appears living, as indeed do the other figures. To this work Titian affixed his name. In the second picture . . . there are numerous figures of Loves and beautiful children in various attitudes: the most beautiful among these is one who is fishing in a river, and whose figure is reflected in the water. This greatly pleased the Duke, as did the first picture." It was the distinctly Cadorine background of the unfinished Bellino picture, however, that gave Titian the opportunity to show how thoroughly he had studied his own mountain region, sketchbook in hand, and with what grace and ease he adapted it to such a scene of wild celebration as this. Behind the trees edging the clearing where Bellino grouped his hilarious myth towered the rock of Pieve di Cadore, with the castle upon its rugged peak, the far-off, almost lacy outlines of mighty Antelao, the scattered little houses of Sotto Castello clinging nervously to the rock under the castle's frowning shadow. This work is not clearly cognizable as Titian's, but as the picture is studied the links which bind Titian to Bellino, the sixteenth to the fifteenth centuries in Venetian art, are easily discernible. Besides all this, the landscape is clearly signed.

Duke Alfonso rewarded his painter "very largely," according to Vasari, who also says that at about this time Titian became a friend of Ariosto the poet, and was given praise in the *Orlando Furioso* as the honor "not only of Cadore but of Venice." Crowe calls attention to the fact that the first edition of the *Orlando* made no mention of Titian. The year was 1516. The poem, which issued that same year, had been a long time in the hands of the printers, and it is entirely possible that the two geniuses had not met or barely knew each other at the time the poem was revised and ready to be set in type. In the second edition, which appeared sixteen years later, Ariosto devoted a stanza to the painting fraternity in his Thirty-third Canto, ending with the names of *"Bastiano* [Sebastiano del Piombo], *Raffael e Tizian ch'onora Non men cador, che quei Venezia e Urbino."*

At this point Lafenestre brings an interesting observation to bear upon Titian's method. He seems from this time on, as was pointed out briefly in the preceding chapter, to have cultivated the habit of beginning as many pictures as possible. After they were solidly sketched and their proper color notes touched in, he would let them remain untouched, sometimes for long periods. In every case, once he had the essentials of a picture permanently caught, he would not finish the work except in the secure quiet of his own studio. There, by close study and thought, he would slowly perfect composition and refine color and technique as far as it was possible to do so. The final step was to set the canvas or panel in the exact spot for which it had been designed, and to retouch and complete it only after it was ensconced in its particular frame. This is a picture in itself, a graphic likeness of greatness taking infinite pains and achieving the results that only such care could assure.

From the delightful landscape against which Bellino's drunken celebrants gambolled, to his own continuation of the same story and thence to the powerful and utterly different *Assumption of the Virgin* ordered for the church of the Frari as he was finishing his work in Ferrara, is a leap exceedingly few painters have ever been able to accomplish with even moderate chances of success. Titian took it as a matter of routine. The genius of the man was so universal as far as art was concerned, his imagination so fluid and his reverence for beauty and appropriateness so keen that he could turn from one subject to another with as much enjoyment as facility. It may be, indeed, that the habit he had begun to observe as a custom, of keeping many pictures in an unfinished condition, was partly the source of his remarkable power and that fresh, vivacious touch appearing in almost every one of his canvases. He had, in other words, something at hand to work upon which was always practically virginal and stimulating.

John Addington Symonds, in that volume of his great *Renaissance in Italy* devoted to *The Fine Arts,* says in leading up to his comment upon the *Assunta* [Assumption]: "To seize the salient characteristics of an artist whose glory it is to offer nothing over prominent, and who keeps the middle path of perfection, is impossible. . . . Titian's art [is] a golden mean of joy unbroken by brusque movements of the passions—a well tempered harmony in which no thrilling note suggests the possibility of discord. In his work the world and men cease to be merely what they are; he makes them what they ought to be: and this he does by separating

what is beautiful in sensuous life from its alloy of painful medita-
tion and of burdensome endeavor. The disease of thought is unknown in his kingdom; no divisions exist between the spirit and
the flesh; the will is thwarted by no obstacles. When we think
of Titian, we are irresistibly led to think of music. His Assumption
of the Madonna (the greatest oil painting in the world, if we except Raphael's Madonna di San Sisto) can best be described as a
symphony—a symphony of colour, where every hue is brought into
harmonious combination—a symphony of movement, where every
line contributes to melodious rhythm—a symphony of joy in which
the heavens and earth sing Hallelujah."

With Symonds' praise as a background, it is easier for us to
grasp the mastery of the picture by comprehending the conditions
of turmoil and unremitting annoyance under which Titian painted
it. We also, with both these things in mind, discover fresh cause
to reverence the superb mental poise and undeviating craftsmanship with which the artist executed the details of his perspective,
the laying on of his colors and the final bringing of all into an
exquisite accord of symmetry and color. Shortly after his return
from Ferrara to his Venetian studio, Titian took this order, calling
for a large painting of the Ascent of the Virgin, for the high
altar of the church of Santa Maria Gloriosa dei Frati Minori, for
which Father German, prior of the Franciscan convent of Santa
Maria de' Frari, ordered a magnificent marble frame. It was a tremendous picture measuring approximately twenty-two feet six
inches in height by eleven feet eight inches in breadth (6.90 by
3.60 metres), a heavy wooden panel braced and stayed against
the stress of time. The mere physical labor of painting such a
great object, with the constant climbing up and down the necessary
scaffolding, was enough to give the most vigorous painter all he
wanted to do for a long time.

But Titian was unique in his unwearying labor and his gusto for
as many commissions as he could obtain. He accepted the order

even while he was still hard at work on a number of unfilled
orders for the Duke Alfonso. Naturally, the accomplishment of
such a demanding work required so much of his time and effort
that his lesser commitments were delayed. The *Assunta* was not
formally shown in place to the public until March 20, 1518. In
the meantime Alfonso and his diplomatic agents at Venice kept
Titian constantly in hot water. The astonishing correspondence
and conversations which kept the pot boiling during these two
laborious years have been reported so faithfully by Campori we
can follow, practically day by day, the vicissitudes which must
have caused even the placid mountaineer to tear his hair and sometimes wish he had never heard of Alfonso d'Este.

The Duke, full-blooded and choleric, a genuine lover of art and
accustomed to the exercise of unquestioned authority, by turns
raged and wheedled. The wise and cautious Titian handled him
with the tact of a diplomat, promising fulfillment, putting him off,
evading him in various ways. It was not only his pictures that the
irascible Duke wanted completed. He was a noble of sudden no-
tions. One day he called upon Titian to demand without warning
a design for a handsome balustrade such as he had just seen and
admired. Titian hastily sketched a design, thought better of it, and
supplemented his first idea with another outline, sending both.
This was on February 19, 1517. In the letter that accompanied the sketches he also said: "As for the Bath Your Most
Illustrious Lordship has demanded, I have not forgotten it but
am working at it daily, and when you wish to see it, I will send it
to you without delay." Lafenestre thought that by "Bath" Titian
meant a bathing scene full of nymphs or beautiful women. Gronau
believes the picture meant must have been the *Venus Anadyomene,*
now in Bridgewater House, London, otherwise known as the
Venus with the Shell, of which we shall see more.

Shortly after this we find the Duke paying "the painter" through
the Venetian banker Teofilo Lardi seventy-five *livres* for one com-

mission and forty-eight more for a "horse in bronze," doubtless an antique. With the coming of 1518 the Duke had apparently given up all hope of persuading Raphael to come from Rome to decorate his study. Titian was so obviously the man to gratify the Duke's curiously mixed tastes in art, which ranged from the purely sensuous to the deeply religious, that he turned more impetuously than ever to the Venetian Master. Many of his letters were delivered by his agent, Jacopo Tebaldi, who reported in faithful detail all his visits to the busy studio in San Samuele. While all this was going on, and Titian was submerged in a welter of portraits, sketches, designs and whatnot, to say nothing of his huge panel and a lot of slow and tedious diplomatic letter-writing, the *Assunta* was finished, placed in its marble frame, given its final scrupulous revision by the Master's hard-to-satisfy hand, and at last, on St. Bernardino's Day, March 20, 1518, revealed to throngs which jammed the church.

The final weeks spent upon the picture were a sore trial to both painter and patrons. Prior German, or Zerman, confused and extremely uneasy by what his untrained eyes told him was all wrong, plagued Titian constantly by his inspections and queries. The painting, meant to be seen from the floor of the nave, was to hang high above the altar, partly in obscurity, partly in a soft light. What the monks could not understand was why, when they looked at the monstrous thing on a level, its proportions seemed so absurdly exaggerated, its manner so grandiloquent, its movement so theatrically vivacious. This was not at all the sort of thing they had anticipated from a great master; not in the least like anything in the nature of an Assumption of the sort to which they were accustomed by works of the calm, philosophic schools of the previous century. In spite of elaborate explanations they were so dissatisfied, and so worried, Ridolfi declares, that Titian threatened to keep the painting himself and was mollified only by Prior German's halting apologies.

On the great day, so busy had rumor been, the church was even more crowded than was expected. In the throng were two men of major importance: Marino Sanuto, the dry, loquacious annalist of the Republic, who recorded the showing in his notes, and the Emperor's ambassador Adorno. The latter immediately offered to buy the great panel for his imperial master, the vast congregation joyously acclaimed it, and the previously dubious monks, seeing their treasure at last in the proper lighting and perspective, realized they possessed not only the largest but the greatest painting the city had ever seen. Its effect was instantaneous throughout the world of culture, and Titian, however highly he had been esteemed before, was now hailed as the supreme painter of his School. At one stroke it elevated him to that small company of genius sought out by the very greatest in other fields, and so overwhelmed him with demands for his work that he could give attention only to the most important. Alfonso of Ferrara was not slow to realize this, and the haughty tone he had hitherto taken with Titian was touched with a new respect and rendered with more appeal.

In the technical sense the painting is a remarkable exhibition of the virtuosity of the artist in gauging his perspective and, despite the heavy foreground, directing the attention to a sharp focus in the center of the tri-partite scene. Titian, though the rules of pictorial composition had not in his day been studied and rationalised completely, instinctively knew that he must have a definite center of interest in his canvas. Since his theme was the ascending Virgin, she naturally formed this visual center. In order to obey the physiological rule which is the basis of this truism—that the eyes are at least semi-independent instrumentalities that perceive without being actually ordered by the will to observe—he assisted them by the use of the simplest of all means: lines leading the vision directly to her. In the foreground, at the very foot of the picture, the Apostles are tightly grouped, every one of them straining upward. Above them the magnificent giantess soars serene in the middle of the

painting. When the eye attempts to go farther, it is instantly
checked by the horizontal line made by the figure of God, who is
looking down, and above Him by the arc of cherubim at the top
also all gazing downward. Thus at one stroke the artist achieved
not only his center of interest, but that utter simplification without
which the work fails. Not a line, a figure or an item of any sort in
the entire painting but adds to the sum total of effect. And finally
in his balancing of masses, his distribution of lights and shadows,
his effortless and easy arrangement of space, and his glorious color
he produced that harmony which is the supreme test of excellence
and which Symonds has hymned as symphonic. The *Assunta* is a
work which, seen in its proper position and lighting, has in it no
physical reaction of weariness or discomfort to the beholder. It is
strange, considering how erudite Edward Hutton was, that when
he studied the *Assunta* where it now hangs in the Academy, he
should not have recognized instantly it is improperly hung, garishly
lighted, completely unsuited by its ambient. He said it left him
cold, and he passed over this glorious achievement with a few
words. If only he could have seen it in the place for which Titian
painted it, suspended in the mellow semi-gloom above the high
altar in the church, its strong colors warmed and softened by the
dim and hazy illumination, the great, sharply cut figures of the
Apostles reduced by the perspective to their normal human proportions, the whole picture eloquent as a psalm! Dolce reports that
Titian's contemporaries found in the *Assunta* "the formidable
grandeur of Michael Angelo with the charm and beauty of Raphael,
and the very colors of nature."

If any picture can be said to have "made" him, the *Assunta* certainly made Titian. Orders poured in upon him from all sides from
nobles, prelates, kings, wealthy collectors and amateurs of painting. Besides all this, his innumerable unfinished canvases ripening
in the studio and periodically examined and retouched or finished
with the meticulous care he never scanted, made a tremendous

Photo by Alinari

PIETRO ARETINO (*Left*) AS THE MAN OF GENIUS AND (*Right*) AS THE BASER ELEMENTS IN HIS NATURE PREVAILED

From the Kress Collection *From the Mellon Collection*

Both by courtesy of the U.S. National Gallery of Art

load of work, on top of which scowled the Duke of Ferrara, demanding his pictures in no uncertain terms. How any genius in such circumstances could keep his head, not scamp his work, and continue accepting commission after commission with unperturbed equanimity is a testimonial to the steadiness of Titian's nerves and the tremendous virility and physical prowess of the man who continued to follow this sort of feverish activity most of his life.

Whatever the public or his nonofficial patrons knew about the reasons for the apparently inexcusable delays the painter permitted, the fact was that Titian had one extremely serious matter on his mind. On July 13, 1518—in other words, soon after the *Assunta* had made him what we of today would call a world figure—he received a stinging rebuke from the Signoria. After digesting the report of the Salt Office, which had been quietly investigating, the Signoria informed Titian bluntly that within eight days he would begin painting the promised battle canvas and carry it on until it was finished, with the threat that if he did not another artist would be assigned to do the work, and Titian would have to pay the bill. Those steely nerves apparently did not quiver. With all he had to do for Duke Alfonso, huge altarpieces for churches in Brescia and Ancona, and an *Annunciation* for the Cathedral in Treviso through Canon Brocardo Malchiostro, Titian plodded steadily on, unhurried and apparently heeding the threat of the Signoria only as a part of the routine annoyances to which his readiness for orders had long subjected him. Evidently he went to work to some extent upon the picture, somehow pacified his other clamorous patrons, and meantime accepted still another commission from the impatient and even yet frequently hostile Alfonso.

How many pictures the Duke had ordered while Titian was in residence at Ferrara we do not know. We do know that he finished none there which he undertook at the time, but worked on them later in his studio. His portrait of Alfonso, a noble work, was certainly one. The *Worship of Venus* and the first *Bacchanal*, both now in Madrid, were probably others. It seems very curious that Titian was not ordered to paint the Duchess, who was as beautiful as her reputation was evil. Ridolfi says he did; but not a word exists in the records at Ferrara to prove that the lovely Lucrezia Borgia ever sat to the Master. Crowe points out the significant fact that the Borgia name was anathema to all decent Italians after the death of Pope Alexander VI, and the Ferrarese were anxious to forget the means by which they had laid claim to the cities of Modena and Reggio. It is entirely supposable in such circumstances that a Borgia portrait of no matter how beautiful a woman would be ignored for a time, and later, when again exhibited, shown merely as that of a great lady whose name unfortunately had been forgotten or lost.

Duchess Lucrezia died in 1519. On September 29 of that year the Duke in a rage wrote his agent Tebaldi: "We thought the painter Titian would eventually finish our picture. We see that he holds it in no great esteem and does nothing about it even yet, so we wish you to go to him as quickly as possible. Tell him for us that we are amazed that he does not seem to wish to finish this painting, and that he completely fails to make an end of it; otherwise, we shall feel great resentment and show him what he shall have deserved from someone who in his turn deserved to be well served; and make him understand that I am not of those who can be deluded. Talk to him firmly, because we have decided that he must finish the work he began, according to his promise; and if he refuses, inform us. Give me an immediate statement of his decision."

Titian's response to this tirade was to make a trip to Padua, and on his return in October, to tell Tebaldi that when the Duke's picture was near enough completion to warrant it, he would take it with him and finish it on the spot. Infuriating man; yet indispensable! On October 22 he leisurely embarked on a boat which took him up the Po to Ferrara. In all probability the picture

he took with him to finish after he had himself seen and gauged the
spot where it was to hang and studied the way the light would fall
upon it in the Duke's office, was the famed *Bacchanal* now in the
Prado Museum in Madrid. The correspondence of 1518 between
patron and artist, and the record of Tebaldi's conversations with
Titian, indicate almost certainly that this was the subject for which
the Duke had furnished a rough sketch and detailed instructions.
It depicts a wildly gay, bibulous revel in a delightful landscape,
with some of the participants already overcome, two of them dancing, some pouring the wine or drinking, and others lying quietly on
the grass conversing. In the foreground is a nymph who has thrown
off her robe and lies completely nude and drunkenly asleep, while
a cunning child beside her pulls up his little shirt and looks down
with complete indifference to the fact that the sleeper is being at
least thoroughly splashed. The scene is a page straight out of
Catullus, a paean of feminine beauty touched with Rabelaisian
humor. Like its companion pieces for the Duke, the *Offering to
Venus* and the *Ariadne and Bacchus,* of which more in a moment,
the *Bacchanal* breathes freely the Greek joy of living; but the light,
the color and the poise, as well as the surprising rhythm of the
picture, are pure Venetian. Lafenestre points out at this juncture,
with truly Gallic keenness, that the drunken nymph so completely
delineated in the foreground and the fully dressed beauty holding
out her cup to be filled while displaying a violet on her breast are
no indication of any base interest on Titian's part, since "at the
epoch of the *Bacchanal* Titian, recently married, seems . . . to have
been a very regular husband." Could anything be more delightful
or more French than that description? "We know," Lafenestre
adds, "the probable date of his marriage, the certain date of his
widowerhood; but we do not know the family name of his wife; his
life as a bachelor is unknown to us, but his life as a widower con-
serves all the appearances of impeccable correctness."

The other two pictures of this great suite which completed the decoration of the Duke's study begun by Bellino's wall frescoes, struck somewhat the same note though inspired by different sources. Once they were finished and in place they remained in the castle until 1598, when Cardinal Aldobrandini, the Papal Legate, removed them clandestinely against the vigorous protests of Caesar d'Este, Duke of Modena. The latter had renounced his sovereign rights at Ferrara, but retained his property rights, and made a fully justified outcry when Aldobrandini stole the paintings and took them to Rome. There they remained on full exhibition in the Ludovisi Palace until 1638, studied by artists from all over the world. In that year both the *Bacchanal* and the *Offering to Venus* were presented to the King of Spain by Cardinal Ludovisi. Only the *Bacchus and Ariadne* remained in Rome, where it graced the Aldobrandini and Barberini galleries until the English collector Buchanan bought it in 1806 and twenty years later sold it to the National Gallery, where it remains today.

All three of the subjects of these works were furnished by Duke Alfonso. They spoke as eloquently as only Titian could speak of the enthusiasm sweeping all of Italy for the classics, and especially for the previously forgotten poets of Greece and Rome. Lafenestre believes also that throughout all one can perceive the "pagan inspiration of Ariosto, then working with ardor on the *Orlando Furioso*." First of the trilogy was probably the *Offering to Venus*, whose theme is clearly drawn almost literally from the Greek philosopher-poet Philostratus.

The dominating figure in the scene is a statue of Venus, draped from the waist down, standing upon a pedestal before a great rock or cliff, from whose foot a sparkling rivulet gushes out clear and cold. In the right corner at the goddess' feet are two female votaries of the lush type of beauty Titian loved to depict. Through the entire central part swarms a crowd of tiny winged Cupids, the incarnation of grace and loveliness, playing, caressing one another,

THE VIRGIN WITH SAINTS CATHERINE AND JOHN AND THE
INFANT CHRIST

THE MADONNA DEL CONIGLIO, OR VIRGIN OF THE RABBIT

Courtesy U.S. National Gallery of Art, Mellon Collection

MADONNA AND CHILD AND THE INFANT ST. JOHN IN A LANDSCAPE

squabbling, tossing apples, eating them, shooting their arrows, even flying through the lower air. To the left lofty apple trees, with the colored fruit showing plainly, are being despoiled by Cupids hovering like human hummingbirds. The landscape stretches away into an exquisitely delicate background under a softly tinted summer sky whose warm, clear air is so perfectly imagined as to be almost sensible. Commenting upon this canvas Lafenestre remarks: "It is with the naif simplicity of an ancient Greek that Titian remade, without changing anything, this antique scene. Before the grace of the little ones as before the beauty of the women this mountaineer, sane and perfectly balanced, protected by a grave and constant love of nature against the corruption which surrounded him, found himself as simple and as frank as the primitive artists of Ægina and Athens. No other painter of the Renaissance was either so natural or so completely pagan, in the noblest sense of that term, as Titian in his profane pictures. In the naked children as in his nude women there is never a trace of a shamed convention nor of a shameful intention; it is life, it is nature, composed and expressed in the fulness of their force, the glory of their fullest bloom, in the unconsciousness of their perfection." Every great painter since then, and each of hundreds of minor ones, who has used children in his work, has copied and imitated and despaired over this vivid masterpiece.

The *Offering* might well be called a poem of infantile beauty, just as the *Bacchanal* is a lyric of feminine loveliness and abandon. The *Ariadne and Bacchus* is also a pagan theme, but with a clearly Venetian interpretation, for while it murmurs of the poems of Anacreon and Sappho, Catullus and Ovid, its joyousness and motion, color and rhythm are distinctly peculiar to the art of the lagoons. Here the story is told with a dash and freedom that can not be found by the closest reading of the Veronese Catullus who described, fifteen centuries before, the finding of Ariadne on Naxos

by Bacchus. Into his canvas Titian poured not only all the detail
the poet had given, but the suppleness of his own fiery imagination.
The amorous god leaps impetuously from his golden chariot, drawn
by two very tame leopards, toward the terrified princess, who gath-
ers her robes about her and tries to run away from the deific vision
descending upon her. Here is the ugly brown satyr with snakes
writhing about his leg and body; the second satyr, with his thyrsus,
the lower leg of a calf in his raised right hand; before them both,
the baby satyr, dragging by a cord his bloody toy in the shape of a
freshly severed calf's head, while his little dog faces him barking
protest. The cymbal-playing nymph beside the largest satyr and her
companion with a tambourine in the background are as vivacious
as any of the figures in the other two paintings.

In this twentieth century we express unbounded admiration for
the incalculable treasures of beauty such patrons of the arts as the
late Andrew W. Mellon, Peter A. B. Widener, Samuel H. Kress
and others have gathered at infinite pains and cost from the far
corners of culture. All this is utterly desirable and praiseworthy,
especially the decision of the collectors in each case to present their
groups to the National Government for the benefit of the world in
posterity. But imagine the difference between collecting and buy-
ing as specimens works painted at different times for different men,
and the action of such a petty lord as Alfonso of Este. He deliberately planned his private study to reflect his personal wishes in
the greatest and most brilliant art of his time, with its walls frescoed by Giovanni Bellino, greatest of the great at that time in the
north. When the Duke could not prevail upon Raphael to accept
his commission, he selected Titian, who was already bordering
Giovanni's fame, to execute not only these three great canvases but
many others, including portraits of himself, of the beautiful Laura
Dianti, his mistress and later his second wife, and of the poet
Ariosto. What a room that must have been! Even if only the
three largest canvases could find a place in it beside the frescoes,

what mingled pride, satisfaction and calm must have permeated the soul of the Duke as he gazed upon them. In such a study, its lights and shadows falling upon paintings expressly designed and hung to be so illuminated, no man could remain unmoved, and we can well understand why Domenichino (Domenico Zampieri) wept when such treasures were taken to Spain.

And then, on March 20, 1523, Doge Antonio Grimani died.

CHAPTER NINE

Fame and Power

With the death of Doge Antonio Grimani the complexion of affairs in Venice underwent a profound change politically. Titian, as usual in the very thick of things, entered upon that phase of his career which eventually brought him more than the irascible patronage of petty lordlings. It gave him the entrée to the imperial court, brought him the respect and friendship of the Emperor himself, after him the favor of his dour son Philip, and made him more than ever sought after by all who followed the attitude of the great.

Doge Andrea Gritti, who succeeded Grimani, had long been a warm admirer and friend of the painter. Sixty-eight years old when he ascended the ducal throne, as the summit and crowning achievement of as melodramatic a career as could well be imagined by an adventure novelist, one of his first acts was to demand of Titian the portrait the artist was bound by law to paint of him for the Republic. Gritti was a shrewd politician also. Wishing to leave a subtle impress of his policy in the Ducal Palace he ordered Titian—this was in September 1523—to execute a large fresco of *St. Christopher* at the foot of the staircase leading from his private quarters to the Senate chamber. Considerably more significance hid beneath this command than appeared on the surface. Doge Andrea had for some time secretly cherished a strong leaning toward the French party, but he dared not risk offending the Emperor Charles V.

He could not possibly express his sentiments publicly, and he was obliged for reasons of political exigency to contract an alliance with the Emperor. In such circumstances he found it expedient to have a votive fresco of St. Christopher painted which would also be a commemorative picture celebrating by inference the entry of the French army into the town of St. Christopher, not far from Milan, the imperial stronghold. Such statesmanlike acuity in protecting his personal interests without giving obvious evidence that he was doing so, was typically Venetian. Titian quickly finished both pictures, and as a result of further interest on the Doge's part was ordered in May of 1524 to redecorate the little chapel of the Doges, then undergoing renovation.

Of course while he was fully engaged on these works he had to neglect the notorious battle picture in the Hall of Great Council, besides leaving untouched the privately ordered canvases waiting in his studio. Here one lord wanted his picture finished instantly, there a wealthy amateur clamored for his mythological scene and a dignitary raised a storm because his frame full of nude beauties was not ready. The Marquis of Mantua, a new patron and "protector," sent Titian by the hands of Braghino Croce di Coreggio, his chamberlain and ambassador to Venice, a magnificent doublet to induce the artist to complete a portrait already commenced, which the Marquis wanted without delay. For once Titian seems to have bestirred himself on behalf of an individual, for on August 15 of that same year the Marquis acknowledged receipt of the painting. Whose portrait it was we do not know.

Meantime Duke Alfonso was plaguing Titian through his emissary, the indefatigable Tebaldi. Apparently the canvas now in dispute was one the artist held unfinished in his studio. To complete it after all the work had been done that was possible at home, he would have to carry it to Ferrara for the hanging and the subsequent finishing touches. Patient and serené as usual, Titian endured these fresh "assaults" with apparent equanimity for several months in 1523. Lafenestre gives a graphic sentence worthy of remembering about the matter. "From the beginning of 1524," he says, speaking of Tebaldi, the Duke's agent, "we find him attached to the painter's flanks and harassing him without respite to get him to embark for Ferrara." Titian was suffering from fever at the time, and a trip through the marshy delta of the Po was a risk not lightly to be considered. Nevertheless, on March 13, though scarcely able to be about again, Titian told Tebaldi he would make the journey if the latter could procure a medical certificate to the effect that a change of air would do him good. What happened we do not know. Perhaps Tebaldi could not bribe any physician because of the eminence of the patient. Perhaps Titian, if the certificate was forthcoming, found some ingenious way to hold back. In any case it was not until November 29 that Tebaldi, to make absolutely sure of "this devil of a man," had a barge brought almost to Titian's doorstep. This time the painter kept his promises, for we know from the account books of the castle that he was in Ferrara during January 1525, when an ounce of azure was sent to him from Venice for use in completing certain pictures for the Duke. Then he probably went on to Mantua, returning to Ferrara in February.

Five years before he had been presented to the Marquis Federigo Gonzaga in Venice, but it was not until 1523, when the young lord had acquired some stability on his uneasy throne and some experience of art, that he decided to send for the painter. As Mantua was the nephew of Ferrara, Titian risked nothing by accepting commissions from both. It was also probably during this period of the middle twenties that Titian painted an astonishing number of pictures besides working on the battle scene in the Ducal Palace and carrying out personal orders from Doge Andrea Gritti. It may have been during this time that he did the portrait of the scholar Mosti, a familiar of the Duke Alfonso and one of his witnesses at his marriage to Laura Dianti who, though she may have been of peasant birth, had both the spiritual and bodily grace to be a fit mate for the haughty Duke. Crowe's solemn doubt, on seeing the portrait reputed to be of herself and the Duke, "whether a girl, beautiful indeed but simple in attire, could be the mistress of a duke like Alfonso" is so ridiculous we suspect the Englishman of being very hard pressed for something to say about an exceptionally lovely portrait. He seems to overlook completely the painter's license to garb his figures as he wishes, and we are more inclined to agree with the estimate of Vasari, to whom it appeared as a "stupendous portrait."

The aged Doge, despite his preoccupation with affairs of state, did not overlook his friend the painter. On April 24, 1525, he promoted Titian's brother-in-law, Matteo Soldano, to be chancellor at Feltre, and put his father, Gregorio Vecelli, in Soldano's place as inspector of mines. Unfortunately, we have very little documentary evidence of the years between 1521 and 1526, except for the records of some few pictures. We know the *Ariadne and Bacchus,* the paintings in the chapel of the Doges in the Ducal Palace, the large fresco of *St. Christopher* in the same edifice, the *Virgin and Six Saints,* generally known as the *Virgin of San Niccolò* and the magnificent *Pesaro Virgin,* all fell within these years. But we cannot, except by circumstantial evidence, account in the same period for other celebrated works, among them the *Annunciation* in the Scuola di San Rocco, the *Entombment* now in the Louvre, the Darmstadt *Sleeping Venus,* the *Venus Anadyomene* in the Ellesmere Collection in London, and the world-famous *Flora* in the Uffizi Gallery in Florence. Besides these which are known the world over, Titian seems to have produced during these same fecund years of achievement, a considerable number of portraits of individuals which, by reason of their style and finish, can almost certainly be declared contemporary with the better-known canvases and panels.

An inexcusable mutilation of the entire upper arched part of the *Virgin of San Niccolò,* cutting off the Dove of the Holy Spirit, whose rays only are partly visible, has shrunk both this glorious work and its full intention. Notwithstanding this it remains, by virtue of both color and style, one of the marvels of the Vatican, where Clement XIV placed it. Titian himself regarded it as of such great importance, since it was a work in which the theme compelled him to unify the severe beauty of traditional classic figures with the magnificence of a high-keyed luminosity, that he himself drew the designs on the wood blocks which Andrea Andreani engraved for subsequent printing. It is worth notice that the painter did not follow in any way the design which made him famous in the earlier *Assunta* in the Frari, and have all his six saints gazing upward toward the Virgin. Instead, St. Catherine at the extreme left looks down as though she were trying to select a place to step, while at the right corner St. Sebastian is staring down absorbed in the arrows that have pierced his side and thigh. Vasari says of the Sebastian, which excited breathless admiration among Titian's brother painters, that it was "exactly copied from the life without the slightest admixture of art; no efforts for the sake of beauty have been sought in any part: all is as Nature left it, so that it might seem to be a sort of cast from life, it is so fleshly and real."

Continuing our own analysis, St. Francis with his back turned to the beholder looks at the blank wall in the background, St. Anthony of Padua across the scene toward St. Catherine, and the aged St. Peter from behind gazes down at the opened book held by the magnificent and imposing figure of St. Nicholas, whose features are clearly somewhat reminiscent of the *Laocoön*. Titian had in his studio a cast of the recently executed model of that famous sculpture which Sansovino had made for Cardinal Domenico Grimani. St. Nicholas, it is true, gazes upward, but away from the vision soaring directly behind him. Notwithstanding the high enthusiasms of Vasari and Dolce for the "force of the style and the breadth of execution," the present writer cannot quite persuade himself that Titian here achieved the strength and unity he manifested not alone in the *Assunta* but in other works. Blashfield declares it "somewhat monotonous and lacking in dominating motive." Gronau, on the other hand, is enthusiastic, especially regarding St. Sebastian, quoting approvingly Dolce's report of Pordenone's exclamation, "I believe Titian for this nude form must have used real flesh instead of colours!"

The apex of Titian's fame and genius as a painter of religious presentation or votive canvases is his superb *Madonna di Casa Pesaro,* painted for the same "Baffo" he had shown in 1503, more than twenty years before, praying before St. Peter for victory on the eve of sailing against the Turk, for the glory of Christianity—and his own pocket. Now, in 1526, Titian gave perfect expression to what Crowe calls the "noblest combination of the homely and devotional with palatial architecture—the most splendid and solemn union of the laws of composition and colour with magic light and shade." Though Bishop "Baffo" conquered the Turk, it took him a good thirteen years to make up his mind to return thanks to the Virgin and St. Peter in the church of the Frari. Possibly it required that length of time to make secure the Pesaro family's heavy investments and other interests in the Levant. Whatever the reason, and that there was an excellent material one we may be certain, he finally turned as a matter of course to the Cadorine who had so splendidly depicted his devotions prior to the risky voyage. No one could have reasoned from that first Pesaro likeness that the young man who displayed boldness and breadth in his treatment would in less than a quarter of a century reach such a height of expression and flowing, easy power in every subtle aspect of his work.

The great canvas, which still hangs in the Frari for which it was done, is a tremendous advance over any other presentation picture, and surpasses even the *Assunta* in the sense that it is more Venetian and far more personal. In it Titian dared to create a setting for his figures so colossal it would, in the hands of any lesser spirit, have completely crushed the celestial and human figures enclosed by it. The temple pillars soar into the empyrean; the mere plinths from which they rise are as lofty as the pedestal supporting the Madonna. St. Peter, at her feet to the right as we look at the picture, interrupts his reading, holding his book open with his fingers. The Pesari kneel on the floor in the left foreground—Benedetto, who died in 1503, three other adult members of the family, including "Baffo" in front, and a handsome lad. Opposite them the group that has St. Peter's attention fills the right lower corner: an armed knight who holds aloft the flag of the Church, marked as victorious by the spray of laurel on its staff, while a turbaned Turk, dark and uneasy, bows to him as a captive, and a tonsured prelate kneels facing the Madonna. St. Francis displays his stigmata joyously to the Child, who gazes raptly at him, and, almost lost in the shadow behind, St. Anthony hovers benignly. Above all, two cherubs on a cloud between the pillars hold up a massive wooden cross.

Titian spent either six or seven years in bringing this canvas to perfection. The portraits are highly individualized—even that of Benedetto—each one displaying a different emotion. A strong family likeness appears in them all. The bored youngster, not in the least interested in the specious devotions of his elders, turns a fascinatingly frank and curious face away from ceremonial to life, and gazes directly at the beholder. Lafenestre finds the group full of the most serious qualities of Giovanni Bellino and Giorgione, but with greatly added suppleness of form, and more freedom and allure of treatment. Crowe, while implicitly recognizing all this, goes deeper and discovers infinite varieties of subtlety in decomposing the lights and shadows which balance the painting so beautifully, making a "sublime unity that shows the master who created it to have reached a point in art unsurpassed till now, and unattainable by those who came after him."

Representations of religious themes such as this of course bear much the same relation to fact as grand opera does to life. We must never forget when examining such a work that it was never supposed to have any reality. Every Venetian if he thought about such matters at all, which is most improbable, knew perfectly well that dead men do not come back to life, nor living men visit Heaven and return to earth. If Bishop "Baffo" Pesaro was actually while still alive to be admitted to the presence of the heavenly hierarchy, what was the Turk, that paynim, that hated "infidel," doing in such irreproachable company, even as a captive? An allegory is of course the reply to any such comment, a symbolic representation only. But suppose for a moment than an artist of today should paint a splendid, glowing picture showing the president of a great corporation kneeling in prayer in Heaven while his family obediently accompanies his devotion with theirs, and the head of an embittered labor union, bound hand and foot, bows scowling and helpless beside a column. What would the painter attract beyond some amused attention, a few gibes, and not much of either. The difference is in our thinking, in the spirit of the times, not in the theme. We of today refuse to accept overt artifice as a factor in our daily lives, even when presented in allegorical form. Nevertheless we can and do admit its vitality in the past; and we delight in the power of such a creative titan as Titian to give epic expression in form, color, light and shadow, sheer beauty, in a word, to that which men have always known never touched and never can touch reality.

The feeling of the Venetians was so strong for this it amounted to a passion, a holy zeal. Symonds, if we may quote him again as the philosopher of art and the historian who has most profoundly understood Venetian character and emotionalism, sees clearly and expresses the underlying reason for all this. In describing the decoration of the Ducal Palace, which is the outstanding example of Venetian prodigality in art, he wrote that the conditions of life in

Venice "inclined the individual to accept life as he found it. Instead of exciting him to think, they disposed him to enjoy, or to acquire by industry the means of manifold enjoyment . . . to create a monument of Renaissance magnificence was the task of Venice. Without Venice the modern world could not have produced that flower of sensuous and unreflective loveliness in painting which is worthy to stand beside the highest product of the Greek genius in sculpture. For Athena from her Parthenon stretches the hand to Venezia enthroned in the Ducal Palace. . . . The halls . . . are walled and roofed with pictures of inestimable value, encased in framework of carved oak, overlaid with burnished gold. Supreme art—the art of the imagination perfected with delicate and skilful care in detail—is made in these proud halls the minister of mundane pomp. . . . A more insolent display of public wealth—a more lavish outpouring of human genius in the service of State pageantry, cannot be imagined. . . . Religion in these pictures was a matter of parade"—no less real than the faith of the Sienese and the Florentines, let us say, but content to exist as one function among many functions.

It is in a badly lighted place in this palace that we find the huge fresco of *St. Christopher,* already mentioned. To see the picture one must stand on the stair-landing and look back into the semi-darkness, which Titian gauged so remarkably the color and character of the composition are instantly apparent. The Saint, a Herculean figure with the Child gaily seated on his shoulder, wades against a mighty current across the shallow lagoon, with the towering campanile shimmering in the far distance. Christopher wears an expression of astonishment as he gazes upward at the unanticipated weight of the divine Child, who points to Heaven, and steadies himself with a heavy pole which he thrusts forcibly against the muddy bottom. As Crowe points out, the technical execution of composition, drapery, colors and atmosphere clearly indicate the painter of the *Madonna of San Niccolò;* and if the artist disappoints us somewhat by his color, which in the fresco is darker and less transparently brilliant than in his oils, we can understand this because we so thoroughly realize Titian to have been for many years a painter in oils almost exclusively. The harshness—even, one might say, the almost flat quality—of the coloring here is due to his relative inexperience with the medium, not to any lack of genius or to any falling back in skill.

There is, however, one material defect to the picture which must instantly strike any seaman. To brace against the strong thrust of a current or wind, one not only leans against it, but uses his pole or oar to thrust from behind against it, as one might use a third leg for stability. For the purpose of harmonious composition no doubt, Titian set his pole in such a way, slanting diagonally across the Saint's leaning body, that its entire force is being exerted against the straining of his muscles and *with* the current and wind. No living creature could make progress in such a manner. In nautical terms, his use of the pole as it is painted takes the user "all aback," and the tremendously powerful Christopher would either stand still or fall over backwards were he to try it. It has often seemed to me, after noting similar inaccuracies in many paintings and drawings, that artists, who are supposed to be keener observers of life than laymen, either frequently do not see vitally unconvincing elements in a composition or, if they do see them, are so fettered by their own conceptions of their work as a whole as to be unable or un-willing to exchange clear error for convincing fact. Crowe, evidently not possessing any knowledge of the ways of water and heedless of the common principles of equilibrium, did not notice this defect. On the contrary, he declares the *St. Christopher* to be one of the works which Titian's followers Paul Veronese, Paris Bordone and Lorenzo Lotto probably studied most attentively, adding, "and it is not improbable that we may thus ascribe to this period the connection which united these artists in the relative positions of master and disciple." Bordone, indeed, he declares in his *Madonna with Saints* in the church of Sant'Agostino at Crema "takes almost bodily into the picture the *St. Christopher* of the public palace."

It would be difficult to find a sharper or more apposite criticism of the composition of Titian's *St. Christopher* than hangs at this moment in the Metropolitan Museum of Art in New York. In one of the splendid Italian rooms is a large and horrible fresco of *St. Christopher,* credited to a follower of Antonio Pollaiuolo, and executed during the final quarter of the fifteenth century. The picture is theatrical, affected, dreadful in color, and everything a Titian is not. But this unknown painter poised his big, powerful saint as leaning against the strong current creaming about his legs, and his heavy staff is slanted with the slope of his mighty body against the thrust of the water. Bad as the painting is, it is superior to Titian's infinitely better painted Saint and Child in respect of hydrodynamics. This Christopher is in no danger of falling over backwards.

The *Annunciation* in the Scuola di San Rocco marks a distinct advance in technique over the same subject painted for Treviso a few years before. In the later picture Titian displayed a broader handling and finer simplicity, with perhaps less youthful tenderness. Clearly the maturity of the artist was growing. The serenity of the Virgin kneeling at prayer testifies to that. Crowe finds one serious defect in the picture, with the words: ". . . the piece would be more perfect if the angel who hops into the terrace on a cloud was not presented in a dancing motion, which gives a worldliness to the composition inseparable, it would seem, from Titian's treatment of this theme." Being funny at the expense of Titian is bathos.

There is much in these paintings of Titian's transitional period to make the student thoughtful. Possibly the one which best exemplifies the change subtly going on in the painter's mind is the famous *Flora* in the Uffizi Gallery at Florence. It seems almost in itself to mark the transition between his more delicately youthful touch and conception, which in a way bound him to what has been called his "timidity," and the full, robust manner of assurance which came with his realization of his own matured powers. The subtler delicacies of his earlier figures disappear from this point onward. We notice it especially in his nudes and in some of his portraits. There is no lack of characterization, but the corporeal weighting of most of the figures shows Titian was seeing his models as themselves fully adult. In the case of *Flora* this is strikingly evident. This is no unsophisticated young girl, innocent and waiting to be aroused, but a woman in the fullest bloom of her loveliness, all aware of the meaning of life and entirely capable of securing her own interests. As in the case of the picture of Laura Dianti and Duke Alfonso, tradition calls the *Flora* by the same name: *Titian's Mistress*. It hardly matters now what she was. The vital thing is that the painter has given us with all his power a vision of sensuous beauty that is unforgettable.

It is very much worth while in connection with the labels falsely given some of Titian's pictures, and the reckless guesses as to the painter's personal habits, to glance for a moment at the testimony of Aretino who, as we shall see farther along, formed one-third of the astonishing Triumvirate that played so interesting and important a role in Venetian artistic life. Aretino was probably the outstanding blackguard and rascal of the entire Italian Renaissance, and his friendship with Titian was the one pure and decent thing we can record of him. His letters, written with appalling frankness and an evident enjoyment of the salacious, never refer to Titian except in terms of a respect which borders upon actual reverence. The utterly cynical and spicy note he wrote to Sansovino, the third member of the celebrated clique, in January 1553, is typical, and shows Titian as invariably far more reserved than his friends. Aretino scrawled: "I'm sorry I suggested that you leave the girls there, because I'm built of such stuff that I torment myself with them. But not Titian! *Omnia pecunia falsata sunt,* says the pedant.

What astonishes me about him is that, let the girls be whom they may, when he meets them he is courteous, he makes his manners by giving them a friendly kiss, he amuses them with a hundred other juvenile follies, but he never goes beyond that. And we," adds this sordid rascal, with perhaps a touch of genuine envy, "ought truly to correct ourselves by his example." Again and again, in other letters, Aretino excuses himself for not inviting Titian to a dinner or other party, "because this time my feminine company is too bad."

If we may judge by the usual technical criteria, Titian about this time painted a considerable number of nudes, among them the Darmstadt *Venus,* the *Venus of the Shell,* the Madrid *Venus.* Since success breeds imitation invariably, the real Titians were eventually followed by a host of copies, many of which have since masqueraded as originals by the Master. Crowe deals roughly with a number of the better-known examples, flatly classifying them as the work of the Venetian and Bolognese Schools, one by Padovanino, a dubious Sassoferrato, a disciple of the Schools of Bassano, and Tintoretto. So much retouching and patching has been done that in practically none of the authentic examples of this type is the characteristic beauty of Titian's style now visible.

The Bridgewater House *Venus Anadyomene (Venus of the Shell)* is a variant of the always popular Venus theme. It completely fulfills Symonds' remark already quoted that Venice was producing that "flower of sensuous and unreflective loveliness worthy to stand beside the highest product of the Greek genius in sculpture." Crowe disagrees pointedly with this and declares that Titian, with even such a theme as this to inspire him, "could not imagine anything sufficiently elevated to compare with the antique, and he produced at best one of those creations which recall Greek art in its externals without impressing us with a sublime purity."

Perhaps if we once more look behind the obvious into another field of Greek art we shall see the reasons which were clearly responsible in part at least for Titian's making what he did of this remarkable picture. Some four hundred years before Titian was born the scholiasts and antiquarians patiently picked over the débris of the fallen world of classic Greek letters, and gathered with loving care the epigrams and poems they found into the several volumes of the Greek Anthology. In it the flower of Greek wit, intelligence and culture blossomed afresh in a garden of such richness, beauty and variety as but relatively few of the Greeks themselves had ever known. Aldus, the Greek scholar-publisher of Venice, who gave new life in Europe to all the best of Hellas by issuing un-numbered volumes of the classics, undoubtedly printed all or parts of the Anthology. Titian himself may not have read— probably could not read—the Greek text, but his fellow members of the Aldine Academy certainly could, and any one of them would delightedly have rendered the soft music of the Greek for him into the equally musical slurrings of the Venetian dialect.

As one reads the Anthology today he sees instantly that it affords explicit and obvious proof of the source of Titian's inspiration for this great picture. In Book XVI—I quote from Paton's translation facing the original Greek—Antipater of Sidon in Epigram 178, "on the Aphrodite Anadyomene of Apelles" wrote: "Look on the work of Apelles' pencil: Cypris, just rising from the sea, her mother; how, grasping her hair with her hand, she wrings the foam from the wet locks. Athena and Hera themselves will now say, 'No longer do we enter the contest of beauty with thee'." Archias, in 179, on the same theme, phrased it more succinctly: "Apelles saw Cypris herself brought forth by the sea, her nurse; and so he drew her, still wringing with her fresh hands her locks soaked with the foam of the waters." In Epigram 180 Democritus took a somewhat different note by particularizing: "When Cypris, her hair dripping with the salt foam, rose naked from the purple waves, even in this wise holding her tresses with both hands close to her white cheeks, she wrung out the brine of the Ægean, showing only her bosom that indeed it is lawful to look upon; but if she be like this, let the wrath of Ares be confounded." Two more epigrams, by Julianus, Prefect of Egypt, and Leonidas of Tarentum respectively, add to the significance of Titian's work by their evidence of his familiarity with them. Julianus put it: "The Paphian has but now come forth from the sea's womb, delivered by Apelles' midwife hand. But back quickly from the picture, lest thou be wetted by the foam that drips from her tresses as she wrings them. If Cypris looked thus when she stripped for the apple, Pallas was unrighteous in laying Troy waste." And Leonidas: "Apelles having seen Cypris, the giver of marriage blessing, just escaped from her mother's bosom and still wet with bubbling foam, figured her in her most delightful loveliness, not painted but alive. With beautiful grace doth she wring out her hair with her fingertips, beautifully doth calm love flash from her eyes, and her paps, the heralds of her prime, are firm as quinces. Athena and the consort of Zeus shall say, 'Oh, Zeus, we are worsted in the judgment.'"

Certainly it seems clear as we study the canvas that not only was Titian familiar with all five epigrams, but that he wrote the immortal sixth with his brush. He saw his Venus standing in the sea, which rises halfway up her fairly heavy thighs. Beside her a scallop shell floats on the ripples lightly. She is wringing out her magnificent hair, the ends of which still trail in the water. As she bends over slightly to handle her hair the more easily, she turns her head and gazes, not at the spectator, as Crowe mistakenly asserts, but off slightly to the left. Her eyes are full, bright and wide open, her face completely unperturbed. What the English critic decries as an air that is "more conscious than innocent" is evident. Gronau points out that her beauty "may compensate for the fact that she is wanting in the conscious majesty of the goddess." Yet as one ponders over the picture and its splendor, are not complete self-assurance, beauty and knowledge the prerogatives of pagan divinity? What Apelles may have done with the same theme we know only from the epigrams in the Anthology. We do know what the sculptors of the Hellenistic period did with the goddess. We know that gradually, as the Olympian hierarchy became more familiar to man, his thinking changed regarding his divinities. The old austerity and unapproachable qualities waned, and in their stead came a more human ideal, with, if you will, a corresponding voluptuousness which nevertheless was lovelier when analyzed than mere mortality. Titian must be judged by the standards of his time, not by the standards of the ancient Greeks. And who is there to say that the glorious color of the Venetian School, for all its lack of deep and penetrating thought, has not given more human beings ideas of beauty and the ideal than the rigid and austere philosophies of the older Florentine School?

It is a relief to turn from the purely carnal to such a striking work as the *Entombment* of the Louvre. This picture made its slow way from the castle of the Marquis of Mantua to the royal collection of Charles I of England, and after his death to that of Louis XIV of France, to be placed eventually in the Louvre Museum. This is one of those extraordinary works every separate part of which manifests the very highest competence and fluency in art, yet which as a whole is more arresting than convincing. Raphael's treatment of the same theme surpasses this in both its complex lines and balance, but Titian's conception is the one that holds the spectator best and remains longest in memory because of its marked diversity of the individuals and elements, its subtle coloring and the strong action that characterizes it. Titian was seldom conventional in his working out of any theme, and fortunately for him Venice was the one city where variation in the handling of religious subjects was regarded with tolerance, if not approval. As a result he dramatized powerfully many a composition that in other hands would have lacked all the vividness he was able to infuse into it. The *Entombment* precisely illustrates this.

In the foreground Nicodemus at the right and Joseph of Arimathea at the left support most of the weight of the dead Christ, John the Evangelist in the rear passing one arm beneath His shoulder and holding up the sagging arm with his right hand. Behind to the left the Virgin and Mary Magdalen offset the heavy foliage in the upper right corner. Each figure is nobly drawn in itself. The painter's hand had so learned to obey the mind and the eye that each individual character is depicted with an effortless ease and eloquence that is liquid, spontaneous. It is only when the beholder's eye is satisfied with the general effect, his mind filled for the moment with the rich color and subtle, tenuous lighting, that he begins to analyze each part and test the whole for logic and unity.

Here the artist's fluency betrayed him. Nicodemus, as he bends with his back to us, grips the gravecloth at the Christ's hip. Opposite him Joseph has his left hand under the knees and the cloth, and holds the loose end of the cloth in his right hand. Under the weight of a large and muscular body such as that of the majestic figure of the dead Saviour, every line of that cloth would be stretched to the tightness of a steel rod. As Titian painted it no strain showed. The position of Joseph, kneeling on a block of stone, is such that he could scarcely support the heavy legs and maintain his balance. To use an architectural figure, while all the parts are correct enough in themselves, they are decorative rather than functional, and have no true organic purpose. Something besides the three men must be supporting the weight that seems almost to float between them. The stress we should observe easily is simply not there at all. The highly dramatic figures of the two Marys at the left, expressing each in her own way the suffering of the hour, are much more than the bit of highly colored and splendid *fornitura,* which is Crowe's contemptuous wave of dismissal for them. The tragic scene would not be complete without them, and to add to the intensity of the effect what could be more highly imaginative than to have the Virgin, herself immaculate, clasped in and partly leaning upon the grieving embrace of the Magdalen? The finely delineated differences of expression shown in the two faces are remarkably keen and psychologically sound, and while the Marys are subordinated to the four central figures, being made bystanders instead of principals, the picture simply could not have been painted without their presence. If they are "furniture" we must revise our opinions of many a noted painting.

In his long and detailed commentary on this canvas Crowe emphasizes the debt Titian owed to Giorgione by attributing to his influence the "picturesque form and wind-blown hair of the Evangelist," adding that Palma Vecchio is recalled clearly in a "certain moulding of face and limbs, in shallow depressions of stuff in drapery, and in contrasts that bring before us varieties of weather-beaten flesh in males, and pearly skin in women." In his very next sentence the Englishman declares roundly that neither Giorgione nor Palma ever did anything to compare with this, and that so far as expression of high feeling and passion are concerned, no one of the Venetian School could compare with Titian.

There are often many right ways of doing a thing, one of which at least has been done before. Shall we say then that because a man arrives whose genius told him certain things are best suited to his mind and manual expertness, he should not do them because they faintly suggest the work of another man now dead? And shall we say of the painter's progress little more than that he eventually "lost the impress" of the art of a predecessor? It might be fairer to remark that as he grew in artistic personality and character his spiritual stature developed correspondingly, until no method he had studied in his youth and early maturity was adequate to the full expression of his always ripening genius. Notwithstanding its defects, the *Entombment* represents Titian at his Venetian best, and brings to a triumphant close the period of progress which so auspiciously began with the noble figure of the Christ in *The Tribute Money*.

CHAPTER TEN

The Triumvirate:

Titian, Aretino, Sansovino

SPRING and the month of May in the year 1527 were a dreadful time for Rome. What happened affected Titian without changing the course of his life, drove Sansovino out of the city where he was both successful and popular, making him flee for his life, taking shelter in the safety of Venice, and settled forever the destiny of Pietro Aretino, the world's first new commentator and outstanding blackmailer. The amazing clique these three formed and what it accomplished for each constitutes as strange a story as the history of art contains.

Pope Clement VII, by name Giulio de' Medici, was a weak and vacillating man, a politician who had his moments, a patron of the arts and letters, but not the strong character the Roman Church needed at one of the most critical of the crises of its tempestuous career. It was not long after he came to the papal throne in 1523 that Clement began to breathe hard under the weight of the triple tiara he had assumed and would wear until his death in 1534. The international political and military conditions were grave and full of menace. Francis I of France and Charles V of Germany and Spain were waging their frightful dual royal over the possession and destiny of the valuable Duchy of Milan. Rome had neither the vision, the patience nor the backbone to maintain the neutrality

nd strict aloofness Clement had at first decided upon as his offi-
al policy.

Wavering and timorous, naturally predisposed toward Catholic
rance as against Protestant Germany, but pulled by Catholic
pain, the Pope drifted into the camp of Francis. When Pavia
aw the French monarch a captive and his army broken, it was too
ate to pretend. Charles was not a man to be easily deluded. The
esult of the battle was the forcing of Clement into a treaty with
he Emperor on April 1, 1525. The "overweening arrogance"
f the Spanish contingent in the Empire, however, soon sickened
he Pope of his forced alliance, and back he went into the French
roup again. A year later, on May 22, 1526, he went still fur-
her, in a step so fatal he was to rue it all his life, adhered to
he League of Cognac, and joined the Italian city-states in their
truggle against the spreading Spanish hegemony. Perhaps we of
oday are harsh in judging his blindness: it is easy to judge when
ne has all the results of the mistakes as guides. We know enough
f what was going on to realize the pressures being exerted upon
he unhappy Clement, the lack of any intelligence system to inform
im as to the military competence of the enemy, the lamentable
aucity of capable Italian leaders, the difficulty of reconciling con-
licting Italian purposes, jealousies, claims, and so on. His position
vas difficult in the extreme. Action was demanded, and he acted.

The storm burst upon the Eternal City with a fury never ex-
eeded in warfare in so-called historic civilized times except, perhaps, until Nanking was put to the torture by the Japanese. On
May 6, 1527, the imperial armies which had poured down across
he Apennines roared across the Campagna, led by the Constable
de Bourbon. Before they reached the city on the Tiber they were
met by Ugo de Moncada, the Viceroy of Naples and special ambassador of the Emperor to Rome. Spurring furiously, he galloped
up to the imperial ranks and demanded the commander. "You
cannot touch Rome," was the import of his message. "On behalf

of the Emperor I have just signed a treaty with the Pope. I
pledges the safety of the city."

Bourbon shrugged. "My troops will not listen," he answered
and the army rolled on. Soldier that he was, whatever he thought
the Duc de Bourbon was the first man on the scaling ladder.
flung against the city walls near the Vatican. Before he could se
foot on the top of the wall he was hurled back, dead. The storm
ing was over in less than a day, and then followed nights and day
of such horror as only those who have seen war at first hand car
visualize and dare not describe, such unrelieved horror as only ar
army let loose in conquest can perpetrate. So terrible was the
treatment of the fallen city that the worst the savage hordes of
Alaric, and those of Genseric after him, both of whom successively
sacked the city in the fifth century, could not compare with it. Ever
the sack by the troops of the Norman adventurer Robert Guiscard
in the eleventh century was mild beside this devastation, in which
fire and sportive torture and murder made a desolation where even
the rats could not live except upon the dead. Clement was taken
prisoner, and confined for seven maddening months in the Castle
of Sant' Angelo, from which he went into exile at Orvieto and
Viterbo. He regained his throne through the political sagacity of
Charles only on October 6, 1528, a heavily chastened man.
His capital lay in ruins around him, the population of Rome was
gone to the four winds. Almost like a second Romulus, he had to
build a new city. Not until another year had elapsed did he succeed in making his peace with the taciturn Emperor at Bologna,
where, late in the fall of 1529, he was given the monarch's help in
restoring the Medici dynasty's despotic rule in Florence.

Of the two creative artists most directly affected by the fall of
Rome, and thus eventually placed in contact with Titian, Pietro
Aretino had left the city some time before, and was in Mantua.
The other, Jacopo Sansovino, the sculptor and architect, escaped
somehow. Vasari says only that "this ruin, amidst which so many

DOGE ANDREA GRITTI

POPE PAUL III

men of genius came to an evil end, compelled Sansovino, to his infinite loss, to depart from the city, and he took refuge in Venice, whence he proposed to repair to France, where he had been invited to enter the service of the King. But while he halted in Venice to provide himself with necessaries, having been despoiled of all, the Doge Andrea Gritti, a true friend of distinguished men, was told that he was there, and desired to see him; the rather as Cardinal Grimani had given him to understand that Sansovino would be just the person they wanted to restore the cupolas of San Marco. . . . The Doge therefore caused our artist to be called, and receiving him very favourably, after many conversations he gave him to know what he wished, or rather entreated, him to find a remedy for this misfortune, which Sansovino promised to do."

As a firm friend and patron of the arts, the Doge was personally responsible, in all probability, for bringing together two such noted men as his old friend Titian and this new one whose distinguished record in Rome made him the natural choice for the repairs to the cathedral. The remark of Cosimo de' Medici the Elder in reply to a criticism of his indulgence of a wild exploit of Fra Filippo Lippi was indicative not only of the morals of Cosimo's time but of the equally lax conduct of the next century. "The vagaries of great men," the brilliant Florentine merchant prince and banker said drily, "should be forgiven, for they are celestial creatures and not beasts of burden." It was entirely natural, accordingly, for Doge Andrea to sponsor the red-headed, ugly, reputedly dissolute Florentine-Roman and foster the friendship between him and the grave, conservative Titian. Through all the tales of wildness and dissipation with which the records and legends are filled, there runs also the substantial account of enduring work accomplished. It is hard to see how a wastrel could produce such notable and so many major works and be truly dissipated. The buildings and decorative statuary Sansovino designed and created have a solidly material existence. We can examine them in detail. The stories of the wanton lives such men are supposed to have lived do not generally stand the test of a careful scrutiny.

Jacopo, born of a good family in Florence named Tatti, was laid in his mother's arms in January 1477, according to Vasari, though a footnote to the biographer's text by Blashfield declares the baptismal registers in Florence record that Jacopo d'Antonio di Jacopo Tatti, or del Tatta, was born in 1486, the son of Antonio the mattress-maker and of his wife Francesca. Temanza thought Sansovino was born in 1479, but we may stand on the official record, which makes the sculptor Titian's junior by nine years. Born with a keen mind, the boy quickly proved that neither mattress-making nor letters was to be his field. Encouraged by his mother, he began studying design, and showed such clear promise that his father reluctantly consented to let him follow his artistic leanings.

About that same time the sculptor Andrea Contucci, of Monte Sansovino, near Arezzo, set up a *bottega* or studio-workshop in Florence, and to him the lad was apprenticed. Andrea not only liked and encouraged the boy, but saw in him the necessary qualities for greatness and did everything in his power to help him. "The attachment between these two," Vasari says, "was indeed of such a character that being almost like father and son, Jacopo was no longer called De' Tatti, but Sansovino, and as he was then named, so is he now and ever will be called." The story of Italian art is full of such nicknames. Seldom, however, did the recipient of such a title do it greater honor, and work after work came from his hands with a grace and ease that earned him an enviable reputation among his brethren in the arts in Florence. One of them, Antonio da San Gallo, then the second architect of Pope Julius II, took the youngster off to Rome with him, and Sansovino was at last fully launched on the career that was to give him rank among the immortals. No less a person than Raphael was the judge of the contest in which the boy submitted a model of the *Laocoön* which easily carried off the honors. Rome at that time was the focus of the world's outstanding artistic genius. Raphael, Bramante (the Pope's chief architect), Perugino, Signorelli, Pinturicchio and many another were all busily at work there, and Sansovino threw himself into his tasks with a fervor that produced immediate and permanent results. Models, sculptures, carvings in wood, the tremendous triumphal arches erected in the city in 1514 for the arrival of the new Pope, Leo X, restorations and reconstructions of important edifices, both religious and secular, and finally the design and erection of elaborate buildings flowed in a swift and unceasing stream from his busy mind. No man, however brilliant, can maintain such continuous work and on so high a plane of quality, and fritter away his powers in profligacy; so it seems as if Sansovino's true record, at least until he reached Venice, clears him of a large part of the charges laid against him. The age was amoral, and we do not expect immaculacy of such a man; but common sense tells us his work came first always, the dubious luxury of the ignoble afterward. Doge Andrea Gritti found nothing wrong with him, and the genius with which he attacked and solved the problem posed by the weakened condition of San Marco as soon as he reached the Most Serene Republic resulted in his appointment as official architect of the State at a generous salary.

The meeting with Titian probably came very soon after he arrived. As the painter was always generously inclined toward artists in any field, and especially toward younger men, he was cordial to the newcomer and respected his talents. The first steps toward the formation of the Triumvirate that became world-famous had been taken. The third member, Pietro Aretino, impavid, blustering, quite as much the genius as his two compeers but unlike them devoting all his terrifying powers to selfish or evil purposes, had found Rome distinctly too hot for him before the catastrophe of May 6, and had gone to the relative safety of Mantua. He left there also under a serious cloud, but with a substantial cash gift from the Marquis Gonzaga, and stepped ashore on the Molo of

Venice on March 25, 1527, forty days before Rome went down in fire and blood. Sansovino, and he had been friends there, and it was to him that he went at once. Jacopo presented him to Titian, and a scant three months later the artist had immortalized this new friend on canvas. Still a little later Sansovino gave the Triumvirate immortality by introducing portrait heads of Titian, Aretino and himself on the great doors of the Sacristy of San Marco.

This close-knit group was a psychological impossibility, yet it exercised a profound influence all over Europe until death broke it up. Titian, the cool, grave conservative, concentrating on producing only the nobility of sheer beauty, could not possibly be the intimate of a gay, careless technician whose art and skill frequently outran his intelligence, and of a monster in human guise whose brilliant mind made a fetish of slander, blackmail and vice. Yet Titian was the daily companion of both Sansovino and Aretino for more than a quarter of a century, and because his own character was as rugged as the rocks of his native Cadore, he remained serenely unmoved and untouched by any of the vicissitudes of the architect and the orgies indulged in by the poet. It is possible also to pay tribute to the other two members of the Triumvirate, since deep in their souls they recognized the untarnished fibre of their companion, accepted gracefully his refusals to participate in any wantonness, and at all times accorded him the respect due to a noble nature.

The more we know today of Aretino, the clearer it becomes that, in the words of Hutton, to deny that he was a monster would be to "belittle him." Scholarship never deliberately attempts such an anomaly. The answer to all our questions regarding him lies in the character of the age that produced him as the most preternatural example of everything it conveyed. His ebullient genius, bitter and unsparing wit, uncanny apperception of the public reaction to his pasquinades, and the fact that he discovered and put to the basest uses the publicity we of today call the Press, gave him such

FRANCESCO MARIA DELLA ROVERE, DUKE OF URBINO

ELEANORA GONZAGA DELLA ROVERE, DUCHESS OF URBINO

power that he could and did dare often to pit himself unaided against pope or emperor. So confident was he of his own position that he boasted in one of his letters: "My own genius is enough. Let others worry themselves about style and so cease to be themselves. Without a master, without a model, without a guide, without artifice I go to work and earn my living, my well-being and my fame. What do I need more? With a goose-quill and a few sheets of paper I mock myself of the universe."

We can only surmise the effect this tremendous personality must have had upon the keenly sensitive painter. Roeder puts it that "Aretino divined in Titian what Titian divined in him—the soul of matter. The painter was fascinated by a model who excited all his powers because he himself possessed them so abundantly— veracity, voluptuousness, virtuosity. . . . Again and again Titian returned to that portly figure . . . never satisfied that he had plumbed the secrets of its broad bravura, its superabundance of vitality, and its jovial aroma. He painted everything," exclaims the author in his *Man of the Renaissance,* "but the smell of the man. But the smell was the soul, and it was lush and elusive."

Peter the Aretine was born during the night between Holy Thursday and Good Friday, which were the nineteenth and twentieth of April, in the year 1492, in the mountain town of Arezzo, as he himself declared in his famous *Letters.* Was the year significant; did the wail of the newborn infant in the night mark the dividing line between an old and outworn world and a new and struggling one? Lorenzo the Magnificent had already marked the year by his death, ending that period of the fresh exuberance of artificiality that went out forever with Botticelli and his imitators. The Genoese Columbus a few months later (October 12, 1492) was to step ashore on the New World, and by his discovery in the name of Spain revolutionize man's conception of his ambient. So perhaps the new baby in that little town straggling about the slope of the Tuscan hill was marked by destiny to stand between the two worlds, partaking of the nature of both and giving both much to remember.

Tradition until lately had it that Aretino was a bastard, born of a gentleman of Arezzo named Luigi Bacci and a common prostitute named Tita. Research, however, notwithstanding Aretino's own shameless half-admission ("They say that I am the son of a courtesan; it may be so"), proves that he was entirely legitimate, the child of Luca the shoemaker or cobbler and of his wife Tita, both natives of Arezzo. Luzio the research scholar, digging in the State Archives at Florence some years ago, discovered the truth of the matter when besides other documents he found and published the letter of one Medoro Nucci, a quondam friend, who now addressed an insulting letter *"Allo Aretino Pietro de Lucha calzolaio—*To Peter the Aretine, son of Luke the cobbler." Aretino was tremendously upset by it, and sent the letter to his patron of the moment, Cosimo de' Medici, with a letter of his own which tried to cover his confusion with braggadocio: "I say that I glory in the title he gives me to demean me, since it should teach the nobility to procreate sons like him whom a cobbler has begotten in Arezzo. . . . I was born there of a mender of shoes." As for his mother's character, we need only turn to the correspondence between the poet and Vasari. At the repeated urgings of Aretino Vasari finally painted a portrait of her, taken from a picture of the *Annunciation* in the church of Sant' Agostino, in which Tita had posed for the likeness of the Virgin. Like Pietro, Giorgio Vasari was an Aretine, knew the old church and its picture well, and said of it: "The face of the Madonna is the portrait of the mother of Pietro Aretino, the famous poet."

The man's callous indecency in encouraging the world to think him illegitimate and then boasting that though he was the son of a workman he had the soul of a king, was very Italian and entirely characteristic of his attitude toward life all his days. He boasted that he never needed to lie because he enjoyed telling the truth, and it was enough. Examination of his long and malodorous career bears that out so far as his written attacks on noted men went, what he said in them was true enough for the most part, and gave them some exceedingly uncomfortable hours. Aretino's baseness was in selling out one patron for another, better one, and in accepting rewards from more than one at the same time, attacking each in the cause of the other. Always he skated on the thinnest of thin ice; never did he enjoy the entire respect of anyone except perhaps the poor, to whom he gave lavishly. But the great, roaring, tempestuous volcano of a man had infinite charm for his cloak, a heart as large as his burly body, and a mind so keen and alert the finest expressions of it are among the classics of his era. Part of Titian's fondness for him was probably due to the very difference in their characters. The older man could secretly smile at the bubbling enthusiasms of the younger, value the ruthlessly honest criticisms and appreciations of his painting—since the Aretine had had some training in art as a young man—and profit by the biting, satirical comment of the practiced turncoat on political affairs and the misconduct of high officials everywhere.

How a man who boasted that he had never been to school, had neither Latin nor Greek, and was a vagabond and an acknowledged parasite all his days managed to acquire terrific facility in writing his own tongue is something of a mystery. We know Aretino managed that not inconsiderable feat very early, for part of his boyhood was spent in Perugia as apprentice to a bookbinder. Apparently, despite the slanderous *Vita dell' Aretino,* written by the false Berni to slander and vilify him, Pietro remained in Perugia until he was about twenty-four years old, coming to Rome in 1516, and remaining there living a kaleidoscopic existence until 1525. Soon after he reached the Eternal City he took a minor position in the vast establishment of the fabulously rich and powerful Sienese banker, ship-owner and merchant, Agostino Chigi. There in his villa, today known as the Farnesina, Pietro had the tremendous stimulus of seeing and listening to the conversation of practically every great man of the early sixteenth century—Raphael, Jacopo Sansovino, Giulio Romano, Giovanni da Udine, Sebastiano del Piombo; the scholars and poets Bembo, Paolo Giovio, Accolti and Tebaldo, to say nothing of scores of others, among whom was the Pope, Leo X, himself.

Undoubtedly all this time he was cultivating his muse, learning by using acute ears and an abnormally acute intelligence to evaluate the gossip and news flowing freely all about him. Of his own writings at this period we have not a scrap; but evidently by the time he left Chigi's service for that of the Pope he had established a thoroughly bad reputation and was widely feared. Rossi says in four terse lines enough to assure us of that—

> *Fa sol che l'Aretino ti sia amico*
> *Perchè gli è mal nemico a chi l'acquiste.*
> *Io ho più volte viste le sue rime ...*
> *Dio ne guardi ciascun dalla sua lingua.*

> Make sure the Aretine is your friend
> Because he is a bad enemy to whomsoever acquires him.
> I have seen his rhymes many times ...
> God guard everybody from his tongue.

Still in his twenties, the future scourge of Princes had made a strong start. His complete story is the reverse of the Horatio Alger fiction of the past century, for Aretino prospered by his viciousness, not his virtues. Penniless and hated he came to Venice where, after living richly and riotously, penniless and hated he died. He had invented what amounted to daily journalism in the letters he circulated widely, making himself so hated and feared that the papal general manager (*Datura*) sent an assassin who attacked him one morning as he was riding homeward about two o'clock, maimed his right hand and gave him such a deep chest wound he almost died, keeping his bed for several months of tedious convalescence. The two bright, clean things in his life, so far as we know, were his devotion to his daughter Adria, of whom he was passionately fond, and his love for Titian. The Master called him the *"condottiere* of letters,"* shrewdly estimating both his moral and practical values in a single scorching term.

Notwithstanding its obvious contradictions and differences, the Triumvirate not only held together solidly, but proved a mutual benefit association of vital importance to all its members. Each of them realized this phase of its existence tacitly. Aretino asked Titian to paint him, and Titian did, in a splendid portrait now lost. Pietro promptly sent it as a gift to his erstwhile patron in Mantua, with such fulsome praise of Titian that the painter profited. Again and again Aretino advertised his busy and prideful friend, and commissions for paintings resulted with gratifying frequency. It was he, indeed, who procured Titian's introduction to the Emperor Charles V and thus initiated the patronage that resulted in widening Titian's fame and brought him the knighthood of which he was so proud always that he often signed it on his finest canvases. When Aretino's noisy open house became so crowded and tempestuous he could no longer think or write, he fled to Titian's quiet studio; and the Master often came to the mansion on the Grand Canal to paint because Aretino's great north room was beautifully lighted. Something of the same sort of relation existed between both men and Sansovino; and when, in 1529, Sansovino's new Library in the Piazza partly collapsed because of the weight of ice and snow upon its roof, and Sansovino was immediately thrown into prison, it was Aretino and Titian who interceded for him and not only got him out but within about a year had him restored to his former post as city architect. In a word, each was useful to the others in a practical way, and each enjoyed the others socially in an age when perfection of external forms, completely cynical hardness and security of intellect, and an egoism so vitiating it made the soul its own self-prisoner, took the place of the stern, less welcome virtues which had vanished like morning mist.

During the three or four years following the sack of Rome, Titian made trips to Ferrara and Mantua and executed a number of canvases for Duke Alfonso and for the Marquis Gonzaga, his nephew. But the painter's main preoccupation was not so much the orders Aretino's advertising brought him as the normal requirements of various religious corporations in the city itself. Most important of all this type of painting was the contest initiated by the brotherhood of St. Peter Martyr, whose main altar was in the church of Santi Giovanni e Paolo. The Fraternity wished a great picture of the saint's murder to preside above their worship. As not only was Palma at this time high in the public esteem, but the younger Pordenone, whose art education had been gained under Titian, Giorgione and Palma, now felt sure he could compete with his elders, the monks felt themselves unable to select the best man for the task. Accordingly, they opened the lists, and Titian, Palma and Pordenone sent sketches for public exhibition. The award fell to Titian early in 1528, Palma died before the end of the summer, and the badly chagrined Pordenone lived to nurse the corroding hate of a disappointed competitor. Twice, indeed, did Titian triumph notably over his former pupil: once with the *Peter Martyr,* again with a picture in San Giovanni Elemosinario. Pordenone's hatred grew, and eventually the two were open enemies.

During the two years Titian required to complete the work, Sebastiano del Piombo, who had formed his maturer style in Rome under Michael Angelo's direct influence, spent several months in Venice, staying until March of 1529. It is easy to imagine with what eager interest the Venetian painters must have welcomed him, and how his strength as a designer and draftsman impressed and changed them. Then, during autumn of that same year, the "divine Michael Angelo" himself, driven from Florence temporarily, spent several months in the city of the lagoons. Sebastiano alone would have made a difference in the Venetian conception of form, and when to his influence was added that of the overwhelming prestige of the greatest artistic genius the world has ever known, we have but to study the *Death of St. Peter Martyr* to realize how the greatest of the Venetians was affected and how strikingly, without for a moment surrendering his individuality, he expressed all he had absorbed from the Florentine master. "We may note in this," remarks Crowe, "the origin of the feeling which prompted Tintoretto at last to write over the door of his workshop:

" '*Il disegno di Michelangelo, e il colorito di Tiziano.*' "

The masterful painting no longer exists. It was burned up in the fire of August 16, 1867, and the one hanging in its place in the church is a copy executed by Cardi da Cigoli. We know the original, however, from innumerable reproductions and copies. Crowe, who himself studied the original before the fire, declared the loss to art caused by its destruction is "irreparable because neither copy nor print can give an idea of a masterpiece that deserved to be called sublime." As Vasari described it, "it is the most renowned of any that Titian has *yet* executed" [my italics]. The German scholarship we have for years been taught to respect as so meticulously accurate and thorough has in the hands of Gronau gone badly astray in his discussion of this picture. Notwithstanding the clarity of Vasari's statement, Gronau declares the picture "was the grandest masterpiece Titian created in his whole life, the most perfect, the most admired, the best designed and the best executed." Those superlatives constitute a damaging indictment of the author for carelessness and hyperbole. Vasari said in perfectly simple words: "In the air are two nude figures of angels descending from Heaven in a blaze of light by which the picture is illumined: these are most beautiful, as is indeed the whole work, which is the best and most perfectly finished, as it is the most renowned of any that Titian has *yet* executed." Gronau is by no means the sole offender in such matters, but the difficulty of determining, when sources disagree, who is correct when original documents cannot be examined, is frequently insurmountable.

Briefly, this masterpiece has all the quality of what today we call in photography a quick "action shot." The painter captured the most violent and deadly action possible to human beings. To the left the martyr's companion monk, frightened so badly he is no longer human in expression, is running away as fast as he can, and trying at the same instant to ward off the murderous attack with wide-flung uselessly waving hands which indicate his despair and terror. Peter the Martyr is prostrate on the ground, his left hand and forearm raised to fend off the fatal blow if possible, his left elbow half raising him from the earth. Over him poises the burly figure of the assassin, sword raised, on the point of sending his blade home. High among the trees behind descend two cherubs, one extending the martyr's palm. All this, however, is merely the groundwork. The true artist steps in where the recorder of fact ends, marking the immeasurable difference between the intelligence of the mind as limned by the trained, obedient human hand, and that of the photographer's mind which can be obeyed within purely physical limits by instruments and chemicals functioning by inflexible rules.

Titian had not, as we know from previous experience, been fitted to give such a subject as this its due expression until after he had had the benefit of those months of association with Michael Angelo and Sebastian del Piombo, and Symonds' criticism of his art in general, that it was not thoughtful, is disproved so far as this painting goes by the stormy drama it presents. These are not men "as they should be" but men as the world believed and knew many of them to be in an age when tragic events were commonplace. Crowe's statement is much more apposite: "In this picture above all others Titian reproduced the human form in its grandest development, yet still within the limits which define nature as contradistinguished from the preternatural conventionalism of Michaelangelo. . . . He tempered every excess by a constant appeal to the reality, and he knew so well how to modify strain by balanced play of light and by gradation of tone that a natural effect was the consequence." The background of the forest itself is dramatized, and the almost visibly writhing forms of the trees are fully in the spirit of the action, while the distant hill country landscape gives the spaciousness needed to make the atmosphere convincing, and the armored procurer of the murder with his servant testifies to the veracity of the scene by turning among the trees to go away satisfied.

There are in this, as there certainly were in the *Entombment,* several weak points, but the violent drama of the whole covers them from all but acute technical observation. Artists from every country for centuries studied the picture, and the famous *Dialogue on Painting* written by Dolce opens with the remark by Aretino that two weeks before he had found himself captured by the solemnity of the church of Sts. John and Paul, over whose altar Titian had pictured the death of Peter Martyr in a painting so heroic and masterful "that it could be well said in truth to be on a par with nature." This altarpiece, Gronau points out, was the last one of such major works to which the painter had for almost fourteen years devoted his best efforts. As the most powerful of them all it made a fitting climax, and a triumphal one, to the period which now abruptly terminated with his introduction into the wider field of world activities as represented by such imposing figures as the jovial Francis I of France and grim Charles V, two antipodal personalities each in the grip of the same general persuasion of his own fitness and divine right to rule and to conquer.

Some time during October of 1529 Pope Clement VII sadly started for Bologna to make his peace with Charles V, who was on his way from Spain to meet him. We have already noted the reconciliation, and the restoration of the Medici in Florence. But to these we must add now the suggestion of the magnificent pageant of the imperial and papal courts at the Bologna festivities, which, as Crowe slyly observes, "half-concealed the passions and intrigues of statesmen and princes." Legend has it that Titian was invited to the occasion. Crowe says: "It would have been strange had he been asked to Bologna at the opening of the conferences which were to decide whether Venice should remain at war with the Emperor or not;—less strange had he been sent for after the ratification of peace on Christmas Eve of 1529." If we could only learn to exactly what extent international affairs directly affected Titian's career, we could clear up a great many still obscure points and understand many things for which no adequate explanations are to be found in any of the documents we know. Such knowledge would also enable us to understand, perhaps, the temporary ruptures of several interesting relations which were resumed again after some time had elapsed.

Federigo Gonzaga, Marquis of Mantua, who had been a friend, admirer and patron of the artist since Titian was formally presented at his court in January of 1523, was in studious attendance upon Charles during the Emperor's entire stay in Italy. The natural supposition is that Mantua would have presented his friend to his sovereign. Apparently nothing of the sort transpired. Vasari says plainly—and in this we can probably trust his veracity—"In 1530, when the Emperor Charles V was in Bologna, Titian, by the intervention of Pietro Aretino, was invited to that city by Cardinal Ippolito de' Medici, and there he made a magnificent portrait of his Majesty in full armour. This gave so much satisfaction that the artist received a present of a thousand crowns for the same. Out of these he had subsequently to give the half to Alfonso Lombardi the sculptor."

Many of Titian's admirers in the past have been loath to admit that such a consummate rascal as Aretino could have had a real influence on Titian's fame and prosperity. They point out that the artist was already in his late forties and a famous master when the poet from Arezzo first met him. That is all quite true, but it does not go quite far enough. Titian was fully mature, and he was known as a great master. But his fame was confined to Italy. Chubb points out in his fascinating life of the Aretine that the poet very quickly made the painter the fashion. Ruling princes became convinced by his eloquence that if they desired immortality Titian must paint them just as certainly as he, Aretino, must celebrate their greatness in his writings. And then, indirectly through the Cardinal, he managed the introduction to Charles. A letter of his to Titian about it urges him to go, and not to consider whatever the Emperor gave him as being adequate. Clearly Aretino was shrewd enough to realize that for Titian the first payment meant little; his real reward would come later in the tremendous prestige the imperial favor would create. Gronau supplements this with the statement that the Mantuan Ambassador to Venice complained in the Senate about the Emperor's niggardly ways, declaring that when his master the Duke (formerly the Marquis) took Titian so that he could do a portrait, Charles rewarded him with a single ducat only, and the Duke felt in the circumstances he could do no less than give Titian an hundred and fifty ducats from his own purse. Granting that the story may possibly have some foundation, though it seems very dubious, we wonder whether such a magnanimous gesture on the Duke's part was entirely honest, or inspired by the very natural fear that Titian would tell Aretino, and later that the poet might make capital out of it with blistering publicity at some especially inconvenient moment for the Duke.

Vasari tells the amusing story of the division between Titian and Lombardi of the thousand *scudi* the Emperor ordered paid to the painter for the portrait in armor, and the painter-critic Blashfield appends an explanatory note drawn from a life of Lombardi. According to this account Lombardi, who was a sculptor, went to Titian and begged to be allowed to enter the presence of his

Majesty, whom he very much desired to see close at hand. He would act as a color-boy, taking the place of one of the young men Titian employed as his assistants. The good-natured painter, suspecting nothing, agreed, and as he liked Alfonso did not think of watching him. During the sitting Lombardi took a position directly behind Titian, and modelled a miniature portrait in a medallion of gypsum. As Titian concluded the sitting, Lombardi finished his own work and slipped the small case containing it up his sleeve. Charles stepped forward and demanded to see what he had been doing. While Titian stood aside amazed, Lombardi humbly laid the picture in the Emperor's hand. The likeness pleased him so much he asked if Lombardi would have the courage to attempt it in marble. "Yes, Sacred Majesty," the nervous sculptor answered. "Do it, then, and bring it to me in Genoa," commanded the monarch. What Titian thought, and what he probably said in explosive Venetian dialect, when he understood that he must give up half of the Emperor's largesse to the man who had tricked him, can be imagined. Worst of all from his standpoint was the fact that when Charles saw the finished marble he was so much delighted that he gave the fortunate sculptor three hundred *scudi* more. However much Titian may have felt aggrieved at the time, he had no reason afterward ever to feel that he was not fully appreciated by Charles.

The barriers that always surround royalty had been broken down, and the painter returned to Venice with his unfinished canvas, which represented his imperial sitter in armor, to complete it at his convenience. Sturdy mountaineer that he was, merely veneered with the manners of the city which was treating him so generously, Titian probably felt less self-conscious in the presence of the man who was already so close to controlling the destiny of the world than most men except Aretino would. Charles was also a strong man, and for all his belief in his divine right, he knew the frame of mind in which strong men like those of his own kingdom of Spanish Aragón viewed their monarchs. For a long time the

Aragonese formula in swearing in a king was: "We, who are as good as you," and ended with the clear threat of impeachment if the king proved unsatisfactory to them. So Charles respected the big, bluff man behind the easel who did not make any attempt to flatter or prettify his unwholesome-looking sitter.

No sooner was Titian back again in his studio than he was drawn into a competition for a small picture for the church of San Giovanni Elemosinario, already mentioned; and again Pordenone was not only his competitor but the bad loser of the contest. "Whatever care and pains Pordenone took," Vasari observes coldly, "he could not equal or even approach the work of" Titian. Then the latter was commissioned to paint an *Annunciation* for the church of Sta. Maria degli Angeli, and when the church authorities refused to pay the five hundred crowns at which the painter priced his work, he accepted Aretino's advice and sent the canvas as a gift to the Emperor. At least, that is Vasari's version. Blashfield remarks in a note on the incident that Titian sent the picture to the Empress, but confirms Vasari's statement that the delighted Emperor in recompense sent the painter two thousand crowns. Crowe adds that the painting was destroyed in Spain. Pordenone, according to Vasari, had some small consolation by being retained to fill the place left vacant by the sending of the *Annunciation* to the Empress.

Titian was nothing if not industrious. His readiness for orders and the adroit super-salesmanship and diplomacy of Aretino kept him as steadily at work as any unimaginative businessman. There never was a time when, in modern phraseology, he did not have a considerable "backlog" of unfilled commissions. Before he settled his squabble with the Brotherhood of St. Peter Martyr about the price to be paid for his work in Santi Giovanni e Paolo he was working at several canvases for the Marquis of Mantua. The latter's Venetian envoy, Giacomo Malatesta, reported to his master on February 5, 1530, that the canvas showing the Madonna with

St. Catherine and another of "nude ladies" were well along toward
completion and would be delivered respectively at the coming of
Lent and at Easter. A third, depicting bathing women, when Malatesta reported was in the sketch stage only, but the portrait of the
Marquis in armor was almost finished. Vasari said of the latter
that "the Duke appears to breathe," so lifelike was it. It seems
strange to us of today that Vasari should have been so slipshod in
recording the works of a man of such unremitting effort as Titian
Again and again in other, later, sources references occur to
pictures the Florentine never mentions or accounts for by inference. His chronology is not always accurate, either, and his descriptions sometimes tend to be confusing. On the other hand, he
names other paintings later critics do not mention.

While Titian was in Mantua, after he had completed the portrait of the Duke he executed one of his brother the Cardinal, and
when that was hung, he painted a series of eleven medallions of
the Twelve Caesars meant as decorations for one of the rooms
in the Castle designed by Giulio Romano who, when the eleven
were done, himself did the twelfth of the series and painted a story
from the "Lives of the Caesars under each head." All the medallions were taken to England in 1628, and later presented to the
Spanish Ambassador as a gift for his royal master. Later they completely disappeared. As they are no longer in existence and form
a highly controversial subject of which the details are of no particular interest here and now, it is more to the point to consider
the painting for the little country church of Pieve di Cadore,
Titian's birthplace, in which the Master is supposed to have pictured himself as an acolyte. Blashfield apparently thinks, with
Crowe, that Orazio, Titian's faithful second son and principal assistant, painted the likeness of his kneeling father.

As in the case of many other works of Titian, the *Virgin with
St. Catherine* seems impossible now to identify positively. Crowe
declares it to be identical with the *Virgin and the Rabbit* now in

the Louvre, and Gronau compares it both to that picture and to the London National Gallery canvas of the *Virgin with the Youthful St. John and St. Catherine*. A replica of the London picture is in the Pitti at Florence, but it curiously omits the boy St. John, who is included in the London canvas. The omission makes the position of the Virgin's hand meaningless, since it is extended, as in the London copy, to receive the flowers the boy saint offers. Aside from this, the attitudes of the English and German critics are almost antipodal regarding Titian's success in this presentation of the theme.

Gronau dismisses the picture with chill disrelish: "The whole scene gives an impression as of simple people happy in the enjoyment of the beautiful and rich nature about them. The divine element has been superseded by one that is merely human." Crowe, on the contrary, is enthusiastically human: "As St. Catherine stoops to the Virgin she holds the infant Christ in a muslin cloth, and the child looks half merrily, half shyly at the rabbit, catching at the saint's face to make sure of near support, and making signs of half distress with one of its hands. Palma has made us acquainted with various manifestations of homely feeling in his 'Holy Conversations'. Titian here watches life with an equal and yet more sensitive insight, refining upon that which is merely familiar by bringing before his admirers figures which they revere, in the sweetest and most graceful converse. Trust as displayed in nature is put before us with such singular elevation, in a medium so enchanting from its tone and air and vegetation, that it vies with the more severe sublimity of works embodying the highest ideals of form. . . . We ask ourselves indeed . . . whether an arist with only fleeting ties could have created such a masterpiece; and the answer seems to be that nature here gushes from the innermost recesses of a man's heart who has begun to know the charms of paternity, who has watched a young mother and her yearling child, and seized at a glance those charming but minute passages which seldom or ever meet any but a father's eye." Perhaps, as we study the contrasting statements, the two men are after all not quite so far apart as they seem on a single reading.

No replicas seem ever to have been made of this picture, but the one most similar to it in spirit, the *Virgin's Rest in Egypt,* was much copied, and with varying success. These replicas are still in possession of the galleries in Modena, El Escorial in Spain, Stockholm, Sweden, and Berlin. The rabbit Madonna was one of many canvases Titian executed for his princely friend the Duke of Mantua. He naturally was a deeply interested participant in the Bologna festivities and intrigues surrounding the visit of the Emperor. When Charles and Clement left—the Emperor riding out on March 23, the Pope on March 31, 1530—Mantua saw an opportunity to engage the favor of the imperial household for himself. During his stay in Bologna Charles had more than once accepted the hospitality of Count Pepoli, whose wife had an exceedingly attractive lady-in-waiting named Cornelia. Charles's chief political secretary and confidential man of affairs, a gentleman named Covos, had seen and fallen in love with her. To win Covos's favor, and so beyond doubt through him influence the Emperor, Mantua sent a hurry call to Titian, begging him to come to Mantua at once to paint the girl's portrait. Not content with that, he sent also for Giovanni da Bologna to make a statue of her, so that Covos might have the most convincing evidence possible that his interests were dear to a very free-handed and sympathetic lord.

Titian, in his usual dilatory fashion, did not reach Mantua until July. He brought a letter of introduction to the Countess Pepoli from the Marquis Gonzaga, giving him the highest praise and begging her permission for the taking of the portrait. Giovanni the sculptor had arrived a few days before, and the two masters met at the entrance to the Pepoli palace. Giovanni was furious. There followed two amazing letters to the Duke, one from the incandescent Bolognese, who had immediately gone back home in a passion, the other a characteristically calm and calculating proposal from the imperturbable Cadorine. Canon Braghirolli published them both in his *Unpublished Letters,* and Crowe and Cavalcaselle carried them in an appendix.

Giovanni da Bologna's tone was testimony enough to the fact that he was both ill and angry, for his words were hardly such as one addresses to a reigning prince possessed of very considerable power. He wrote:

"Most Illustrious Lord:

"As per instructions of Your Excellency, it was understood that I take the likeness of the Cornelia. I was sick abed at the time, but as soon as I was able to, I dressed, got on a horse and went to the house of the Lady Isabella. There I found Messer Titian, who said to me that Your Excellency had ordered him to do what I had come to do. I ask nothing more than that Your Excellency keep faith with me. I had a swollen jaw, and all my teeth, as he [Titian] could see, chattered in my mouth because of the fever I had caught on the Tè. I admit having left without license, but God knows I had intended to remain in Mantua for the three festivals. However, I cannot go against Heaven. At any rate, if I live and am healthy, I hope Your Excellency will think well of my services, the more so since you will see me in Mantua at the commands of your Illustrious Lordship, to which I reverently bow and recommend myself.

"In Bologna   "The Bolognese, servant
"1 July, 1530.   of Yr. Ill. Lordship."

Notwithstanding its character, the letter must have made the Marquis-Duke laugh by its helpless rage. Titian's letter probably made him smile, but for a different reason, and then feel well satisfied that he had so intelligent and masterful an artist at his disposal. Titian wrote:

"Most Illustrious Duke:

"This lady, otherwise Cornelia, is not here in Mantua. The Lady Isabella has sent her to stay at Nivolara for a change of air, as she is ill, and they say she is somewhat bewildered by the illness; nevertheless, she is better. Understanding this and doubting that I could accomplish much, besides being myself seriously affected by the great heat, and being unwilling to become completely ill, I have done nothing further, thinking thus better to serve you to your greater satisfaction. These gentle ladies have so impressed me with her beautiful features that I am eager to paint her so that whoever knows her will say I have done her portrait often. For this reason I beg Yr. Exc. to have sent to me—I will show you the result in about ten days—at Venice the picture that other painter did of the said Cornelia. I will send them both back to you, and Yr. Exc. can compare them for yourself and see how I wish to serve you in this as in everything else as long as I live. Once Yr. Exc. has seen my picture, if there is anything wrong with it I shall be glad to go to Nivolara to remedy it, but I do not believe that will be necessary. I kiss Yr. Exc's hand.

"In Bologna,   "Yr. Exc's servant
"12 July, 1530.   Titian V."

Three days later Titian was back at home in his Casa Grande, ill himself. Less than three weeks later the great blow of his life fell when his wife Cecilia was struck down. How he took the bereavement was told by Agnello, the Duke's envoy in Venice. Writing the news to the "Magnificent Messere Jo. Jacomo Calandra, Ducal Secretary and Castellan of Mantau," he said simply on August 6: "Our Master Titian is utterly disconsolate at the loss of his wife, who was buried yesterday. He told me that through the trouble in which he was involved by his wife's illness he was not able to work at the portrait of Cornelia nor at the picture of the nudes that he is doing for our Illustrious Lord, which will be a lovely thing and which he believes he will have finished this month.

Master Titian wishes to know how our Signore is satisfied with his *St. Sebastian* recently sent him, an ordinary performance compared with the nudes, and which he gave him merely for entertainment and as a proof of the service he wishes to render him."

Ciani tells us that Titian in his trouble appealed immediately to his sister Orsa for help. His young children needed a woman's care, and he could give them only the most casual attention because of his own half-sick and overworked condition. Orsa Vecelli responded promptly, came down from Pieve and whole-heartedly spent the rest of her life taking care of her famous brother and his family so devotedly that Aretino could canonize her in one of his glowing letters as "sister, daughter, mother, companion, steward of the household." But regardless of Orsa's loving care, the old home in San Samuele could not be the same without Cecilia. Besides, it was shut in and cramped, and the painter's free spirit but aging, weary, only half-well physical body needed space, air and light. Titian decided to move.

CHAPTER ELEVEN

Biri Grande and a New Life

In 1530 the Most Serene Republic was little like the Venice of today. Its heart, lusty and full-blooded, beat about the once open, tree-shaded meadow flanked by the Cathedral of San Marco and the Palazzo Ducale. Between Cathedral and Molo or gondola landing-place towered the huge Campanile. But the long and beautiful structure of Sansovino's great Library had not yet been more than imagined on paper. The buzzing swarms pouring into and out of the Piazza from the Merceria beehive saw the vast pile of the Procuratie Vecchie, just completed, and opposite, on the south side of the square, the Hospital of Doge Pietro Orseolo beside the Campanile. The irregular congeries of low buildings also on the south side formed additional offices for the Procurators. These old structures were eventually to be torn down because they spoiled the appearance of the Piazza as much as the disreputable-looking hostelries which occupied the site Sansovino had just been given for the erection of his Library.

As is true of all other great capitals, Venice grew spasmodically, at first without plan or purpose other than the desire of its inhabitants to be as close to the foci of their lives as possible. The natural result was the dense overcrowding of the districts closest to the

Cathedral and the Ducal Palace. Even the slum quarter was close at hand, and so small is the area that most of the distances to various important edifices may be measured in hundreds of yards from the Piazza. The San Samuele quarter, about halfway between the Rialto and San Marco, was typically congested. The heavy, sluggish air stirred not at all through the tall, ill-ventilated houses during the torpid Venetian summer which, as all of us know who have experienced it, can be tropical in intensity and all but unbearable. Titian in 1530 was fifty-three years old, burdened with a sad heart in addition to a tremendous load of work, and felt that he must move to some brighter, airier and more refreshing location, away from the noise and the crowds, the stifling atmosphere and the accessibility that must have added to his problems by leaving him a prey to visitors of every shade of distinction.

Crowe and Cavalcaselle are apparently wrong in saying that Titian lived in the San Samuele mansion until after his wife's death. G. Saccardo, in the *Archivio Veneto,* T. xxxv, pp. 405-7, Pt. 2, fasc. 70, 1888, publishes the words of the Council of Ten regarding the Duke of Milan's former house, and two records of the dreaded Signori di Notte which prove his case. Saccardo said, adapting from Lorenzi: "Crowe and Cavalcaselle (*Life of Titian*) interpret badly the decree of the Council of X. In that, in 1515, they ordered the restoration of the House formerly of the Duke of Millan in San Samuele where he [Titian] *has the models of the pictures he is to make in the great Council* [Saccardo's italics]. The distinguished authors give too much importance to this fragment, and go far afield in leaving us to believe it treats of Titian's residence, whereas it was not intended to speak of anything but the painter's studio. . . . It was all a pretty romance. Three years before going to live in Biri Grande Titian resided in San Polo" in the house of a family named Tron. The statement is further proved by the minutes of the Signori di Notte (reg. 22, c. 29), which speak of Titian as "*Magistri Tutiani, pictoris habitatoris in confinio Santi Pauli in do-*

mibus de ka Trono." Police records such as this are very apt to be accurate so far as residence is concerned.

It is interesting to note in connection with the error about housing that the records cover two criminal cases indirectly involving the painter. Both were indictments for murder. In each case the victim was a servant of Titian. Neither one has ever, so far as available data go, been satisfactorily explained. The times, of course, were tumultuous and human life had small value, so there is nothing unusual about assassination. It may have been merely a matter of the unhappy victim having paid undue attention to some woman, which was the commonest cause of violence. On the other hand, since the identification of the victim in each instance was by naming him as a servant of Titian, the painter may have had a quarrel in which an innocent servant was killed as a sharp warning to the master. Such things occurred.

The first crime was committed in 1528, when Titian had removed from San Samuele and was living with his sister Orsa and his children in the Tron mansion. The minute of the Signori di Notte, in stilted Latin, reads: "Nobleman Ser Baptista Quirino, son of the late Nobleman Paul Quirino of the district of St. Thomas, inculpated the month of November MDXXVIII as having wounded the late Aloysius de Cypro, at that time a servant of Master Titian the painter, inhabitant of the district of St. Paul in the house known as Ca Tron. He wounded him with the point under the left eye, so that he migrated from this life. On the 27th May, 1530, was banished and posted the said Baptista Quirino."

The second murder occurred in 1566, when Titian was eighty-nine years old, and living in Biri Grande. By this time the great artist had become so universally famous there was no need to say who he was, as the minute of the authorities shows. What makes the second case more curious and interesting is that the second victim was a mountaineer compatriot as well as a servant. The account reads, freely rendered from the Latin: "Nicolò da Venesia, formerly known as Battista Ranpogna, charged by imputation with the death of the late Mathio, Cadorine, servant of Titian, was remitted to the Signor Zudesi de Propio the 4th of February, 1565." The date is Venetian Old Style. In our reckoning it was 1566. Astonishing enough to turn up unexpectedly two exactly similar tragedies, thirty-eight years apart, in the life of the same man, neither one of them explicable and neither one even to be guessed at by anything else we know of Titian's otherwise peaceful existence.

How the painter conducted his house-hunting, with the first murder so close in the background, and whether he had any help in it, we shall probably never know. It is reasonably safe to assume that he discussed it at some length and again and again with both Sansovino and Aretino, since the three were *compari* or intimates. It may, indeed, have been Sansovino who remembered that the patrician Ser Alvise Polani had, three years before, in 1527, built a splendid mansion in the Biri Grande district on the far northern side of the city, close to the water. Although it was barely half a mile distant from San Samuele as the gull flies, it was far enough away to be in practically the open country. The location was about midway between the churches of the Gesuiti and SS. Giovanni e Paolo. Ser Alvise had called the building the Casa Grande, and Titian executed a curious lease with Polani's son-in-law, Messer Leonardo Molin, covering at first only the upper floor and later the entire building and its spacious grounds. Examination of that one document tells a great deal more than the mere dry fact of the rental.

On September 1, 1531, according to Cadorin, Titian, his sister Orsa and the family moved into their new suburban quarters, probably with a sigh of satisfaction in the fresher air, the extended views, and the freedom from annoyances. The house stood somewhat back from the edge of the wide lagoon to the north of the city, and was flanked by handsome gardens extending partly along the water's edge. As Crowe and Cavalcaselle describe the building, which they personally visited in the years during which it was still shown to the public, "The basements were let to various tenants, whilst the upper storey, composed of one large apartment and several smaller ones, was entered by a terraced lodge, to which there was an ascent from the garden by a flight of steps. From the garden the view extended [over the little cemetery island, in the near foreground of the lagoon] to Murano and the hills of Ceneda, between which, on favourable days, the peak of Antelao, the tutelary dolomite of the Cadorines, might be seen against the morning sky. We can fancy such a garden and such a house having peculiar attractions for Titian, who would find there constant memories of his native Alps, rural surroundings, and complete freedom from the noise of traffic."

We can imagine with what relief he would think of the two boys, Pomponio and Orazio, and their little sister Lavinia, a wee baby in Orsa's arms, as frolicking in the sunny garden instead of having only congested streets for their airings. He could look up from his easel also and feast his eyes on the sheen of the ripples that matched the finish of the colors he laid on masterfully with brush and fingers. In the intervals between his frequent journeys back to Cadore he could take comfort in seeing from his eyrie what he so often drank in through closer contacts. His choice was a happy one, and he never regretted it, for though he was out literally in the country, he was still close enough to permit the continuance of the closest relations with his friends and patrons. As a result, the Triumvirate flourished with an even greater zest, and we know from one detailed description the impression that the house, its master and his friends made on distinguished visitors.

Titian renewed his partial lease several times, and then, in 1536, because in part he was dissatisfied with the tenants who held the lower floors, he rented the entire dwelling. One source declares that certain ladies of the evening, of whom Venice had more than enough in Renaissance times, offended the painter not by their profession but by the boisterousness of their entertainments. So he leased their apartments, rented them to quiet burghers, and had peace again. In 1549 he bought the property outright and for the rest of his life spent much time and money on improving it. His son Pomponio sold it all in 1589. Unfortunately, we know very little about the interior of the house and its furnishings. Communicative to garrulity about his uncompleted commissions and the moneys due him, Titian was as silent as Molmenti's traditional Venetian about other matters. All we know with any certainty is that he had innumerable canvases in his studio at all times, ranging from the completed works he kept on hand to give as presents to men of rank and value, to studies, sketches and partly finished pictures on order; also that he had received many beautiful and costly gifts, some of which undoubtedly enriched his surroundings.

At the time Titian went to live in Biri Grande the Fondamento Nuovo or new sea-wall had not been built, and no ugly clutter of artisans' and laborers' homes obscured the painter's view. The suburb, indeed, was a fashionable one, and in the evening, as soon as sunset had cooled the air, the lagoon filled with gondole, pulsed with music from lyric voices and instruments. The Latin grammarian Francesco Priscianese, who was a dinner guest in the gardens of the Casa Grande, has left us in his dusty old *Grammar* a vivid impression of what sort of life the painter and his friends lived in apparently almost idyllic conditions. On August 1, 1540, the Roman, who was visiting in Venice, where he had hopes of having his *Grammar* adopted by the schools, was invited to dine and accepted gladly.

"I was invited on the day of the Kalends of August," he recorded, "to celebrate that feast they call the *ferr'agosto*—why I do not know, though it was discussed a good deal during the evening—in the delightful garden of Messer Tiziano Vecellio, an excellent painter, as is known by everyone. There were gathered there with the said Messer Tiziano, since like seeks like, some of the most re-markable personages in the city: chiefly Messer Pietro Aretino, a new miracle of nature. Next to him, Messer Jacopo Tatti, other-wise known as Il Sansovino, as masterful a copier of nature with his chisel as is our host with his pencil; and finally Messer Jacopo Nardi [a warm friend of Titian, a scholar, and member of a cele-brated Venetian family] and myself; so that I made a fourth [guest] among so much wisdom.

"The sun's heat was still considerable, though the garden is shady, and we put in the time before the tables were set out in ad-miring the lifelike figures in the excellent paintings with which the master's house was filled, and in rejoicing ourselves with the singu-lar beauty and charm of the garden, which moved us all to admi-ration. The place is situated at the extreme limits of Venice upon the sea. From it one overlooks the pretty little island of Murano and other pleasant spots. When the sun had set this part of the sea was thronged with gondole full of beautiful women, and until midnight as we feasted, the night resounded with singing and the music of various instruments.

"Messer Tiziano's garden is so well laid out and so beautiful and praised by all that it recalled St. Agatha to me and made me wish to see you again, so much so that it was hard for me to realize whether I was in Rome or Venice. At last the supper was served, not less well planned than it was bountiful. In addition to the most delicate viands and choicest wines, we had all those delights suited to the season, the guests and the feast itself. We had just reached the fruits for dessert when your letters arrived, like some fruit of a new and delicious kind. . . . I read them before all . . . and because in praising the Latin tongue the Tuscan was rebuked, Aretino became furiously angry. If we had not prevented him, I think he would have put his hand on the spot to one of the most cruel of invectives, crying out hotly for paper and a pen, though he kept right on doing a good deal with words. At last, however, we quieted him, and the supper finished in gaiety."

It was Aretino, always the man of news, good or bad, who eventually told Priscianese that his *Grammar* had actually been successfully adopted by some of the local schools. The same newshawk five years later warmly congratulated Messer Jacopo Nardi on the publication of his translation of Livy, dedicated to the Marquis of Vasto. These pleasantly convivial gatherings were held often at Aretino's house, and not infrequently women were among the guests, sometimes ladies, oftener the models Titian and Sansovino used, with a sprinkling from Aretino's harem, who lived in his mansion. We have already seen what Titian's attitude was on such occasions, and the relative gravity of his conduct as compared with that of the boisterous littérateur and the red-bearded, bulbous-nosed sculptor.

Today the Casa Grande is no longer in a fashionable quarter, it has no view of any sort, and it is no longer a private residence. With the construction of the Fondamento Nuovo and the building of houses and other edifices near by the character of the district completely changed. The newer buildings blocked any vista, the Casa Grande itself became part of a solid row of houses, and the loggia entrance from the garden was torn down. Many of the near-by creeks were filled in, contours were changed, a road was laid out along the waterfront, and houses put up beside it until the older mansion was entirely enclosed, its charm forever gone. It is not worth the time and trouble to seek out the location now: the glory of Titian lies elsewhere.

Wise enough to have learned the lesson that without work life is empty and a mockery, Titian toiled steadily at his painting regardless of both his impaired health and his empty heart. We do not know whether he was the type of man who can really love but once, and having loved must always walk quietly alone in despair when the loved one is taken; but from the energy with which he threw himself into every artistic activity and the complete absence of any hint as to interest in any woman in any way, it seems fair to assume Cecilia dead still held her place in his heart to the exclusion of everyone else. It is a pleasant thought; and he was a brave and gallant gentleman who, in an age whose profligacies were notorious, wore the guerdon of his dead love as proudly as he later wore the chain and spurs of knighthood. As Kipling said of Lord Roberts, Titian did not "advertise."

While he was living in the Ca Tron in San Polo, Titian became still more melancholy about the benefice that had been promised him by the Duke of Mantua for his oldest son, Pomponio. How this promise was made or what led up to it is not certain, but it seems that Aretino may have had a hand in it. Heath says that the *Madonna del Coniglio* (*of the Rabbit*), painted for Duke Federigo Gonzaga, was what caused the promise, though he does not give any evidence to support the statement and Crowe does not mention any such commission. Certainly the Aretine knew all about it, and pointed out to Titian the benefits it would bring him personally before the boy was old enough to take up the rich curacy of Medole himself. So on September 27, 1530, we find the Venetian representative of the Duke, Messer Benedetto Agnello, writing to the Castellan, Messer Calandra, at Mantua: "It is several days since I have seen M. Titian, but from what I understand, his health is not yet good. When I called upon him the other day, he told me that he would make a quick recovery if the news came to him that our Lord had given him possession of the benefice of Medole, because that would brighten up everything, and that his indisposition is caused by his melancholic humour."

It is no wonder that Titian felt himself in a most uncomfortable position. When the promise was made he unwisely put the boy into clerical dress, and all Venice knew what was expected. When the confirmation failed to come for a long time, and the painter re-

membered how conveniently short princely memories sometimes
were under the pressure of circumstances, he felt he must either un-
frock Pomponio himself or secure the comforting fulfillment of the
Duke's word. As in many other cases nothing happened for
months, and on July 12, 1531, almost a year later, he wrote personally to the Duke to express himself more or less bluntly. Crowe
gives the letter, originally published by Pungileoni and reprinted
by Cadorin, in these words: "I have been expecting the bull of the
benefice of Medole which your Excellency gave me for my son Pomponio last year, and seeing that the matter is delayed beyond
measure, and what is worse, that I have not received the income of
the benefice, I find myself in a state of great discontent. It would
be greatly to my dishonor and infamy if my boy should be forced to
change the priest's dress, which he wears with so much pleasure,
after all Venice has been made acquainted with the gift made to
him of this benefice by your Excellency." Two weeks later he wrote
in a very different tone. The Duke meantime had written him of
his approaching marriage, and confirmed the gift of the benefice.
Titian was apologetic for not having read correctly previous letters,
which were not clear, congratulated the Duke on his approaching
nuptials and prayed for his everlasting happiness, then thanked
him warmly for the expected gift. On September 7, 1531, Agnello
wrote his master briefly: "I have given the bulls [confirming the
curacy of Medole] to M. Titian, who expressed the greatest
pleasure and could not say enough. I also demanded that he
immediately finish the pictures he has promised Y. E., as your
debtor, and get them off to you quickly." Crowe is sarcastic and
contemptuous regarding this episode, condemning Titian unspar-
ingly. "There is something painfully comic in the letters in which
Titian treats of these matters bartering his skill as a painter for the
fat returns of a Lombard curacy." They do not make happy reading,
it is true; but the times were those of promises made to be broken,
of total expediency, of cynical flattery for any purpose. If Titian

seemed to cringe and scrape before dukes and cardinals and such, those very dignitaries did exactly the same things before their superiors in rank—kings and popes and emperors—and for the same exact purposes. If we judge, we must have all the facts, and it is unjust to single out one great man for the pillory because he comported himself according to the rules of the game as all men then understood them.

The ten years following Titian's removal from San Polo to Biri Grande were busy and eventful ones. Federigo Duke of Mantua remained his most important patron, and the most influential one. The painter sent him a *St. Jerome* early in 1531, and in the letter acknowledging it the Duke ordered a Magdalen, "as beautiful but as tearful as possible." Both the Duke and his mother had an interest in this, as they meant their picture to be a bribe to the Marquis del Vasto, who was in a position to do much for Mantua. Crowe says the Duke was so pleased with the picture that he immediately ordered a replica of it for himself. Davalos, or the Marquis del Vasto, seems to have received the original. When the entire Mantuan collection was removed to Venice, a Titian *Magdalen* in it was listed as a copy only. The painter liked the subject, and the Duke of Candia, Francesco di Pietro Morosini, writing to F. Lollino at Venice in 1601, said the painter had declared he had earned more than two thousand *scudi* painting the repentant saint. When he painted the first one, and what became of the del Vasto example no one knows. According again to Crowe, the earliest existing example is the one painted, probably, for Duke Francesco of Urbino, now in the Pitti Palace. It is one of the loveliest studies of the lush type of feminine beauty the Master ever set upon canvas in his familiar glowing color, and merits all the praise that has been lavished upon it. Yet it was hastily accomplished—begun March 18; finished, including the varnishing, April 12, 1531—and is an idealized reflection of nude grace and sensuous charm rather than of a penitent saint. The subject was a highly popular one, and

Crowe reports that "the friends of this form of art were so numerous that copies could not be made fast enough for them, but the
copies were not executed by Titian, seldom even by his immediate
disciples." Some of the copies, he adds, "are quite unworthy of
Titian's name."

Another of the Gonzaga pictures that is missing is the *St. Jerome*.
This saint and his very placid-looking lion proved another favorite
subject with patrons, and everyone recognizes the stern old grey-
beard with the stone in his hand, glaring at a crucifix while the
lion stares at him in a puzzled fashion, and a skull on the ground
near by carries its own message. Most of the copies are weak,
and few if any are by even Titian's immediate followers. The
Master was too fully occupied with his three principal patrons to
think about copying.

First of all he had to consider Doge Andrea Gritti, to whom he
owed so much, and whose official needs kept up a steady pace. Aretino was becoming increasingly important to him as the man who,
more than any other in Europe, was listened to by the very highest;
and in return for the valuable advertising Pietro gave him, Titian
sounded his friend's praises in both speech and letters, and worked
for his advantage in many influential quarters. Federigo of Mantua
remained constant, and his demands were unceasing. Last of all
the grim old hunchback Francesco Sforza, Duke of Milan, whose
favors came through the Castellan of that fortress-city, Maximilian
Stampa, had to be given serious attention. Again Aretino had a
hand in affairs. In October of 1531 he sent as gifts to Stampa a
gem in the form of a medallion carved by Luigi Anichino, a lapidary who was close to the Triumvirate, a crystal mirror and buck-
lers, and, by no means least important, a picture of the boy *St. John
the Evangelist*. The Aretine waxed lyrical in the letter with which
he accompanied the gifts, going so far as to say that the lamb beside the boy saint was so lifelike it would make a ewe bleat. It is
not unlikely in such circumstances that Aretino was responsible for

the paintings Titian executed less than three years later of Stampa himself, of Duke Francesco, and of the child bride Charles V gave the old monster in 1534.

These and many other paintings of the period might almost be called casuals in comparison with official commissions such as the splendid canvas of Doge Andrea Gritti kneeling before St. Mark and the Virgin, who were attended by a whole court of saints: Bernardino, Alvise and Marina. According to the diarist Sanuto, who filled scores of fat tomes with dry records of what he daily heard and saw of life in the city, much of it a mere parroting of the unimportant but with an occasional invaluable paragraph, a popular story of the day accounts for the presence in the picture of these particular saints. In his 55th volume, under the date of October 6, 1531, Sanuto wrote: "And it is commented that among these three saints there arose differences as to which one had elected the Doge. St. Bernardino declared he had been elected on my Day. Santa Marina declared he was elected because he recovered Padua on my Day, the 17th of July. St. Alvise said I bear the name of that Alvise Pisano, Procurator of St. Mark, who was the main cause of his selection. St. Mark, hearing of the squabble among the saints, brought them all before Our Lady with the Doge to settle the matter of the election to the dogate of his Serenity. That this fine picture by Titian the painter is very beautiful was the comment made by all whom I have wished to memorialize."

During the winter of thirty-one Titian probably went back to Cadore for a much needed refreshment in the cold and bracing mountain air, on one of his periodical vacations from the lagoon, and with the coming of summer was once more in Mantua. In the meantime Emperor Charles V had been a very busy man. After Clement VII crowned him at Bologna, Florence was the only Italian state in rebellion against him. But to the north France had spurred on the dreaded Turk to invade Hungary and take Austria if he could. The Emperor had to make extraordinary exertions to get

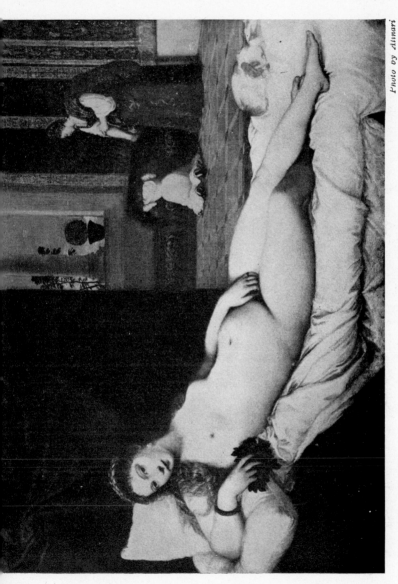

THE VENUS OF URBINO

ogether an army to march against the Moslem invasion. In the
interim, conditions within the Church made it essential to renego-
tiate several matters, and Charles was forced to persuade the Pope
to call a general council, promising himself to meet the Pontiff at
Bologna as soon as possible. By summer the Turk was driven away,
and in November Charles, with a formidable staff of generals at
his back, arrived and turned over the management of Italian affairs to his favorite Covos, Commander of Castile.

This gentleman, as will be remembered, was fond of pictures,
and no sooner was he known to be the man responsible for practically everything in Italy except in the Papal States than intrigues
for his favor began. He was all but smothered under hospitalities
and bribes. Alfonso of Ferrara ordered his agents to win Covos at
any price, and Titian was called upon to make good the attempt
with a fine painting. From all this the Duke of Mantua stood aside
because the Emperor had already done more for his domains than
for those of any other Italian lord except Sforza. Instead of paying
attention to Covos, Mantua wined and dined and flattered the Emperor personally. Charles was barely there when he demanded to
see the Gonzaga art treasures, and the Duke led him in triumph
through the newly decorated parts of the castle, and especially
about that room, the Sala d'Armi, where he kept his finest pictures.
Raphael, Titian, Andrea del Sarto and a good Fleming were all
there. Charles studied them with the keenly appraising eye of the
connoisseur, and was so impressed by Titian's likeness of the Duke
that he said he must have a portrait of himself by the same masterful hand. The Duke dashed off a hurry call to Titian on November
7, and followed it the same day with a second note, increasing his
urgency and asking him to bring along some fish. The painter,
however, did not leave Biri Grande for Mantua, but in his usual
leisurely fashion followed the imperial court to Bologna.

It has been twice shown already that Titian was able to ride the
often swirling political tides of the day, and he did so now. For

the past two years the good-sized cities of Reggio and Modena ha‹
been occupied by imperial garrisons, and the Emperor was unde‹
cided whether to turn the towns over to the Pope or to the Duke o‹
Ferrara. Alfonso desperately wanted them to strengthen his de‹
mesne, and had sent his most capable and trustworthy representa‹
tives to Bologna to try to secure them. The man who could turı
the scales was Covos, and Titian, as the man who best knew exactl›
the values of Alfonso's choice collection of art, was immediatel›
in demand. Charles himself discussed the matter with the painter
and Titian and Covos held talk after talk. Apparently Titiar
became restive in the circumstances, and to keep him quiet, Covo:
arranged that he paint the Emperor's portrait. Meantime he
Covos, drew up a long list of the pictures Charles most desired fron
Alfonso, presented it to the Ferrarese envoys, who suggested Titiar
as the man best fitted to advise about the matter, and were bluntl›
told that whatever else they might do, they must see to it that the
portraits of the Duke himself and of the Emperor were sent at once.
Other pictures were involved, Titian was again drawn into the
debate, and in the end Covos made his point and the pictures were
sent, with a letter from the despoiled Duke asking if there was
anything else he could do.

At this point one of the familiar discrepancies enters the story.
Vasari's statement is clear that Titian's admission of the sculptor
Lombardi to his sittings of the Emperor occurred in 1530. Crowe
declares it could not have happened then because Charles in 1530
came to Bologna from Genoa on his way to the Alps, whereas in
1533 he came from Germany to sail from Genoa on his way to
Spain. Today it does not matter when Lombardi tricked Titian, and
whatever the truth about the sculptured bust, Titian's 1533 portrait was a masterful one. Charles was not a naturally prepossessing
man. He used to say of himself that being ugly by nature, and being
always painted as uglier than he was, he often pleasantly disappointed people who expected to see him worse-looking than his

portraits. Titian did not attempt to correct and make beautiful what nature had seen fit to give his imperial sitter, but he did succeed in investing Charles with a majesty which was most compelling. As Aretino phrased it, he gave the Emperor eyes that disclosed mercy tempering justice, and a brow marked by "virtue, fortune, wisdom, majesty and grace." The imperial skin was pale, the eyes blue, hair a sunny auburn, and moustache and beard red. His Majesty was dressed for the occasion in a rather simple court costume, with a black velvet *béret* having a white feather in it. Today much of the color and beauty of the portrait is gone because of repainting done to cover injured places.

When he reached Barcelona the Emperor gave remarkable proof of his satisfaction by issuing a patent of nobility to Titian dated May 13, 1533. It names the painter as "Count of the Lateran Palace, of our Court and of the Imperial Consistory," with the title of Count Palatine, elevated him to the rank of Knight of the Golden Spur, and granted him all the rights, privileges and appurtenances of his degree of official standing, including that of admission to the imperial court. The painter's children were also ennobled to the same degree as those of families with four generations of noble forebears. Titian in his new honors had the right to legitimize the illegitimate offspring of anyone below the rank of Prince, Count or Baron, to appoint notaries and ordinary judges, and to wear the symbols of his position, the golden spurs, chain and sword. Not since Frederick III had created Gentile Bellino a Count Palatine had such honor been conferred upon any Italian artist, and Titian was justly proud of his recognition. The patent distinguishes the Emperor hardly less than the recipient, for the reasons Charles gave for the appointment show not merely what he thought of his now official painter and his friend, but testify to his judgment in art and character. The two men became so close that once the Emperor picked up a brush Titian dropped, and when the courtiers murmured Charles replied that Titian was worthy to be served by

Caesar. The stories told of the relations of the two are many, probably the most famous being of the occasion when the courtiers were astonished at the knighting of Titian. The Emperor looked them over grimly. "I can create as many lords as I wish," he growled, "but only God can make a Titian." That story has had so many variants in so many different periods regarding so many different personages it is at the very least dubious, but as the old Italian proverb runs, *"Se non è vero, è ben trovato*—If it isn't true, it should be." One wonders whether the poet Joyce Kilmer may have had the saying in mind when he wrote his greatest lines—

> "Poems are made by fools like me,
> But only God can make a tree."

One of the most important pictures painted at this general time was the group portrait of the Marquis del Vasto, otherwise Davalos, and his wife, Mary of Aragón. He was a distinguished soldier, in command of the imperial forces in Lombardy, and Charles called him in 1532 to Vienna, to serve under the command of the Duc de Croy against the Turk. He and all the other military leaders knew that the last time the Ottoman had invaded Europe, he had taken eighty thousand Christian prisoners, almost all of whom were sold as slaves. The women went into their captors' harems and the children were useful in a number of ways. The Marchioness was not happy about her husband going into battle against such an enemy. But Davalos came back safe, and promptly suggested to Titian a painting in which he would be shown with his wife at parting, but comforted by allegorical figures of Love, Victory and Hymen. The canvas is in the Louvre today, and we can admire the skill with which Titian accomplished his difficult task.

Mary del Vasto, quite as beautiful as the sister whom Raphael had painted, is represented brooding darkly. Her breast is partly covered by a snowy diaphanous muslin, a yellow veil partly hides

Photo by Alinari

PRESENTATION OF THE CHILD VIRGIN IN THE TEMPLE

Photo by Anderson

THE ALLOCUTION OF THE MARQUIS DEL VASTO

her shoulder, and a rich green mantle offers glowing contrast with the red of her skirt. Bare-armed, she holds a crystal orb which symbolizes the fragile quality of humanity. Fully armored, ready to go, Davalos stands behind her, his hand on her breast, staring straight into space. Cupid holds his arrow, Victory bows in salutation, and Hymen, farthest in the background, holds high his traditional fruits and flowers.

Both Gronau and Crowe doubt that this picture is a true portrait of the pair. Where the original is no one knows. Gronau declares that "the importance of the picture as a work of art will in no wise be diminished when we confess we cannot explain its meaning in words, more particularly as, for a composition in colour and for the grouping, it is one of Titian's finest works." The English critic, after some rather childish prudery about indelicacy, gives the painting fulsome praise. "As an allegorical creation and as a work of a potent master of colour, Titian's canvas is one of the most entrancing that was ever created. There is such perfect sweetness of tone, such a rich strain of harmony in tints, such a solemn technical mastery—that we can do no more than look on and wonder. . . . Titian, perhaps, had the general aspect of his sitters, Davalos or Mary of Aragón, in his mind, but he transformed them with a grand conventionalism of which he alone had the secret, and we gaze on the lovely faces, the slender and elegant hands, the ductile and pulsant flesh,—the eye wanders past the brighter forms into the tender gloom of the background and finds something to admire at every glance. That this should be the portrait of Davalos which Vasari describes there is every reason to doubt."

During this same period Titian painted the Cardinal Ippolito de' Medici in Hungarian costume—the one now in the Louvre is rated as a copy—one of Aretino, another called the *Allocution* which represents Davalos with his son Ferrante addressing his troops, and several others. The *Allocution* was taken to Spain and long since vanished. Belonging also to about this same time are a number of copies made for other personages who wished the allegory repeated with modifications to suit their particular requirements. Some of them were done by Titian, in haste and carelessly, Crowe reports, showing that he attached small importance to either the orders or the patrons, but mostly by such methods that while they reveal the Master's touch, they could be considered more in the light of pot-boilers than as contributions.

As soon as he could manage it, Titian escaped to the sun-drenched studio in Biri Grande, where he toiled assiduously to complete his portrait of the Emperor and to finish up the altarpieces, already mentioned, for San Giovanni Elemosinario that had caused Pordenone such heart-burnings. As this particular church was ruled by the Doge himself, so far as patronage was concerned, and its high altar was completed October 2, 1533, it was eminently fitting that the principal picture should be the work of the official painter of the dogate. The subject itself was dull enough.

St. John Almsgiver, who was bishop and patriarch of Alexandria, was not a saint who had done or been anything sufficiently spectacular to make himself known to art as an inspiration. In the hands of a lesser genius than Titian the picture would have been an ordinary bit of ecclesiastical furniture. But it was in exactly such uninspiring cases that the flame of the painter's remarkable gifts burned the highest and clearest. He seated his bishop on a raised pedestal or podium above marble steps. On his desk are the Gospels, which he has been studying. Beside him an acolyte or attendant page holds up a ceremonial cross. At the foot of the steps kneels a ragged beggar, his tatters in sharp contrast to the bishop's white surplice and episcopal cope over a glowing red robe.

The action is in the movement of the bishop-saint, who turns from his reading, gazes down at the mendicant and drops a gift into his extended hand. As Symonds remarked in general terms of him, when Titian chose the middle road of a broad perfection in which composition, color, theme and treatment balanced so perfectly as to leave no preponderance to any aspect of the work, it is impossible to criticise. Crowe's ascription of the power of the canvas to the influence of Michael Angelo and its debt to Raphael in the figure of the beggar may be justified by the extremists, but it seems reasonable to assume that a man who was in his middle fifties and who had been painting with ever-growing power and success for more than forty years, would by this time have reached a point of individuality at which he expressed his own clear thought only. If it chanced in certain features to resemble the work of others, it is much more likely that the resemblance was fortuitous, not imitative. And it must not be forgotten for a moment that Titian as yet had never been in Rome or seen any of Michael Angelo's work except in cartoons and reproductions on a small scale. This picture, like so many others, was mutilated. Originally it was arched at the top. Now it is square, with an added section at the foot; yet despite this desecration it remains one of the best productions of Titian's mid-channel period.

It would be impossible to tell from the painter's works during this time that he was even aware of the stormy political tides running high throughout the Peninsula. Intrigue, plot and counterplot pitted Clement VII against his own handiwork in helping Charles to unite Italy. Alessandro de' Medici offered Aretino, whether in ridicule or not we cannot say with any certainty, the noble Strozzi Palace in Florence as his home if he would only come there, and Ippolito sent him a letter breathing of golden chains and cash. Constable Montmorency on behalf of Francis I of France said his King was sending the poet a golden collar, and General de Leyva notified him that the Emperor was giving him a pension and a cup of gold. Aretino in all this whirl of excitement managed to write his famous play of *The Courtier* and keep his "glorious Titian" and "the stupendous Michael Angelo" always before the eyes of his friends and patrons.

Wars and intrigues meant nothing to the artistic soul; neither did the fact that many of his patrons were bitterly inimical to one another. With the likeness of Charles still unfinished in his studio, the painter began to work at a portrait of Francis, his arch-enemy; but where Caesar had sat to his portraitist, Francis had to be imagined with only a medallion as a guide. Crowe believes, indeed, that Titian probably never saw Francis, adding that the three pictures of him (one to keep in his own studio, one for Francis, and one for the Duke of Urbino) permit us to make a real test of "the skill of the master in representing persons whom, it is more than probable, he never saw."

Another portrait of this period painted without seeing the sitter was that of the Duchess Isabella d'Este of Ferrara. The personal vanity of women has played a role in many a crisis, sometimes with tragic results. This time the commission represented merely the complacent egotism of an aging woman who wanted a masterpiece of the days of her youth instead of the inferior picture friends of hers already possessed. She borrowed this and sent it to Titian. On March 6, 1534, she wrote the Duke's agent, Agnello, to get the original early portrait back immediately. Crowe says there was no reason why the Duchess should not have sat to Titian, who was often at Mantua, but the reason is obvious. No painter could possibly depict a young and lovely bride with the matronly features of what the years had made of her as his guide. Whatever he thought of the order, Titian did so well by it that two years later when he delivered the new "portrait" the lady was delighted and wrote him that she doubted she had been so beautiful at that age. How different Aretino's blunt description of her as she really was at sixty, "insupportably ugly and repulsively touched up." *Tempora mutantur et nos mutamur in illis* does not seem to apply to feminine makeup. Aretino might have been writing of the disgusting spectacles we see in the streets of every city today.

If Titian had only left us an autobiography, as his contemporary Benvenuto Cellini did, it would be relatively simple to deal with him today. But the conflicting records and fragments, the correspondence, the always questionable fixing of dates for pictures on the basis of technical peculiarities, the few facts that occur in reminiscences of individuals and in public and private documents, make a chain many of whose vital links are regrettably missing. One thing that has never been satisfactorily explained is how Titian and the Duke of Urbino came together; another is why and how he lost the favor of the once warmly friendly Duke of Mantua, Urbino's brother-in-law. Urbino was Francesco Maria della Rovere, nephew of Pope Julius II, gifted with the same diabolic temper, a soldier of distinction, and at this particular time an occasional resident of Venice while serving as commander in chief of the Venetian field armies.

The Duke had had a long and arduous struggle to secure relative safety and stability for his little realm, "so dangerously placed in the center of Italy." Once he was fairly certain his House was secure, he could give the attention to art for which the court of Urbino had long been noted. Naturally, being in the city where Titian towered waist-high above everyone else in the world of art, he was attracted to him. Long before he had heard his name and seen something of his work at Mantua. His wife, Leonora Gonzaga, was Federigo's sister. It was not strange, therefore, that as he became better acquainted with Titian's work he should prefer him to any other painter, and so began a relation which lasted for many years. During that second half of his life Titian executed, so Gronau asserts, at least twenty-five paintings for the Castles of Urbino and Pesaro. Vasari, in 1565, when he visited the Castle, said he saw magnificent portraits by Titian of Francis I, Charles V, Pope Sixtus IV, Julius II and Paul III, the Turkish Sultan Suleiman II, Duke Guidobaldo II and Cardinal Lorraine, besides a young recumbent Venus, the Magdalen already mentioned, and two unusually beautiful female heads, all of them in the Guardaroba at Urbino. No gallery in the world today outside of

Venice possesses such a wealth of color and historical value by a master of such standing, except the Prado in Madrid.

The Duke's first order, given Titian in 1532, was probably never filled completely. He asked for a "portrait" of Hannibal, as accurate as the painter could make it by studying tradition; a *Nativity;* and a figure of the Christ. Titian's hands were so full, however, that the Duke's wishes had to be deferred for fulfillment. Again in 1533 he wrote in the friendliest manner begging for at least one picture, and taking no consolation that his brother-in-law of Mantua had also been put off. Urbino's reply to his representative's statement had a good deal of cogency to it. "I know all about being patient because he is busy," the Duke wrote in substance, "but my brother-in-law already has pictures by him, while I have nothing." After that matters seem to have rested for some time, as the painter was not only busy but spent part of the time in Pieve on a periodical sojourn he never failed to repeat whenever Venice became too stuffy for him. Vasari tells of the visit he paid to Pope Paul III in Bologna, whence he returned by way of Ferrara after having sketched out the Pope's likeness, to be completed in his studio as usual. Cardinal Santa Fiore liked it so much that he ordered Titian to make a replica for him, which was done. In Vasari's time the two paintings were in Rome, one in the hands of Cardinal Farnese, the other held by Santa Fiore's heirs.

It was during this general period also that Titian had a neat little task of a diplomatic nature to carry out for his fellow townsmen. While he was in Pieve his cousin, who bore the same name, Titiano Vecellio, was attending the county fair at Bolzano. On his return to his office in Pieve, of which he was Syndic or Mayor, he wrote the painter, "Good Sir Cousin and All But Brother," to ask his influence in helping two Cadorine "orators" persuade the Venetian Signoria to make the commander of the Castle of Cadore, Ser Girolamo Zeno, attend to his duties as a soldier and not engage any further in trading with the notion that he could enrich himself at the expense of his neighbors. Promptly Titian went to work, and though Zeno had powerful friends in the Senate, the painter's personal prestige, friendships, and the shrewdness of the envoys from Pieve succeeded. Zeno was ordered peremptorily to do no trading. Syndic Titiano Vecellio continued his timber and grain business without fear of more than the rivalry of local friendly interests.

The year was an eventful one in many ways. On September 25 Pope Clement VII died, and the House of Medici passed for the moment out of the larger picture of affairs. Paul III, Farnese, succeeded the dead man, and a new stream of influence came into being. A month later, on October 31, Duke Alfonso d'Este of Ferrara died suddenly, and Titian lost one of his strongest patrons and friends. Some months before, on February 7, 1534, to be exact, Duke Federigo Gonzaga gave Titian a letter introducing him to his brother Ferrante, and the artist was asked to paint a *Rape of Proserpine* and another picture intended as a gift to a Spanish noble. The painter's activities during the whole of this year or more are shrouded in uncertainty, and Crowe, after exhaustive research, admits that "all we can determine with reference to one of the former [a portrait of *Cardinal Lorraine,* two pictures of women, an *Allegory* which the death of Alfonso saw still incomplete, and the *Proserpine*] is the existence of a copy representing the *Rape of Proserpine,* preserved as a genuine production of the master. . . . Titian, like Giorgione, had his imitators in different schools. The copyist here reminds us that artists like Paolo Franceschi or Christopher Schwartz might oftener succeed in a close reproduction of tricks familiar to Schiavone or Tintoretto than in a faithful rendering of Titian's sweetness and gorgeousness of tone."

Before the year had passed into history Titian was writing Cardinal Ippolito de' Medici to excuse himself for not accepting that dignitary's renewed invitation to come to Rome. He begged the churchman's secretary to tell the Cardinal of his most dutiful regard, promising to send him a picture which the Cardinal of Lorraine had already seen and wanted. Titian was deeply impressed by this powerful and haughty prince of the Church, who visited him, and also flattered Aretino by a similar call. In each case his condescension had prompt reward: from Titian, a portrait which drew universal acclaim, and from the Aretine a public letter, dated at Venice November 21, 1534, fulsomely praising the Cardinal as a prince smelling more of the purple than of the ecclesiastical habiliments.

It was a typical performance by the two most noted members of the Triumvirate, which was not only flourishing but drew into its confidence from time to time as occasion warranted such companionable spirits as Anichino the lapidary, who has already been mentioned; Serlio the architect, a friend chiefly of Sansovino, and the humanist Fortunio Spira. One wonders with what mixed feelings such a man as Doge Andrea Gritti watched and heard of the convivial meetings, at either Biri Grande or in Aretino's mansion on the Grand Canal. Gritti's portrait discloses a wide-eyed, stern-featured old noble with a tremendous nose, small and shapely but thoroughly flattened mouth, a well-trimmed white beard and moustache, and thick black brows, arched high. The forehead is unwrinkled, but where the eyebrows meet the nose two short, deep creases betray what the expression of that face could be in anger, while the traces of lines etched from nostrils to lips show the sagging flesh of age. Doge Gritti, incidentally, was sixth in the long line of fifteen doges during whose reigns Titian lived. First was Andrea Vendramin, who ascended the throne in 1476, a year before Titian's birth, and reigned until 1478. The fifteenth was Alvise Mocenigo, who reigned from 1570 to 1577.

In between most of the great families of Venice were represented: two Mocenigos, two Barbarigos, two Priulis, two Loredani, a Grimani, a Gritti, a Veniero, a Trevisan, a Vendramin, a Lando, a Donato. Cicogna's catalogue of them, illustrated by engravings from Nani's burin, is almost a complete Golden Book of the power and achievement of the lagoons. Yet as one studies the features of these men who directed the course of the Most Serene, there is such an amazing similarity of expression about all of them that we see again, ineradicable in its highest manifestation, the immortal spirit and character of the pioneer ancestors of the mud flats. In each patrician visage is the same hard, fixed, ruthless determination that led the fishermen to defy the quaking ooze and to build permanently upon it, willy-nilly. Each expression carries connotations of cold calculation, of the shrewdest sort of estimates covering everything in life, of an armored self-satisfaction withal. In studying such characters it is simple to understand Venetian success in a world composed of rivals who lacked some essential quality that gave these characteristics their force and efficiency. The wonder is that Titian, surrounded by them and their fellows in politics and business, all of them bearing the same stigmata and living the same lives, should have been able to paint so many of them as individuals in whom we perceive souls and single personalities.

Notwithstanding their severity and habitual caution, many of these doges possessed the traditional Italian sense of humor. Doge Andrea Gritti shows plain traces of it in his portraits. He showed it also in a characteristically Venetian maneuver slyly directed at the Triumvirate, perhaps, as Crowe fancies, that he might enjoy "setting the confederates by the ears." He had given Sansovino orders this very year—it was still 1534—for the reconstruction of the church of San Francesco della Vigna, and without waiting for the completion of the work had had the Zecca or Mint strike off a medal giving a clean and accurate view of the restored edifice with its cupola and graceful tower. Sansovino was feeling very sure of himself in these days, and had grown slightly careless. The Franciscan monks in charge of the church watched closely as the alterations progressed, and when they became convinced that the actual construction did not follow the plans strictly, made a complaint to the Doge. After considering the matter, Doge Andrea solemnly appointed a commission, consisting entirely of members of the Triumvirate and its allies—Titian, Serlio the architect and Spira the man of letters—with a Franciscan monk, Frate Giorgio, as its chairman. Instead of the committee whitewashing Sansovino, it brought in on April 25, 1535, a learned but windy technical report based upon Vitruvius' principles and finding serious fault with the general measurements of the building and especially with its acoustic properties. How the old Doge must have smiled in his beard when he saw that all three of Sansovino's friends had signed it. But the guilty architect, far from being chastened by such an extravagant and pretentious rebuke, shrugged it off disdainfully and went blithely on riding for the terrific fall he was so soon to take, and from which and its consequences nothing but the love, power and influence of Titian and Aretino saved him.

CHAPTER TWELVE

Difficult Mid-Channel

THE three or four years which followed, ending in 1540, included some of the most momentous happenings in Titian's entire career. Death struck right and left among his best and noblest patrons, Titian himself had to fulfill his long overdue obligations to the Signoria and lost his *senseria* simultaneously, while Aretino committed himself to what in a smaller man would have been counted as treason, and Sansovino began erecting the great Library that was to give him both his greatest fame and almost a death sentence.

The general tenor of the period is indicated by the first occurrence of any importance. For some time past the Emperor had been, as Aretino's letters disclose, asking Titian to come to Spain. Now, with the quick and savage African campaign against the pirate Barbarossa in Tunis to occupy him, Charles wanted the painter to celebrate what he meant to—and actually did—make a resounding triumph. There would be drama and to spare in such a campaign. But Caesar had to content himself with the services of a second-rater, usually known as Vermeyen. His name was Jan Cornelis Vermeijen, and he was born at Beverwijck, near Haarlem, Holland, about 1500. Son of a mediocre painter, he became interested in mathematics as well as in art, and studied engineering. About 1534 he came under the protection of Charles V, and when Titian refused to come to Spain, with the Tunisian campaign looming large in the foreground of possible events, the Emperor decided to take Vermeijen along to depict the incidents of the expedition.

It was a poor substitution, for El Barbudo, "The Bearded One" or, as we should slangily call him today, "Whiskers," accomplished nothing of note. He spent his time partly as a military engineer busy with fortifications, and partly in painting some of the dramatic incidents of the siege of Tunis. From his field sketches he painted permanent record pictures, and worked out series of cartoons for tapestries for the imperial palace in Madrid. Practically all his work was burned up in the fire that devastated the Prado in 1608. But Vermeijen, notwithstanding his mediocrity, acquired immortality. Though he was a very tall man, his beard was so luxuriant it trailed on the ground. The Emperor had a rough sense of humor, and when not too preoccupied by the weight of his campaign, sometimes mischievously trod upon it when with the artist, and the laughing courtiers dubbed the unlucky painter "El Barbudo."

Titian, while the Barbarossa was being disposed of, remained in the comfort and safety of Venice, where, according to Gronau, he excused himself to the Spanish Ambassador Lopes de Soria, on the ground that he could not possibly leave Biri Grande until his brother Francesco returned from Vienna, whither he had gone to transact some important business connected with timber privileges in Cadore. In vain Lopes de Soria urged that the Empress was most anxious to have Titian do portraits of herself and the young Infante Philip. Whatever else his enemies alleged against him, none of them ever accused Titian of being subservient to either royalty or riches. He merely perceived and made excellent use of the advantages accruing from understanding and judiciously utilizing both. When he concluded that the painter was really honest in refusing to obey—the request was an imperial one, and as such was considered as a command—Lopes de Soria tried to hasten

Francesco's return by making a direct appeal to King Ferdinand in Vienna. He even went to the extreme length of promising the King portraits of the Emperor, the Empress and the young Infante. Francesco finally reached Venice early in November of 1534, and Titian, having made his stand on his brother's absence, no longer had a valid excuse for refusing. Reluctantly he made up his mind to go. And did not go. How he managed it none of the historians of the period have so much as hinted. But we know he did not make the long and wearisome journey, and that he painted the portrait of the exquisite Empress from one of her that had been made long before by another artist.

At the same time that this campaign was being waged across the Mediterranean, Titian worked steadily at his various commitments for the Duke of Mantua, unaware that violent death was swiftly creeping up on one of his best patrons. While the Emperor was preparing for his African war, he deferred any decision regarding the ultimate fate of Florence. There were much more vital matters in his mind than settling the local administration and patronage of a duchy which was already completely at his command. But in his train were Alessandro and Ippolito de' Medici, heading the rival Florentine factions, each one certain he could win the Emperor to his belief and interest if only he could block his competitor.

Cardinal Ippolito finally decided that, war or no war, he would go to Naples and so eventually reach the Emperor's ear. When Alessandro learned of his plans through a treacherous servant in the Cardinal's suite, he made swift plans of his own. At Itri, northwest of Naples on the road to Rome, on August 13, 1535, Ippolito was poisoned by his own cupbearer, whom Alessandro had bribed for the purpose. So passed one of Titian's most generous, consistent and cultivated supporters. The Triumvirate was saddened by its loss, but Titian was given little time to brood, if a man of his calibre could do such a neurotic thing. Ten days before the murder, on August 3 to be exact, Duke Federigo Gonzago had written him that he remembered with such pleasure the painting of the Christ Titian had once sent him, that he very much wanted another one, and he wanted it delivered before the feast of the Madonna in September. A month in which to produce a *chef-d'oeuvre!* Moreover, the Duke made very clear, the canvas had to be as wonderful as its predecessor, and one "I could call one of Titian's best." Whether it was ever painted, if so what become of it, why the Duke wanted it at all and why it had to be delivered on such astonishingly short notice are facts all wrapped in the mystery of the unknown past. A really "best" Titian is something we should like very much to study today, especially if it were un-marred by time and the retouchers.

There was no end and no inaction for any of the Triumvirate, however. Aretino was as busy as ever, dividing his days between what he called the "sweat of his pen" and carousing, Titian was painting with his usual impassioned vigor, and the dogged little red-bearded genius Sansovino had all he could manage happily in the starting of his grandiose structure of the great Library in the Piazza di San Marco. They must have had joyous reunions indeed, these three, gathering after the day's toil was over to exchange gossip and criticism, discuss the political happenings of the moment, and enjoy the good food and generous wines with which they regaled their lusty bodies. With such wholly dissimilar character and such dissimilar artistic aims, we may wonder that the three men held together with such permanence. Aretino explains it perfectly in one of his fiery letters. Each one, he wrote, was content to re-main in his own field and not meddle with his fellows. Naturally each criticised the others, but it was all in good part and no one resented expression of moderate opinion. But nobody meddled or heckled, and an attack from without drew the three always closer together in defense. So the association remained as serenely immovable as the Republic of which it was such an excellent indication and image.

Charles V, meantime, had won his African war, and early in the spring of 1536 was on his way back to Europe, planning as he came for a vigorous campaign against the French. Duke Federigo wrote Titian to join him, and together they would meet the Emperor on his way north. This was an invitation that appealed to the keen-witted painter, and early in May he left Venice, joined his august patron and went with him to Asti, northwest of Genoa in the middle of the present Piedmont, where Charles stopped with his huge suite to rest. In these days of air travel, when Naples is only a few hours from Venice, progress afoot and by horseback seems incredibly tedious and wearing. The Emperor was still a young man, in his late thirties, and he probably had more regard for the necessities of his court and his troops than for any need he himself, despite never robust health, might have felt for relaxation.

Court and camp were in a fever of eddying excitement as Duke and artist rode in upon them. Everybody was talking war with France. Ambassadors and visitors of all degrees came and vanished with the flashing rapidity of shuttles. Drums beat and men worked over their weapons. Titian saw Alvise Davila, but for a moment only, and could not even approach Don Antonio de Leyva, who stayed with the overworked Emperor but half a day before he dashed away. Whether painter and ruler met is unknown. Also whether Titian took any orders for portraits during this hectic interlude is something of which we can have no idea. We do know that of Titian's subsequent meetings with Charles at Milan in 1541 and at Busseto in 1543, we have little more information. Not until the artist was summoned to court at Augsburg on German soil, where he began the masterpieces which made the sittings immortal, do we have enough data to realize how close these two antipodally opposite men could become.

Back to Venice came Titian, and on to Provence went the Emperor and his impatient armies. The campaign there was short and indecisive, and Charles came down to Genoa, embarking there for Spain. With him went Covos, his "Comendator Mayor," and the latter's secretaries and confidential agents, Luigi Davila, Gonzalo Pérez and Domenico Gaztelù, all friends, also, of Aretino and Titian. Pérez wrote the poet from his galley anchored off Villefranche on November 16, 1536, and again from Valladolid, Spain, on March 3, 1537, paying the usual florid compliments and assuring Aretino that Gaztelù had already written him that the favor Titian had expected had been done. But Spain was far away, the Emperor busier than ever. Titian waited a long time for the canonry promised him for Pomponio his son, and the pension for himself from the Neapolitan treasury which was not productive of a single *scudo* for many a weary year. All such promises were of dubious value because of the dishonest and treacherous officials through whose grasping, sticky fingers they had to pass. In fact, as late as 1555 Titian complained directly to Charles that his pension on Milan and his grant of corn on Naples had never yielded him anything.

Death struck at the protectors of the Triumvirate before the African and French campaigns, when Duke Alfonso d'Este of Ferrara was suddenly taken in 1534. The Duke's son and successor, Duke Ercole II, while no such judicious art patron as his father, knew Titian had an unfinished portrait of Alfonso in his studio, and as soon as he was installed in his new authority, sent Titian fifty ducats and wished him to complete the picture Alfonso had intended should replace the portrait Covos had carried off to Spain at the command of the Emperor. Duke Ercole had an excellent eye for politics as well as art, for besides the money he sent Titian through his agent, Tebaldi, "the Order of France" with strict instructions that the painter should copy it carefully in the portrait.

The alliance between France and Ferrara was something Ercole meant to give full value, at least in public. On December 15, 1536, Tebaldi wrote the Duke that the portrait was completed, as much like the original "as water to water," and so beautiful he marvelled his Excellency was not impatient to see it. He did not seem to be, for he waited until he came to Venice in the following January. When he had examined the painting himself and was satisfied with its rare quality, he behaved like a duke and paid Titian two hundred *scudi* for it. Afterward the painter told Aretino that he had never been more royally treated. Alas, the picture vanished irretrievably. So did the likeness of Ercole himself, though it remained at Ferrara Vasari said long enough for Girolamo da Carpa to make a very good copy of it.

The distinguished French critic Élie Faure said in that volume of his famous *History of Art* dealing with *The Spirit of the Forms,* that the true theatre of art is "the love of life and the instinct of its vanity." No other painter of any school ever realized that so completely as Titian. He was never concerned with morals in his work, knowing that it was for his brush neither to emphasize nor to try to control human passions, but to give them a sane moderation and to order them. His interest was in uniting on his canvases all that was wholesome and natural, and he sternly bent all his efforts to that goal. We might feel that the disappearance of such paintings as those just referred to constituted an irreparable loss did we not have many others of illuminating quality, and further, did we not realize by this time that Titian was far more than a portrait painter. The universality of his genius not only grasped intuitively the cogency of Faure's dictum in his portraits, but he infused it in glowing verisimilitudes into his representations of mythological subjects, into his great altarpieces and other religious paintings, and into his difficult votive pieces. Whatever he touched with his brush he dramatized; but Titian's drama never sagged into melodrama, never remotely approached histrionism because it was through and through a vivid presentation of truth—and really good wine needs no bush.

However much we may miss the Ferrara portraits, we have a treasure in those of the Duke and Duchess of Urbino, in which it is evident why Titian was so successful and so universally admired for the way in which he "cheated death" by immortalizing his sitters on canvas. In the previous chapter the beginning of the long friendship between soldier and painter was indicated, with its results, and something of the Duke's choleric nature. Francesco Maria della Rovere was the last of the famous *condottieri* or professional military leaders, and the son of gallant, fighting Giovanna di Montefeltro, who dared to defend her castle of Sinigaglia against no less an antagonist than Cesare Borgia. When at last she had to flee, she sent her boy, who had been under the tutelage of Andrea Doria, to France, where he learned the ways of chivalry and the duties of a ruling prince—he was heir to the throne of Urbino—from the great Gaston de Foix, a *preux chevalier*. The lad turned out a very pleasant and amiable young gentleman. At seventeen he murdered his sister's lover. At thirty he attacked Cardinal Alidosio and ran him through quite successfully. Twice in the next few years he had his duchy wrested from him, and twice he carved it back with his sword. All this endeared him to the Emperor as one of the few Italian generals who were not only personally fearless and instant in action, but who had proved by field experience their military capacity. The Venetians loved him for his dashing spirit, his intrepid horsemanship, and his readiness to fight anyone anywhere at any time about anything. Aretino in particular understood and admired him because of his likeness in many ways to Giovanni delle Bande Nere, the poet's old friend and hero.

At the time Titian was ordered to paint him he was commanding general of the Venetian and Allied armies, and a perfect type of the soldier. Short and heavy-set, with curly black hair, a great hawk nose and piercing black eyes, the lower lids of which pouched noticeably on his tanned cheeks, he is shown in full armor with his baton of command. Against the red background the polished steel armor stands out brilliantly, while the tremendous helmet with its fanciful flying griffin crest and white plume at one side on the shelf behind, and the three additional batons of rank—from the Pope, from Florence, and from the Emperor—at the other side make a brave show. The impression is that of a stern, strong man, looking life in the face squarely, expecting little and ready to enforce his rights if need be. But there is much more to the face than mere strength. Subtly the artist indicates the underlying sadness of a man who has seen and done much, and who therefore knows the futility of most worldly achievement. I cannot see the "bile" in the face Crowe finds there, nor is there the guile the features of so many of the Doges display frankly. The more one studies this likeness the more one is inclined to endorse the message of 1538 sent back to Urbino by Giovanmaria della Porta, the ducal ambassador to Rome. He said that at Pesaro, when he was already horsed and starting away, the chamberlain told him he had just received from Titian "the portraits of your Excellencies, so I dismounted and remained standing for a while contemplating their wonderful resemblance, and scarcely could I refrain from kissing their hands, so lifelike did they seem."

Companion portrait to that of the Duke is his Duchess, Eleanora Gonzaga della Rovere, the Duke of Mantua's sister, a mature woman in her thirties. Whether or not Northcote was right in his assumption that Titian had first painted both Duke and Duchess before this time—something not mentioned by Vasari—these two portraits offered the artist a supreme test of skill. On the one hand he had the tanned, rough skin of the soldier and the trappings of soldiering. On the other he had a stately and commanding woman in elaborate costume, with fine skin and eyes, and delicate, shapely hands. Crowe says rather amusingly that she was a "woman of perfect shape but slender figure, with fine cut features and glancing eyes shaded by long and dark eyelashes." It is this sort of loose description which has brought about a good deal of popular disregard for all art criticism and description. The Duchess is rather unusually plain in appearance, without too much intelligence in her features, and no one could tell anything about the slenderness or dumpiness of her figure because she is seated and her voluminous costume conceals her body even while it indicates bulk. The mastery of the painting resides in its treatment and the handling of light and shadow.

Aretino summed up the difference between the two portraits very well when he wrote, after dwelling vehemently upon every detail, that from the Duke's likeness "the life in the flesh and the manliness of soul shining forth" make the happiest sort of contrast with the Duchess, "a chaste and lovely apparition with grace upon her brow and command in her glance." In the technical sense Titian achieved his purpose by delicacy and minute finish in the Duchess and by a bold breadth and strength in the Duke. Aretino's sonnets on the pair, sent to Veronica Gambara, the poetess friend of Charles V and of the Estensi of Ferrara—she had prompted him to write them—set the tone for Venetian acclaim. The pictures proved to be among the best of all Titian's portraits and the great Uffizi Gallery in Florence is the richer for their presence. Vasari's brief mention of them says only that Titian did the portrait of the Duke, "which is so wonderfully beautiful that it was celebrated by Messer Pietro Aretino in a sonnet." Gronau adds that probably Titian took advantage of the occasional presence of the ducal pair on the island of Murano to secure several sittings. Certainly both canvases show the slow expertness of a craftsman who refuses to be hurried, and whose hand discloses mastery only. There is not a weak or ineffective line anywhere in either painting.

The all but incredible number of Titian's paintings, and the complexity of his relations with all manner of men and institutions make it impossible always to follow a truly chronological sequence in dealing with either the man or his works. Moreover, his habit of taking years to finish certain pictures makes them appear in the record many times, to the confusion of dates. Trying to keep pace with the chaotic Italian scene is much like trying to see what is going on in all three rings of a circus at the same moment. By the time we understand what is transpiring in the first ring, the affair in the second may be almost ended, and the performers are leaving the third while a fresh troupe comes bounding in. Titian managed somehow to be in the thickest of the action all the time. From 1536 onward he was painting steadily for the Duke of Urbino, renewing his old friendship with Pietro Cardinal Bembo, and doing portraits for many private individuals. His private work so absorbed his time and energies that he continued to neglect the battle picture for the Ducal Palace which had been first promised many years before, back in 1516.

Perhaps in the consciousness of his own worth and power Titian was beginning to ignore the rivals he had hitherto overcome so readily by the sheer force of his skill and imagination, plus the continuous hard work necessary to produce a steady flow of pictures. Whether or not that was so, the horizon was closing down upon him. Venice was beginning to think that, as he had turned out less than half a dozen pictorial compositions to something like forty portraits during the past five years, he was after all nothing more than a good portrait painter. Public opinion in Venice had a way of reaching very quickly to the ears of the authorities even without the aid of the indefatigable publicist and gossip Aretino. And now, to complicate matters, a bitter rival who had been away from the lagoons since Titian had defeated him in 1527 suddenly reappeared, famous, confident, eager, and unusually capable. Still Titian paid no attention.

After Pordenone lost the competition for the altarpiece in Santi Giovanni e Paolo which resulted in the magnificent *Peter Martyr* by Titian, he left the Republic and spent the next few wandering years as one of those vagrant creative spirits who preferred to be free and leave their traces broadcast rather than settle in one place. Such men seem to have been inspired much more by the *genius loci* in each town they visited than by any inner imaginative force such as actuated Titian so richly. Italy is full of the traces left by these uneasy creators, whose architecture, painting, sculpture, goldsmithing and decoration permanently enriched a world now careless of the names of its benefactors. Pordenone was typical for years of this ambulant genius. All through Friuli he wandered. His increasingly powerful brush covered here a cloister, there a chancel or choir, yonder a church aisle with frescoes which revealed his strength and taste as a draughtsman on a grand scale. Hardly a town in the hills to the north but had specimens of his work.

Steadily his reputation, as well as his powers, grew. Mantua came to know and value him; so did Cremona. Even distant Genoa was respectful, for the young man's achievements were not confined any longer to fresco but carried weight in every department of the art of painting. A sharp family feud at last made his hill country unbearable and he gravitated naturally toward Venice, where he had already one church completely decorated and the cloisters of another full of his work. Crowe feels that Pordenone at the time he left perhaps also felt a sense of social inferiority to Titian because the Cadorine had been knighted by Charles V; also that perhaps he did not care to work in a city where the older man had so decisively triumphed over him and was more than the predominant Master in art.

Somehow during those wandering years the young painter had acquired from the King of Hungary a patent of nobility himself, with the right to wear a sword and ruffle it with the best. Whether he exchanged artistic work for it, merely begged for it, or bought the patent for cash we do not know. But as he turned to Venice at last he at least had it, and the hour was in many ways a fortunate one for him, as Sansovino's restoration of the Library in the Ducal Palace left it ready to be decorated. The Signiory, distinctly wearied by Titian's dilatory tactics, or his contumacy, whichever it was, welcomed a younger and more amenable painter. Scarpagnini, the architect in charge, under whom Sansovino and Serlio had done the actual work, was ordered by the Council to pay Pordenone ten ducats to decorate the ceiling. But the architect—the same man who rebuilt the Fondaco de' Tedeschi after the great fire—was, like his companions, a friend of Titian, and refused to do so. The Ten apparently respected his feelings, but continued to keep Pordenone busy. In fact, the Ten went so far in the early spring of 1537 as to make special mention in the minutes of their meeting of their approval of what the painter had accomplished. Naturally this did not lubricate the already creaking wheels of artistic life among the lagoons. Pordenone's gratification seems to have been mixed with both hatred and fear of his old conqueror, for he was clearly apprehensive that he might be killed or at least badly beaten, and regarded himself as fortunate that he might legally go armed. As usual, Titian gave not the slightest indication that he so much as knew Pordenone was alive, and made no attempt either in person or by using hired bravos in the fashion of the day, to chastise his enemy.

The minute adopted by the Ten was a mild backhanded rebuke to Titian, but as usual he did not heed it. And then, on June 23, 1537, the Council issued its final decree concerning him, not warning but penalizing their recalcitrant servant. Crowe's translation of Lorenzi's transcription of the original reads: "Since December, 1516, Titian has been in possession of a broker's patent, with a salary ranging from 118 to 120 ducats a year, on condition that he shall paint the canvas of the land fight on the side of the Hall of the Great Council looking out on the Grand Canal. Since that time he has held his patent and drawn his salary without performing his promise. It is proper that this state of things should cease, and accordingly Titian is called upon to refund all that he has received for the time in which he has done no work."

That was not all. Less than five months later, on November 22, another decree appointed Giovanni Antonio Pordenone to paint the picture wanted between pilasters six and seven of the Great Hall: in other words, in the space next to that in which Titian had at last loosed his genius in the effort to regain what his dilatory ways had cost him. One can imagine the fury with which the now elderly Master attacked his task. He could not possibly refund hundreds upon hundreds of ducats, so he had to produce the picture. Meantime his salary or enjoyment of his *senseria* ceased, and he had to defray the considerable costs of the painting from his none too well filled pocket. His reputation, if not his future, was at issue, and with the steely nerves for which he had been noted all his life, he toiled to such purpose that Vasari exclaimed, "The work is wholly copied from life, and is considered the best, most animated and most beautiful picture in the Hall." As Vasari was a cool Florentine not given to overpraising his contemporaries, we may know from that statement the loss the world sustained when this great picture was destroyed in the fire of 1577, the year after Titian's sudden death.

Not the only curious fact about this canvas was the length of time required to set it upon the wall. Vasari calls it the "Rout of Chiaradadda." The commission which authorized the painting in 1516 called for a representation of the battle of Spoleto. This, however, was an imperial victory unpalatable to all good Venetians. When Titian began work he calmly ignored his orders and painted instead the Venetian victory of Cadore, with the triumphant army largely composed of his own fellow countrymen. Doge Andrea Gritti was of course first and foremost a Venetian patriot, and a victory felt better than a defeat as part of the permanent record, so he ordered removed the stilted Latin inscription which had long stood upon the wall under a fresco the new picture completely

DAUGHTER OF ROBERTO STROZZI
(Painted about 1542)

PORTRAIT, SUPPOSED TO BE OF THE POET ARIOSTO

covered. Crowe thinks that as Gritti had always been a French partisan he probably told Titian to "produce a picture which should prefigure the capture of Spoleto but illustrate an action won by Venice against the Kaiser; and Titian doubtless chose the battle of Cadore as one which, on account of his knowledge of the locality, he could paint better than any other."

Whatever the reasons behind it may have been, Titian disclosed in this picture, of which we have many copies of various types, that at sixty years of age his imagination was as fresh, his grasp of essential details as firm, his eye as certain and his touch as unshaken as when he was thirty years younger; indeed, that he was more than ever the master of great composition. Moreover, he displayed sound political intelligence, for while he painted the double eagle of the imperial standard, he dressed the Emperor's soldiers in ancient Roman costume or uniform, and instead of showing the Lion of St. Mark for the Venetian emblem, painted the cognizance of the Cornari family, while not emphasizing anywhere the characteristic appearance of the Venetian troops. To those who could read more than the obvious, the picture was symbolic in the highest degree of Venetian shrewdness and heroism of a successful type in dangerous conditions, and to the vulgar crowd merely a victory without any special political meaning. Even the supposed Castle of Spoleto, blazing furiously in the background, was far more nearly the craggy height of Cadore than what it purported to be. The Venetians on the whole understood very well, and Vasari, alone among the critics and historians, recorded it as the brilliant memorial of a defeat, with General d'Alviano the loser, instead of which Titian painted his greatest victory.

"The soldiers," Vasari says truly, "are contending furiously, while heavy rain is falling on them." His statement that the scene was drawn from life should not be taken to mean that Titian was an eyewitness of the struggle, but rather that the painter caught the spirit of the fight completely. He was wise enough to understand that no painting could possibly record the entire battle or select any one scene as outstanding. So he took the liberty of synthesizing the elements he felt would make the whole picture the most dramatic and effective. The Venetian strategy was sound. By feinting in strength on the imperial flank while the principal Venetian forces slowly fell back upon Alviano's main body, the imperial soldiers were decoyed into a position most disadvantageous for them and favorable to the Venetians. When Alviano had them where he wanted them, his troops sprang forward in a furious charge, and the battle was quickly over. The blazing town in the background, the wild gallop of the leading Venetians across the little stone bridge, the falling imperialist who goes down with his charger, the frightened girl trying to struggle up out of the gully in the foreground, and the figure of Alviano himself being readied by his page as he keenly watches the progress of the fight, carry all the action and suspense such a picture requires. As we study the details we note how impressionistic is its treatment: the armies suggested by only a handful of figures, the few lances in sight giving us the feel of a large force pouring forward into the combat, the imperial troops coming on in the distance indicated by scarcely more than a smudge of shadow with a few vertical lines. For a comparison with a military picture of equal value we must turn to the marvelous *Surrender of Breda* by Velázquez in which, aside from the two central figures of victor and vanquished, the treatment is the same economical substitution of the part for the whole. As an indication of the power of the Master's mind when he had enjoyed two-thirds of his life, nothing could be more valuable than this silent but convincing witness. Ridolfi disposed of the innumerable arguments and comparisons which have arisen since Titian's day by saying bluntly: *"Di questa istoria molte copie si sono vedute, ma scarsamente rappresentano la bellezza dell'originale."* (Of this history many copies may be seen, but they scarcely represent the beauty of the original.) There is small advantage here in going into the disputed point of the identity of the general at Cadore; today his name is completely indifferent to history.

Once the battle picture was accomplished, Titian took the opportunity once more to come to the aid of his birthplace. For some time past Cadore had been disputing a difficult boundary question with the town of Belluno, the case had been referred to the Doge as arbitrator, and that prince had refused to pass upon the case until he had seen a sketch of the terrain involved. Appealed to by his brother Cadorines, Titian suggested to the Syndic of Pieve and his aide Ciani that they conduct Sansovino over the disputed ground. They did so, the architect-artist made a careful outline sketch of the borderlands about the edge of the forest of Toanello on the outskirts of Belluno, and when the Doge saw it, he gave judgment for the Cadorines.

Portrait followed portrait in swift succession now, and the savage political broth grew ever more bitter. Aretino had written Alessandro de' Medici on December 18, 1536, with almost prophetic disquiet, praying that he might escape by God's aid from "the steel and poison of treason." On January 5, 1537, Alessandro was murdered. Six months later—August 1538—the Duke of Mantua again began pressing Titian with commissions and a demand that he finish up the very theatrical series of the twelve Roman emperors and bring them to Mantua. Titian replied that he would do all he could, and that he hoped the Duke would like a "Grand Turk" he was doing from a medal. In September the artist said the emperors series would be delayed because the Duke of Urbino had asked him to accompany him to army headquarters at Pesaro. Death was again in the saddle, this time with a great soldier underfoot. Duke Francesco had been taken inexplicably ill on Murano, and hoped the change of air in Pesaro would be beneficial. But the slow poison that had somehow been given him worked as lethally inland as by the Adriatic, and on October 20 he perished after weeks of agony.

Nine weeks later, on December 28, Titian's protector and greatest friend in high places, Doge Andrea Gritti, died of old age at eighty-three. The painter promptly did his official duty by the new Doge, Pietro Lando, and "took" his portrait soon after his elevation to the throne on January 8, 1539. Like all the other productions of this period that we wish might have been preserved, the Lando portrait was destroyed. None of the twelve Caesars survived either, and with them into mystery went that "Grand Turk," Suleiman.

In the midst of all this work and murder, treason thrust up its ugly and menacing head. During the spring of 1537, while Francis was allied with the Turks against the Christian world as a result of Francis' mad efforts to block Charles V at any cost, and Guido Rangone, the soldier commanding the Papal contingent of the Duke of Urbino's allied command, was friendly toward the French, Rangone's agent in France, Hieromino Comitole, attempted to bribe Aretino. That shrewd member of the Triumvirate was not burdened with any scruples, and listened. The Constable of France, the Duc de Montmorency, through Comitole, offered Aretino an annual pension of four hundred *scudi* if he would write letters approving the policy of King Francis.

Every decent man and woman in Europe shuddered at the mere thought of Turkish atrocities such as had been committed before and now seemed more than likely to occur again. The French King's advisers knew so well the popular detestation of his policy, and the power of Aretino's persuasive pen, that they felt they had to enlist his services. Loathsome as the job was, French gold spoke a language more potent than anything else in the greedy poet's heart, and he accepted. Crowe indulges in some peculiar reasoning in his attempt to minimize Aretino's scandalous conduct by trying to make Titian and Sansovino appear to be tarred with the same brush. The cases were entirely different. Painter and sculptor, in accepting commissions from different patrons who would cheer-

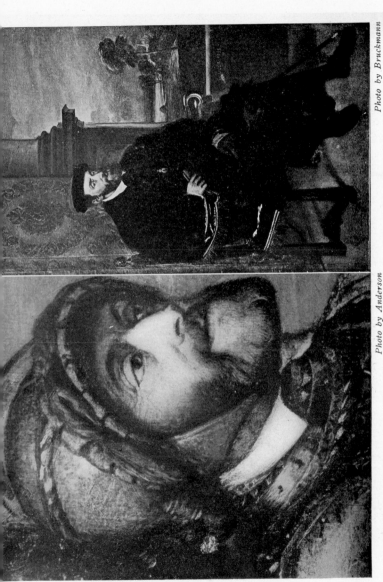

EMPEROR CHARLES V

(Portrait in Munich Pinakothek)

DETAIL FROM EQUESTRIAN PORTRAIT OF EM-
PEROR CHARLES V AT BATTLE OF MÜHLBERG

EMPRESS ISABELLA, WHOM TITIAN NEVER

EMPEROR CHARLES V IN FORMAL

fully have poisoned or stabbed one another, did not by their work try to convince the public of anything except the personality of the patron and his love of art. No political significance could be attached to portraits of the bloodiest of tyrants, to canvases depicting coldly calculating politicians kneeling in Heaven surrounded by saints, or to sensuous renderings of nude feminine loveliness. Aretino, however, brazenly attempted to make the French King's suicidal policy appear to the world as statecraft of the highest order, and the King himself as a benefactor. The arrangement did not last long, and before a great while we find the man who did not slander God only because "I do not know Him," turning against the French monarch with invective as scorching as it was true. What Titian thought of all this is easy to imagine, for the painter's record carries no blemish more serious than that he dawdled inexcusably over the "interminable" battle picture, and we know he rebuked the Aretine at least once for "infamy."

Regardless of what he thought about his fellow Triumvir, Titian had enough to worry about on his own account. Caesar had granted him a handsome allotment on the imperial treasury at Naples, but it did not yield him a single ducat. The Duke of Mantua had given him the benefice of Medole for Pomponio, when he should be old enough to take over; and Titian discovered that its revenues were loaded down with an annuity whose holder beset him most annoyingly for payment. Twice the painter complained to the Duke: in April of 1537, when he asked the ruler to lift the annuity, and again in September two years later, when he declared the annuitant's letters so disturbed him that he could not do his work. Back and forth surged the correspondence. The painter had no money to pay the pestiferous annuitant; the treasury officials at Naples had no money to pay Titian. Aretino wrote to everyone of influence on his friend's behalf, and still nothing happened to ameliorate the situation. Then Aretino went so far as to promise Ottaviano de' Medici that Titian would come to Florence and paint a series of Medici portraits if the Duke would use his influence. Without waiting to find out what might result, he wrote Leone Leoni the Aretine sculptor in Rome, scolding the Pope for not inviting Titian into his service, since the painter's genius was sure to build up "eternal memories of the princes of the House of Farnese." He might as well not have sent a word. Always before Titian had refused every attempt to force him to go to the Eternal City. Now that Aretino wanted him invited thither, no one would ask him. Probably neither poet nor painter realized the unwisdom of this advocacy. So malevolent had the Scourge of Princes shown himself toward almost every personage high in affairs and public life that he was hated and feared, and a little group of satirists, among them Berni and Franco, who were quite as shameless and even more violent than Aretino himself, were savagely lampooning him. In such circumstances Titian could hardly hope for anything through his agency. Fortunately for the painter the Emperor had sent the Marquis del Vasto, that same Davalos already spoken of, to Venice as special ambassador for the coronation of Doge Pietro Lando. As he already knew Titian well, he charged him with a painting which should show him delivering an *Allocution* to his soldiers. Titian accepted readily, told him his troubles, and the Marquis soon straightened matters out satisfactorily. Pomponio was shortly given a new canonry, the imperial Ambassador to Venice was recalled and a new one sent, Pordenone died suddenly at Ferrara in December of 1538, seven months later the Council of Ten decided the aging painter had been sufficiently punished, and by a decree of August 28, 1539, gave Titian back his coveted *senseria* with all its emoluments. Besides this good fortune, Cardinal Bembo, who had been silent a long time, sent a friend to sit for his portrait, and asked Titian to paint another of himself. In the spring of 1540 he wrote a friend to thank the artist for this second canvas, saying he had intended paying for it but was willing to accept it as a gift because he would be able to return the courtesy by some appropriate favor.

Titian did undoubtedly reap a considerable harvest from his work, but the uncertainty of a living much of which consisted of gifts or favors from highly placed and wealthy patrons, must have been distinctly wearing at times. True, at intervals certain of these patrons, such as Emperor Charles V and a few dukes, made the painter substantial allotments from their revenues. When these were paid, the recipient profited handsomely, but as corrupt or inefficient officials frequently stood between giver and beneficiary, long intervals of very meagre living must have resulted except in the case of a man who had considerable reserves upon which he could depend in emergency. One is inclined to wonder how the critics who have so often charged Titian with avarice would manage if their labors were rewarded as spasmodically as were his, and how they would relish being considered base fellows because they protested against unfulfilled or incomplete obligations. Even Lafenestre, in the final chapter of his excellent *Life,* goes to considerable length to press his point, and cites Titian's eagerness for work and his incessant labor after his eightieth year as proof of his greediness. The plain truth, as established by ample evidence, is that he had to work to survive the competition of the strong younger men such as Veronese and Tintoretto. He was a gallant old fighter, and he paid his way every foot of the distance.

Though this Bembo portrait is the only survivor of many such likenesses painted during this period between 1535 and 1540, it hardly ranks, according to Crowe, with several compositions that excited relatively scant contemporary notice. Among these are the lively *Tobias and the Angel,* and especially the remarkable *Presentation of the Child Virgin* in the Academy—twenty-six feet long by eleven feet six inches high—a picture as large as it is arresting in both total effect and detail. Still a third canvas characterized by both its spirited delineation of figures in strong action and the charm of its rich coloring is the *Ecce Homo* now in Vienna.

Crowe enthusiastically calls the huge canvas of the *Presentation* "the finest and most complete creation of Venetian art since the *Peter Martyr* and the *Madonna di Càsa Pesaro.*" A century before, in his sketchbook of 1430, Jacopo Bellino had taken the first step toward a vital contribution to Venetian art. Gentile Bellino carried on and Carpaccio expanded the idea. But it was left for the magnificent Titian finally to grasp completely the potentialities of monumental structure and by sheer overpowering genius to focus attention upon the main figures, seen in their proper perspective and in all the brilliance of color against the duller architectural backgrounds. Jules Levallois, some sixty years ago in his monograph on *Les Maîtres Italiens en Italie,* expressed perfectly the value of such work when he wrote: "Great artistic or literary creations, in stirring, in developing intellectual and moral culture, augment the sum of life as the world knew it before their appearance. They bring in their train an increase of all existence, and this richness, in which plays a divine ray from the Beyond, steadily augments the treasure of humanity."

Certainly Titian knew Jacopo Bellino's sketchbook. But when he was inspired to take the framework and perspective thus created as a skeleton for his own clothing with palpitant flesh, he brought to bear irresistibly all his own love of nature and his boundless experience. The theme was clear: the vital interest must be drawn at the first glance to the figure of the little girl, regardless of her surroundings. Everything must be contributory to her effect. There were an hundred ways in which the picture could be painted, but only one by which it could achieve immortality. Titian chose that one way, building around the shining little figure standing completely detached and distant from all the rest, a scene as quietly dramatic and symphonic as some of his more tragic canvases were stormily detergent.

The room for which the picture was painted was not so large as others in the Scuola della Carità (now the Academy), it was lighted from the left only, and the wall was pierced by two large doorways. With unerring skill the master designed for all these difficulties. The beholder is at ease in the picture with his first glance. At the right the elegant fabric of the temple rises from a massive stylobate. Standing at the top of the interrupted flight of steps, the brilliantly robed High Priest awaits his little visitor in an attitude of benignity with upraised hands. Behind him waits an acolyte with a book, and opposite a tonsured, bearded cardinal in red. Behind both a white-bearded man in a heavy cowl leans interestedly from an opening in the wall.

On the platform dividing the two flights of steps the child Mary in a vivid azure dress steps confidently upward, her left hand extended, a golden radiance surrounding her tiny figure. Directly below her, squatting beside a basket of eggs she has brought for sale, is an old peasant woman completely indifferent to everything but her chances to dispose of her wares to the crowd in the street at the foot of the steps. Down that street we look past elaborate palaces whose windows are filled with curious onlookers, past a ball-topped pyramidal monument across the way, to a typically Cadorine background and sky. Foremost among the spectators is Anna, mother of Mary, watching calmly while a matronly friend points and makes some remark to her, the man behind turns to call to someone in the rear, a tiny dog leaps up to caress its master, and at the extreme left a beggar woman with an infant in arms receives a dole from the hand of a gentleman. Some of the figures are portrait likenesses: we know the names of two at least, Grand Chancellor Paolo de' Franceschi and Ser Lazzaro Crasso. But it is the brilliant color and the play of light and shadow that give the painting its perfect balance and quality. The little Virgin, though she is by far the smallest of all the figures, makes the focal center of the picture because of this delicate and subtle handling of masses and lighting, and the perfection of the perspective. But, to quote the German critic Wilhelm Suida: "It would be presumptuous and perhaps a little stupid to think that the mystery of the effect of a painting by Titian could be interpreted in words." The critic goes on to point out that the disparaging remarks made by previous analysts are all wrong, with the words: "It is of entirely secondary importance that the motif of the stair, in the scene of the *Presentation of Mary in the Temple,* should have been encountered already in a small picture by Cima da Conegliano (at Dresden) because the organization of the two paintings, that of Titian and that of Cima, is completely different." The first remark is the important one: Before genius, words fail. All the technical knowledge of the greatest minds pales before the emotional uplift and gratification that perfection gives us.

It must have given Titian a sustaining secret satisfaction during these middle years of his active career to be able to produce such works as the *Presentation,* which he knew were remarkable and would endure. Unlike his fellow Triumvirs, the painter was so sane and perfectly balanced himself, so stable and easy to live with, so entirely reasonable in all his conceptions, as Aretino testified to a powerful churchman, that the works flowing from his brush reflected these qualities brilliantly. Not all the heartaches and anxiety caused by his son Pomponio's outrageous dissipation and worthlessness, not all the financial difficulties caused by broken or delayed promises, not even the striking of death among his most valued friends and benefactors could change by a hair's breadth the intuitive necessity of greatness to express perfection as fully as possible.

Titian's perplexities were very tangible. As an instance, there was the canvas of an *Annunciation* the nuns of the convent attached to the church of Santa Maria degli Angeli on Murano had ordered. Titian finished it, demanded five hundred *scudi* as his price, and the horrified nuns repudiated their order. The altarpiece stood in the studio, accomplishing nothing, while letters, discussions and every other means failed to secure payment of other long overdue obligations, including those from the Emperor himself. It was the fertile imagination of Aretino that came to the rescue by suggesting that Titian send the *Annunciation* to the Empress as a gift. His reasoning was sound. Isabella was a very devout woman as well as a very beautiful and human creature. She was delighted, and Charles was so pleased he promptly sent the painter two thousand *scudi*—four times what the painter had asked from the nuns. But the imperial largess of earlier dates remained unbestowed notwithstanding. As the jealous competitors of both poet and painter had industriously sown in the public mind the idea that Titian could paint nothing but easy portraits and Aretino write nothing but venomous invective, the latter carried his triumph the one necessary step further and in a published letter told exactly what had happened. How the two friends must have enjoyed their vindication and the irritation of their enemies.

There is no better estimate of Titian's qualities as seen by his contemporaries than the caloric if stilted phraseology of Marco Boschini, the author of that minutely detailed little handbook of the art treasures of Venice published in its second edition in 1574 by Francesco Nicolini. In his introduction to the catalogue, Boschini wrote—as nearly as possible I give his archaic phrasing in its English equivalent: "The Count Palatine Tiziano Vecelli the Elder of Cadore finds himself wreathed about the temples with Laurel, seated upon the Majestic Throne of Painting. . . . Titian truly is the most excellent of all who have ever painted; because his Pencil always brings forth expressions of life. . . . Palma has assured me that in his refinements he paints more with his fingers than with his brush. And truly (so well he thinks), he has good reason for working thus: because, wishing to imitate the operations of the Almighty Creator, which he had thoroughly observed, he saw that He formed the human body with His hands out of earth."

. . . Until now I have spoken of the methods of the marvelous Tiziano, as far as concerns his nudes, which have been a wonder in every class. His babies particularly are so well nourished with milk that they drop from his excellent pencils and are more than alive; in his fabrics he is an excellent weaver, whether in silk, in wool, and in linen above all; in Arms and Armor he was the most erudite worker, though he never labored as a steel-maker. . . . He formed animals which seemed as if Noah had had them and they were coming from the Ark. . . . Truly this Titian will live as long as Nature shall live." Is a great prophet always honored save among his own?

The answer to that rhetorical query is another quotation, this time from the source of so much of our knowledge, Vasari. As he brings his monograph to a close about the time Titian was seventy-six years old, in other words, almost a full quarter of a century before his death while still in full harness: "Titian has always been healthy and happy, he has been favored beyond the lot of most men, and has received from Heaven only favours and blessings. In his house he has been visited by whatever Princes, Literati, or men of distinction have gone to or dwelt in Venice; for, to say nothing of his excellence in art, he has always distinguished himself by courtesy, goodness and rectitude.

"Titian has had some rivals in Venice, but not of any great ability, wherefore he has easily overcome them by the superiority of his art; while he has also rendered himself acceptable to the gentlemen of the city. He has gained a fair amount of wealth; his labours having always been well paid." And then the jealousy of the professional competitor emerges, with the attempt to put on a dry, critical, objective air which cannot deceive any who compare the paintings of the two artists. Says Vasari coldly: "And it would have been well if he had worked for his amusement alone during these latter years, that he might not have diminished the reputation gained in his best days by works of inferior merit, performed at a period of life when nature tends inevitably to decline, and consequent imperfection."

In evaluating Vasari's comment we must remember what he said of the frescoes of 1509 on the Fondaco, and how little he comprehended what Titian was doing. In the same restricted spirit of ultra-conservatism he completely failed to grasp the progressive liberalism of the old-young artist of seventy-six, changing his earlier technique in the studious effort to come ever closer to the secrets of Nature herself. As some of Titian's very finest work was accomplished after 1553, Vasari's criticism shows its hidden spleen clearly.

But we are still in 1540, and still in the fatal circle of influence that clung about the painter and his friends. Once more death struck. Federigo di Gonzaga, Duke of Mantua, after he had ordered Titian to paint the portraits of himself and the Duchess as gifts for Duke Otto Henry of Bavaria, was suddenly called, late in June, to the company of his ancestors. Art had lost a munificent patron and Titian a generous friend to whom he owed the entrée to the Emperor Charles V and all that flowed from it. Crowe remarks: "It is impossible to look back upon the life of this prince without perceiving that he did more than any other to foster the arts and keep up the dignity of the artists of his time. He will always be remembered as the patron of Giulio Romano, Titian, and a host of minor craftsmen. The galleries which he formed, the palaces which he adorned, were second to none but those of Florence and Rome." Between them, patron and artist enriched not merely Italy but the entire world.

CHAPTER THIRTEEN

The Work That Led to Rome

AGE CARRIES with its benefits the grim penalty of loneliness in the loss of lifelong friends who cannot be replaced by new ones, however fine and stimulating. With so many of his former patrons and protectors forever gone, Titian realized the swiftness with which the years were assailing him. He must have thought sadly along the lines Ridolfi expresses so sententiously: "Fortunate Painters, who go out to serve liberal Princes who have that with which to exercise their intelligence. They do not germinate corn in the arid sand nor virtue where it cannot produce worthy effects if not watered by gratitude. Honor serves them for ornament, yes; but comfort gives them existence and food." The painter wasted no time in idle mourning. As soon as the elaborate obsequies of his friend the Duke ended at Mantua, Titian came back to his studio in Biri Grande and picked up his brushes, to work harder and more consistently than ever before, and to continue his effort incessantly to the very end.

It was for the Duke that Titian painted his immortal *Venus of Urbino,* most magnificent of all his similar figures. The subject was a favorite with him, and he repeated it in various forms many times. To those who object to such studies, whether as works of showmanship or for reasons of sentimental morality, it may be emphasized that Titian was a classical Greek in his love of the beauty of the perfect human body. Under his caressing brush such figures revealed themselves with utter simplicity and artlessness, suave and rhythmic, without the slightest trace of any gross afterthought or shamed modesty, as the loveliest spectacle creation can offer to the human eye and mind. Again and again the world has wondered who the lovely model for these pictures may have been. Was she one of the elegant hetairai of the Venice of that dissolute age? Was she, by any chance, Titian's mistress, as has so often been suggested? Might she even have been the Duke's mistress? No one knows. Lafenestre says of her: "What proves in any case that the completely unveiled woman on the couch in the picture at Florence, whether duchess, courtesan or bourgeoise, was a well known person who moved the imagination of the painter strongly, is the fact that we find her peculiarities in a certain number of other figures, nude and draped, notably in the celebrated portrait in the Pitti Palace under the name of the *Bella di Tiziano.*" He adds, of the original: "The *Venus of Urbino* remains, in the order of these plastic conceptions, the most perfect and the most exquisite because it is the simplest and most natural."

This busy year of 1540 saw the completion of the beautiful portrait of Donna Elisabetta Quirini, hailed by a delighted sonnet of Monsignor Giovanni della Casa, who was overjoyed by the canvas. Ridolfi published the original sonnet. Northcote transcribed it and appended his own translation. Both are worth repeating, the original for the liquid music of the Italian, the English approximation for its stilted Victorian quality:

> *Ben veggo io, Tiziano, in forme nove*
> *L'idolo mio, che i begli occhi apre e gira*
> *In vostre vive carte e parla e spira*
> *Veracemente, e i dolci membri move.*
> *E piacemi, che'l cor doppio ritrove*

Il suo conforto ove tal' hor sospira;
E mentre che l'un volto e l'altro mira,
Brama il vero trovar, nè sà ben dove.
Ma io come potrò l'interno parte
Formar giamai di questa altera imago,
Oscuro fabro a si chiara opra eletto?
Tu, Febo, (poiché Amor men rende vago),
Reggi il mio stil, che tanto alto subbietto
Fia somma gloria a la tua nobil arte.

Titian! It is herself—in other guise
 Thy living tints my idol here present;
 See—she unfolds—she turns her beauteous eyes—
 She speaks—she breathes—nay, seems to move intent!
What joy is mine, amid continual sighs,
 Here to regain some portion of content,
 As now on her—now this sweet image bent,
 My doubting heart to find the impostor tries.
But I—shall ever I the inward part
 This heavenly shape's diviner soul pourtray?
 Ah! hand too weak for enterprise supreme!
Help, Phoebus, thou! (since Love o'erwhelms my lay)
 Guide thou my pen, and let the glorious theme
 To fame transcendent raise thy noble art!

The spelling of the Italian text is that given in Freiherr von Hadeln's edition of Ridolfi. It differs somewhat in the orthography familiar in other editions, and especially from that given by North-cote.

Portrait after portrait followed in swift succession. There was borrowing of armor so that the painter could depict accurately the rich chasing and ornament of a great man's military equipment, and pressure to finish the *Allocution,* already mentioned, for the Marquis del Vasto, Governor of Milan. There Titian received from the imperial hand a patent allotting him a yearly pension of an hundred ducats to be paid by the local treasury. He had brought the already famous *Allocution* along with him, and the Marquis was haughtily enthusiastic at the sensation it caused when he exhibited it to his friends at the court. Eventually the canvas was sent to Spain, seriously injured in one of the periodical fires which wrought such havoc among art collections, and was so badly repainted that, as Crowe expresses it, "only with considerable difficulty we discover a touch of Titian's brush. Still, the composition is clear." The painter also probably brought with him a *Nativity* he had painted some time before on order from Ser Giambattista Torniello. That gentleman was dissatisfied with the canvas, sent it back, and Titian did it over with considerable care, introducing his patron as the donor of the picture, intended as an altarpiece for the Cathedral of Novara. It was most unusual for such a thing to happen, and we wonder if Lafenestre's loosely written sentence telling of it can have any substantial background, since Titian was almost painfully careful in finishing his work instead of being a man of whom it could be justly said that a painting was refused "because the first example had been rejected as too negligent."

How long the stay in Milan was we do not know, and since Aretino was momentarily disgraced and not in attendance at court, we know nothing about what the silent painter did day or night, whom he met, what orders he accepted. By October he was back at home, working hard and breaking his routine only with the joyous gatherings of the Triumvirate, now expanded into an "Academy" of which Anichino the lapidary and minor sculptor, Marcolini the publisher and bookseller, and others had become members. The dinners and symposia were held as before either in the Casa Grande or in Aretino's mansion on the Canal Grande. They were very pleasant affairs, and while we do not know exactly what the companions ate, if we may judge of their feasts by what we know of similar gatherings in this prosperous and cultivated class of Venetian society, we may well envy them their enjoyment.

Ordinarily the lagoon dwellers had but two meals a day, and

work began for the Doge himself as well as for the citizenry early in the morning. The first meal was the main one of the day and came at any convenient time between about eleven and noon. Early in the evening came the second and lighter one. Venetian cooking was varied, elaborate and highly spiced. Garlic, onions and all sorts of spices from the East were liberally used, sugar and eggs were plentiful, and beans, peas, cabbage and squashes were on the daily menus, while fish, naturally, was a mainstay. For dinners such as those of the Triumvirate, however, no such simple food served. The rather tasteless fish from the lagoons and near-by waters would be varied by lampreys, smaller eels, trout and even salmon. We have many records of fish being sent by fast courier from the streams and lakes far to the north in specially constructed baskets to keep them as fresh as possible. Pigeons, quail, rabbits, partridges, the famous Bologna sausage and haunches of venison all graced the tables of the rich. Sometimes a large fish would be served whole, gilded from nose to tail. All sorts of tricky cookery were practiced to make the viands seem something other than what they were. Wheat bread was a regular part of every meal on the better tables, the grain that went into it forming a very important part of the Republic's trade. Most of it usually came from the Near East, Egypt and the Barbary States, though once at least, in the great famine of 1268, two centuries before Titian's time, Venetian ships went as far as the distant Crimea to bring back the life-saving grain.

Wine, of course, was on every table. The drinking water of Venice was never too good, and while Titian's mansion at Biri Grande had the usual well in its courtyard and a cistern for catching rainwater, the Master's thirst and that of his guests were mainly slaked by the choicest vintages from the main. Sweets and fruits, of which the ladies particularly were very fond, ended the meal as a rule. Everyone ate heartily and drank deep, and the jovial spirits induced by the good company and the good wines made the evenings merry and often musical. It would be interesting to know whether the feminine guests wore their monstrously high *zilve* or pattens in the house on these occasions. It seems rather unlikely that they did because this type of footwear, built somewhat after the fashion of our modern clogs, was so high and clumsy—Venetian women were stockily built as a rule and quite short, so they used the *zilve* to give them height enough to match their cavaliers—the wearer generally had to have two pages beside her to enable her to keep her footing when she went out of doors. Whatever they wore on their feet, they displayed their charms liberally, and believed that a great deal of facial decoration was much better than none. Casola is reported by Cicogna as eloquent upon such matters.

As the evening drew down, and gondole with their merry occupants drifted lazily across the calm lagoons, through the windows floated the folk songs of the day and the district. Titian probably listened many a time to the plaintive melody of

> *Sospira, cuore, che ragion tu hai;*
> *Aver l'amante e no vederlo mai!*
> *El sospirar vien dal ben volere:*
> *Desiderar e no poder avere!*

Horatio F. Brown, who gives the song in his *Life on the Lagoons,* renders it simply:

> Sigh, heart of mine; good cause hast thou to sigh;
> To love thy Love, and never have him nigh!
> The source of sighs is love, the heart oppressing:
> Desiring to possess and ne'er possessing.

It is easy to imagine the great room in the Casa Grande, softly illuminated by the flickering candle flames that left the Master's canvases in a shadow but shone on the animated faces of the guests as they listened to the distant tinkle of lute or mandolin and the soaring voice of a passionate lyric tenor out in the night. The host, easy and jovial for all the tinge of reserve in his manner as compared with the behavior of his friends, was noted far beyond the borders of Italy for his gracious ways, his ability to converse on any subject, the wisdom and kindliness of everything he said. The women who attended these banquets, though generally not of the highest moral fibre, were many of them far better educated than their hosts. Several of the most noted courtesans in Venice spoke and wrote both Latin and Greek, some were poets of no mean ability, and Aretino wrote of one in particular who had such an air and was so cultivated in speech and manner that he called her a benefactor of all mankind. Not a few were daughters of families of position, some had been and others would end their days as nuns, and all of them, so far as we know, respected Titian and never plagued him in any way. Gossip is so malevolent if the painter had slipped even once we should know all about it. Another point on which the records are completely silent is fighting on these festal occasions. The most exclusive and elaborate dinners given by the most highly placed personages very often broke up in furious quarrels begun indoors, carried on outside, and not infrequently ending in a sudden vicious stabbing or swordplay with fatal results. Apparently the gay parties at Biri Grande and at Aretino's, quite possibly because of Titian's good influence, never reached that stage.

Work, especially the fine and delicate work of a painter, in an age which depended upon candles for its illumination once the sun had gone for the day, was naturally confined to certain hours. So Titian, though he might pen his letters laboriously by candlelight after nightfall, could do nothing in his studio, and the dinners and routs not only took nothing from his productive time but lightened his burden by keeping him fresh and perpetually interested in all the doings of his fellows.

Some time before this the Augustinian monks living on the island

of Isolo in the northern lagoon had Sansovino build them a noble
church, for which Palma Vecchio and Titian painted pictures. During the winter of 1541-42 Titian's *Descent of the Holy Spirit*,
executed for these monks, was in process of completion. Opinions
regarding this canvas vary so widely it is a little difficult to know
exactly what the truth is, none of the comments being too meticulous as to detail. Hutton declares, paraphrasing Vasari, that the
picture darkened and discolored so fast Titian had to repaint it entirely. Crowe says vaguely that the canons of the church refused
to accept it, and that eventually brought about acrimonious litiga-
tion, but, he adds, after considerable technical description, some of
it contradictory, that the work is "bold, free and expressive . . . the
handling betokens a mastery altogether unsurpassable. . . . Titian
is an independent creator" of pictures "pregnant with his—and
only his—grand and natural originality." Lafenestre's comment
is not much more than mere mention. Dr. Gronau, however, goes
into an elaborate discussion of the work, which he regards as being
part of the painter's great artistic legacy to the world, saying clearly
of the several paintings of which this is an important example, that
"it is in them that the Master has left to his country his artistic
testament, those first solutions of the great problems of lighting
which for centuries since have occupied the greatest minds and in
our day have led to new results and violent discussions."

In the *Descent*, which was the first chronologically of the group,
the painter's problem was to cause the rays of golden light from
the Dove to flash down through an almost blinding sea of radiance
and flicker in dancing tongues of flame on the heads of the awe-
struck devotees. The scene is highly emotional, with the differing
reactions of old and young, men and adoring women sharply
marked and each individual characterised with portrait-like exactness. "It is scarcely possible to describe how," says Gronau, "with
such rich variety corresponding to the diversity in the characters,
the light that comes from the Dove gives the tone to the whole.

Yellow and blue predominate, are introduced into the foreground in various nuances, such as golden-orange, grey-blue, and so on, and carried on into the background; the blue, somewhat damaged in several places, rather spoils the effect; the other local colors, such as red or green, are broken by violet or yellow touches of light. A wonderful brightness fills the room, with some strong shadow to help the effect, in the figures of the apostles on either side."

More and more as he progressed Titian concerned himself by the power of his coloring with blending harmoniously the vivacity of dramatic gesture and the energy of the human body in motion. Unlike many other great painters, he remained free from any cut-and-dried system or method which would have restricted his elastic and resilient genius. Each subject he undertook presented its own problem of composition, light and color, and was solved with a freshness of approach that ranged, as Lafenestre judiciously expresses it, "from an extremely simple and almost naive understanding of the plastic and picturesque to a wise research into the most daring and complicated combinations of the linear and of color. The suppleness of his hand during this entire period of his maturity remained incomparable; it was necessary to wait long years still before being compelled to recognize in the ensemble of his works a certain heaviness of aspect, due less to his developed passion for retouching than to the weight of his octogenarian hands."

The other pictures in this remarkable group were *Tobias and the Angel,* the *Presentation in the Temple, David and Goliath, Cain and Abel,* and the *Sacrifice of Abraham.* Vasari placed the *Tobias* in the church of San Marciliano as a work of Titian's youth, which no keen observer of the painter's progressive expertness will ever admit. The Florentine's obvious blunder was to confound this picture with another of the same subject in the church of Santa Catarina. Ridofi dates the former after the San Rocco *Christ at the*

Column and before Titian's journey to Ferrara to "complement the *Bacchanal* left imperfect by Gio: Bellino." Dr. von Hadeln, in a long note on this passage, remarks that Vasari must have meant the picture in Sta. Catarina, and the attribution of the San Marceliano canvas "to the young Titian seems unacceptable." Lafenestre makes point after point regarding the execution of the work which leave no doubt as to its approximate date. Even the little dog that trots along with his angelic and human friends, is "sufficiently like the dog that lies at the feet of the *Venus of Urbino.*" Since small white spaniels are not long-lived animals, that seems to be good evidence against an earlier date by more years than any spaniel ever lived. It also gives the casual observer of a painting a clear idea of the microscopic examination of the slightest detail when noted paintings are subjected to the scrutiny of the experts upon whose scientific verdicts depend authentication and corresponding value.

Three other paintings executed for the Isolo church of San Spirito and now, with the *Descent,* in the church of Santa Maria della Salute, are the ceiling canvases already mentioned of *Cain and Abel,* the *Sacrifice of Abraham,* and the *David and Goliath.* Despite the encomiums of Gronau and Crowe's pages of elaboration, all these works reveal clearly one thing: effort. Completely cutting away from the older conceptions of composition, Titian discloses in these essentially simple yet amazingly complex works such a mastery of the intricacies of his art that we render full homage at the same time that we recognize the straining for effect. Lafenestre points out in a biting sentence this very defect, prefacing his remarks by repeating the inscription Tintoretto painted above the door of his studio as his artistic compass: "The design of Michael Angelo and the color of Titian." "This effort," the French critic adds, "made by one of the great geniuses in whom we had dreamed the union would make ideal perfection, was always an effort, an effort too visible." Titian's forte was not the theatrical poses and overdone muscularity of Michael Angelo's figures, but the more gracious likenesses of men and women radiating charm, the more human persons he could display with "incomparable intelligence and energy as human beings animated by the light."

There is always the temptation, in writing of Titian, to yield to the fascination of his works and describe or comment upon them regardless of their place in chronological and artistic sequence. That is one reason for the hopelessly involved structure of some of the very best works dealing with this Master. The three ceiling paintings for San Spirito are a case in point. While they were painted in 1542, they were not done until after Vasari had come to Venice at Aretino's direct invitation shortly before carnival time in 1541. Moreover, Vasari was soon retained to paint the ceiling pieces for San Spirito, probably through the interest of Sansovino, its architect. Vasari says vaguely that he planned the pictures. Before he undertook that task, the patrician Fraternity of the Calza had planned a tremendous show and celebration for the carnival. Aretino's new comedy, the *Talanta,* was to be presented, and the stage sets and decorative scenes of canvas and scaffolding had to be painted. Venetian custom of the sixteenth century never used local artists for such work, and Aretino, as the most interested person concerned, was permitted to turn to his young fellow Aretine, Messer Giorgio Vasari. That ambitious painter was glad to make his first appearance in the lagoons under such favorable conditions, and worked conscientiously at doing the Calza's *macchine* or settings, decorating a ceiling for Messer Giovanni Cornaro— Titian secured that for him by introducing him favorably to Cornaro—and eventually rough-sketching the ceiling works for San Spirito. In all he was thirteen months in Venice. He ends the record of his stay by saying: ". . . but Giorgio having departed, the three pictures were given to Titian, who executed the same most admirably, having taken especial pains with the foreshortening of the figures." Titian must have smiled a little in his great beard if he ever saw that frigid admission of the amazing skill with which he handled a problem Vasari, for all his acknowledged skill, would probably have reduced to something akin to Correggio's "ragout of frogs" type of foreshortening.

Just before Vasari arrived Titian was engaged upon a portrait of the dead Queen of Cyprus, the lady Catherine Cornaro, clothed as a saint. Whether Titian completely executed the picture himself or merely supervised his associates seems to be a moot point. In any event the picture was copied and broadcast by countless painters for years afterward. It was for this same queen, incidentally, during her stay in Venice in the bitter winter of 1491, that a grand spectacle was presented on the ice of the thoroughly frozen Grand Canal. Majestically enthroned, Queen Catherine watched with interest as a large company of cavalry from the Levant deployed before her and executed spirited maneuvers. That was practically the last time that horses appeared in Venice, and the former custom of riding through the city was completely abandoned.

As we look back over Titian's life it seems as if there never was a moment of it idle or wasted. When he was not painting earnestly he was engaged in some form of business, the purchase and improvement of real estate, helping his fellow townsmen of Pieve in their affairs, or trying to collect some of the moneys due him from patrons. He took what we might call vacations by going back to Cadore for short visits; but even on these occasions which gave him the change of air and scenery he needed, his sketchbook was always with him, and often he took a busman's holiday by painting a portrait or an altarpiece. In the early spring of 1542 he was as busy as usual. Doge Lando gave him an advance of ten ducats on his votive portrait to go into the Sala d'Oro. A month later he received another ten as a binder on an altarpiece for the church of Serravalle, and, between his more pressing labors, he painted a self-portrait as a legacy for his children.

Crowe and Cavalcaselle dug patiently and deeply into the records of all the self-portraits, of which there are several, and were unable to learn very much about them. The one which shows Titian as most youthful is the one now in Vienna which may possibly have been the one painted for Jacopo Strada, the antiquary with whom the painter had such close and extended relations, and whom he painted masterfully. The final one, perhaps, is that splendid likeness in the Prado. There we see the old lion of more than eighty years—Crowe thinks it was probably finished about 1562, when Titian was in his eighty-fifth year—bony, skull-capped, wrinkled, but with noble shoulders held well back, head high and eyes as full of fire and the will to do as in youth. What the thin features have lost in young comeliness they have more than gained in dignity: it is a great man who looks at us from the canvas.

Occasionally the artist painted himself in compositions, such as the *St. Matthew* now in the Salute, the great *Pietà*—his final work —now in the Academy at Venice, and the *Madonna* in the village church at Pieve di Cadore. Veronese placed him in the orchestra in his *Marriage at Cana,* and Palma the Younger in his ceiling picture for San Fantino. Besides these are several others, none of them entirely genuine as they stand. The most striking one is at Cobham Hall, England, a canvas showing Titian seated, in conversation with another bearded and dignified man, generally known as Zuccato. Crowe says of this that "from the thin pigments and rapid decision of brushwork one might guess him [the painter] to be Tintoretto, or an imitator of Tintoretto. Hasty handling, neglected form, and untransparent color are not characteristic of Titian." A real one is the so-called *Titian and His Mistress,* painted probably about 1555. In this the painter stands with his hand on the waist of his daughter Lavinia.

The votive picture of Doge Lando was not finished until some time in 1543, if we may judge by the fact that the final payment for it was made on May 11 of that year. As it was burned up in the fire of 1577, we know nothing about it. In the interim Titian did a beautiful likeness of the boy cardinal Ranuccio Farnese, and another of the ten-year-old daughter of Roberto Strozzi. This latter is one of the loveliest representations of childhood that have ever been put upon canvas. Crowe sets it ahead of anything of the sort ever done by even Rubens and van Dyck. The portrait is high-keyed, the little girl all in white satin, with gold waist-chain and ball, her little spaniel black and white. The child holds a curved bit of bread or cake, and the painter has caught them both just as they looked up at some interruption of their surreptitious feast. Color, lighting, delicate modelling and background are subtle and sweet; so much so that when he saw the picture Aretino burst out with characteristic vehemence: "If I were a painter I should die of despair . . . . certain it is that Titian's pencil has waited on Titian's age to perform its miracles."

The intelligence that served the artist so well also activated the man of affairs. Titian managed his funds with a careful eye to the future, and the slurring remark of Crowe that the painter "was either litigious himself or he had to do with litigious people" is unfair. What drew Crowe's remark is a ducal letter dated April 20, 1542, giving execution for debt in Titian's name against a recalcitrant named Giovanni Battista Spinelli, who was ordered to pay the painter the sum of forty-eight ducats, five *grossi,* and to the court costs of something more than ten *lire.* Why should not a creditor collect what is due him? Titian's whole artistic life was full of delayed or ignored payments, and his patience on the whole was remarkable, even admitting that he did not wish to offend most of those who kept such ill faith with him.

Besides the "sharp" conduct Crowe deplores, Titian was canny in making his small capital safe in judiciously placed investments. We have a contract of March 11 in that same year by which he and his brother Francesco purchased a share in a mill in Cadore from its owner, Vincenzo Vecelli. There was very little grain available to Cadore in 1542, so Titian shrewdly stocked up the magazines after securing an importer's license, drew interest on the vital food reserves while they were in storage, milled a lot of flour and presumably sold it at a profit, which is, of course, not good business sense or benefitting his community as well as himself, but conduct highly reprehensible and something no good American would dream of doing in the enlightened twentieth century.

One of the most striking portraits Titian accomplished during 1542 was that of Ranuccio Farnese, just mentioned. The boy was the grandson of Pope Paul III, Archbishop of Naples at thirteen and cardinal at fourteen years of age. This is one of the portraits on which Crowe and Cavalcaselle go astray. The original is in the Cook Collection in England, and is clearly Titian's work. The delicacy with which the painter has brought out the evil inheritance in the boy's face, the play of light on features and dress, the beautiful delineation of the right hand and the unreadable expression of the eyes, all proclaim not only the touch of the master but the vicious Farnese proclivities.

The nepotism that disgraced the papacy during the reign of Alexander VI Borgia was no less pronounced during Paul III Farnese's rule. His bastard son Pier' Luigi was a criminal, yet his father gave him one after the other the rich and important duchies of Castro, Parma and Piacenza. Piero's two sons and his nephew were all made cardinals at the age of fourteen. The House of Farnese was on the march, and Charles V was dissuaded from making Ottavio Duke of Milan only by the counsels of his most trusted advisers. The political pot was boiling dangerously. The wily Pope had one grandson as a watcher and intelligence officer at Charles's imperial court, another in the same capacity at the gay court of the King of France. At the center of his web of liaison and espionage Paul sat motionless but intensely alert and menacing. Pope and Emperor were equally anxious to meet, finally did so at Busseto, and wrangled for nearly a week over Milan, only to turn aside and go home. The Emperor was furious at being checkmated in his plans. While all this was going on Titian, serene as always, was the guest of Cardinal Farnese.

As an example of the despicable character of the negotiations which faced the painter it is necessary only to cite the attempted bribes. The Cardinal offered Titian a benefice which it later appeared he did not have the right to bestow; Pope Paul, who wanted him to come to Rome, did the same thing, offering him the Piombo, or "seal of the bulls," an office already held by the painter's old friend and admirer Sebastian Luciano, otherwise and more generally known as Sebastiano del Piombo, with the understanding that he pay another artist, Giovanni da Udine, eighty ducats a year. For Titian to snatch away a substantial part of the livelihood of two old friends was unthinkable, and he indignantly rejected the treacherous Pope's offer. That made him all the more anxious to secure the supposedly proper benefice offered by the Cardinal. But that, too, was firmly held. The long wrangle that ensued is too involved for inclusion here. Titian, meantime, had an opportunity to reflect upon the unkindness of a fate which had caused him to make the tiresome journey to court, his production of the portraits of the Pope and of Pier' Luigi, masterpieces in his best manner both, and his lack of absolutely anything to show for his pains.

Titian himself was partly to blame for his troubles. Leone Leoni the sculptor had carefully ascertained that the painter, notwithstanding his home-loving ways, was willing to be persuaded to make the long trip to Rome, and wrote to Cardinal Alessandro Farnese that "Titian, beside his value, appears to all as a very tractable person, mellow, who can be dealt with easily, which is very well worth considering of so rare a man." In due course the Pope invited him to present himself and on April 22, 1543, Titian was in the brilliant throng which celebrated the Pontiff's entry into Ferrara. He followed the court to Bologna, where he became the house guest of the Cardinal, as already stated, and when the Emperor notified the Pope he would meet him at Busseto, Titian again accompanied his new patrons and spent the five days of the conference there, returning with them to Bologna and the Cardinal's house. Before the wrangle over Titian's benefice could be settled, Alessandro felt a touch of fever coming on and abruptly fled Bologna without giving Titian the least warning. The chagrined painter wrote the Cardinal from Venice on July 26 to say he had never passed a worse night in his life than when he found the Cardinal gone, and that if he had not been told next morning, while still in bed, that his benefice had been granted, he would have risked having a bad day and a bad year. The letter was filled with the usual protestations of thanks and affection, but in it lurked a note of doubtfulness and a tone verging upon defiance. So far as any emolument from his trouble was concerned, he might as well have dismissed the affair from his mind on the spot.

It was the world that gained by his effort. The perfidious Farnesi who treated him with such slight consideration won an immortality through his zealous brush all their infamies never could have achieved without it. In the words of the old proverb, in tricking Titian, they had "sold him the skin of a live bear." What the piercing vision of the painter perceived his unerring hand set down upon canvases which speak eloquently to inform millions who would never have heard the name Farnese had they not seen these glorious pictures. Lafenestre ranks the *Portrait of Paul III* "as, in the work of Titian, a *chef d'oeuvre* of the same brood as the *Portrait of Leo X* in the work of Raphael." Titian hardly ever elsewhere succeeded to the same extent in combining so forcefully his splendor of color and solidity of design with the vigor of his observation. The Frenchman's biting comment upon the sitter is classic in its restrained savagery. "All the stubborn duplicity of the Farnese breathes in this bony old man of the long, fleshless hands, from under the heavy shadow of twisted eyebrows darting the crafty and piercing regard of his black eyes. Seated upon a red chair, robed in white surplice, red skullcap and cape, piped with white fur.

with blotched face and long white beard, this priest with the air of a usurer is an apparition at once pale and bloody which cannot be forgotten." Crowe rounds out our impression with equal acerbity: "The quality of life and pulsation so often conveyed in Titian's pictures is here in its highest development. It is life senile in the relaxation of the eyelids and the red humours showing at the eye corners . . . but flashing out irresistibly through the eyeball . . . never was he [Titian] more successful in combining the detail of a Fleming with the softness of Bellino or the polish of Antonello, combining them all with a breadth of plane, freedom of touch and transparence of shadow peculiarly his own."

This picture, which Blashfield, in a note on Vasari's account of it, says is the one painted for the Cardinal Santa Fiore, carries the same story as that told of other portraits of popes. When Titian set it in his window to dry, the fable says, people passing by bowed and doffed their hats, believing it was the Pope himself they saw. Truly, the quality of a portrait is in the painter.

Again and again Titian painted Paul III and his grandsons Alessandro and Ottavio. Several of these canvases are in such bad condition it is difficult to recognize them for what they were. Before considering the most striking of them all, painted in 1546, we must return for a moment to one outstanding composition and several portraits, with mention of a fine *Annunciation,* the altar-panels for the Cathedral of Brescia, and an *Assumption* in the Cathedral of Verona, which Vasari declared to be "the best modern painting in the city."

Busy as he had been during his memorable visit to the predacious Farnesi, Titian was both busier and far better compensated on his return to his studio. There he did the *Assumption* for Verona's Cathedral, and the marvelous *Ecce Homo,* today in Vienna. Back in 1529 a wealthy Dutchman named Martin van der Hann had rendered notable services to King Ferdinand of Bohemia by advancing him large sums of money. The King repaid him by granting him nobility. Well pleased, and probably also quite willing to escape from the atmosphere which had elevated him socially, van der Hann came to Venice with his two sons, Jan and Daniel, established a general business, bought the Talenti palace at the *traghetto* (ferry) of San Benedetto on the Canal Grande, and became a great man after the manner of his kind. His son Jan soon changed his old Dutch name, which the soft-spoken Venetians no doubt found impossible to pronounce, to Giovanni d'Anna, which they could. Then he met and quickly became friendly with Titian. The acquaintance ripened, the naturalized Hollander became Titian's *compare* or intimate, and finally his patron. The first work Titian executed for him was the *Ecce Homo,* followed by Giovanni's portrait and a crucifixion. Both the later canvases have disappeared, but the superb *Ecce Homo* still moves men powerfully.

For this dramatic presentation Titian chose the moment when the irritated and weary Pilate has the naked, broken, scarcely human figure of the Christ exposed to the howling obscenities of the mob. Taking full advantage of the liberal attitude of Venice toward the unusual in religious pictures, the artist dared to show with a perfect fury of conception and power, not the calm, regal philosopher of the *Tribute Money* but this utterly crushed victim of religious prejudice and hate, and a bloodthirsty mob surging about the steps of the palace and off into the distance, yelling and gesticulating. The great canvas, measuring approximately twelve feet wide by eight in height, seems to Lafenestre in its presentation of the figure of Jesus "nothing more than a pretext for the grand deployment of the moving figures throughout the rest of the canvas. It is, in an inverse sense, the same disposition as that in the *Presentation in the Temple;* but instead of a calm crowd watching a charming spectacle, this is an agitated and passionate mob preparing a tragic scene."

Gronau feels, and expresses, the purpose of the picture quite dif-
ferently. After asking if we can wonder at the criticism levelled at
the painting more than once, the eminent German points out irre-
futably Titian's mental processes in designing it. Here all the pro-
gressiveness of the matured artist is at work in sheer drama. The
brush that could so exquisitely reproduce the beauties of nature and
humanity, that could give us martyred Sebastians whose wounded
bodies seemed flesh and not paint, whose Venuses and amoretti
have tremendous seductiveness, now proved it could deal equally
with the ugliest of human passions. I do not agree with Gronau
that "his art had changed its character." It had not changed, as
picture after picture painted in the years to come demonstrated.
This was but a different manifestation of the inexhaustible genius
that grew with every brushstroke; the increasing certainty of the
hand obedient to a mind which never lost its ability to express the
intangible and the unseen with pellucid clearness.

The terrific force of the picture discloses itself slowly as we
study the details, each of which is a contributory stone in the
pyramid of total effect. The faces, we quickly perceive, are most
of them vital portraits of persons we already know. Pilate, who
displays the hapless and battered prisoner to the mob, is, in Gronau's words, "a ghastly mixture of haughtiness and cynicism over
the easily recognized features and figure of the poet Aretino." In
the thick of the press a young mother in a bright dress, holding a
child by the shoulder, is none other than the painter's beloved
daughter Lavinia. Gazing with oriental detachment at the scene
from the back of his charger in the background, a turbaned cavalier
is declared to be the Grand Turk himself, no less a person than the
Sultan Suleiman; while beside him the blackbearded knight in
armor bears a curiously strong resemblance to Titian's old friend
and patron Alfonso d'Este, Duke of Ferrara. With but twenty-
seven figures altogether on his big canvas, the Master has been able

to convey a mob in full cry and tumultuous movement so effectively we can all but hear the disgust of Pilate and the wild howls of "Crucify him! Crucify him!"

Another point of unusual interest to the painting is its prophetic quality, perhaps less generally understood or even recognized. Everyone of course sees the resemblance between the charming Lavinia here and the tiny Virgin in the *Presentation*. Each stands out luminously from the crowd, and each, while a part of it, is completely detached. But there is more, for casting a century ahead, Titian here gives no less a master than Rembrandt the suggestion we find worked out in exactly the same way in the figure of the "pretty little princess straying among the legs of the guards in the *Night Watch*," as Lafenestre expresses it, continuing: "This is not the first time Titian had worked for Rembrandt. In the *Ecce Homo* he even more prepares Tintoretto for the present and Rubens for the future; also this grand canvas, despite certain heaviness of the brush and opacities which could be due to the hands of his collaborators, marks an evolution of his genius most important for the influence it had upon both his contemporaries and successors."

At the same time that he was occupied by the larger canvases discussed Titian, Aretino helping him, never gave up trying to persuade the Farnesi to make good at least some of their promises. But the Pope and his tricky cohorts had something to consider of much more importance to them than pondering the reward of a painter, however great. The tremendous international duel between Charles and Francis, swaying now this way, now that, kept the papal nerves aquiver, the papal policy one of trimming uncertainty in the boiling political and military gusts to the north. In the fall of 1544 the peace of Crépy temporarily quieted things a little, and Titian sent the Emperor two portraits of the Empress Isabella, now dead, which Charles had probably ordered during the Busseto interlude the year before. The letter announcing them

was blunt and personal, not at all like the diplomatic type of communication in which we so easily recognize Aretino's guidance as
to style and phraseology. "I should have liked to take" the two
portraits, wrote the old artist, "to your Majesty in person, but my
age and the length of the journey forbade such a course. I beg
your Majesty to send me word of the faults or failings I may have
made, and return the pictures that I may correct them. Your Majesty will not permit anyone else to lay hand on them." That was
no courtier trying to retain the imperial favor, but the great Master
stating his wishes. Charles, being himself a blunt man at times,
could understand and honor such a letter.

Whatever Pietro Aretino's failings may have been, he never neglected the slightest opportunity to do his utmost for his friends.
Titian's messenger with the two portraits to Don Diego de Mendoza, the Emperor's chamberlain, gave the poet perfect occasion
to let the Emperor know that while he might rule the earth, his
underlings were not afraid to disobey him and prevent his largesse
from reaching Titian. Lafenestre renders the letter, from Volume
III, No. 77, in part as follows: "But of what use that his [Titian's]
pencil labors to rejoice you, and to what good should my pen
glorify you although the recompense promised may well be above
the value of our labors, if the ministers of the imperial treasures
show themselves as thieves? See how nine years have passed since
you accorded Titian your servant a draft on Naples, and so far
from enjoying it, behold four more in which nothing has been
paid of his pension. O glorious wife of Augustus, oh, sainted soul
among the saints, be propitious to us! That God, moved by thy
prayers, may inspire him whom you have enjoyed as your husband,
to the end that he may bring to reality what he has established in
words! I kiss the knees of your Clemency in stupefaction that you,
you who understand how to strike terror into the universe, cannot
secure the obedience of your servitors!" Even for a privileged
international character universally granted freedom of expression

and immunity from punishment for his indiscretions, that was going far—to accomplish nothing.

Other letters of Aretino tell of a young man of letters, Alessandro Corvino, sent by the Roman grammarian Priscianese to Biri Grande to sit for his portrait, which Aretino declared was so marvelous one could see the sitter's pulse beat and hear him breathe. The same month—February 1545—Bishop Paolo Giovio of Como received a portrait of Daniele Barbaro. In March Aretino wrote the new Duke of Urbino, Guidobaldo II, in his usual flowery style, to tell of the likenesses of the Duke's consort, Giulia Varana. July saw still another portrait, that of Marc' Antonio Morosini, which Aretino declared had been so lovingly labored over that the time required to produce it could easily have been marked by twenty other heads if the painter had worked with his customary facility and speed. He added significantly: "If I could see myself in my portrait with that allure with which I look at your image, I should find myself always before it, as a constant mirror of myself."

We could scarcely ask better evidence that Titian was working on his jovial *compare's* likeness. Lafenestre adds this: "This is the evil painting one sees today in the Pitti. The impudent pamphleteer, draped in his robe, displays in it all the vigorous grossness of his broad-shouldered athleticism, with the audacious, knavish expression of his sensual physiognomy. His implacable *compare* had penetrated even to his marrow with customary sangfroid." The poet was not happy about it, for though he had the hide of a rhinoceros and the conscience of a crow, this was such a terrible exposure of his secret self that he bitterly resented it. As a result when he sent it as a gift to Duke Cosimo I of Florence, he took a contemptible revenge against Titian in the accompanying letter. A second portrait, now in the Palazzo Chigi in Rome, avoids the evil dominating the other one, and shows instead a man of middle age in possession of remarkable intellectual powers. Both like-

PORTRAIT OF KING PHILIP II, IN THE RASCH
COLLECTION, STOCKHOLM

Courtesy Cincinnati Art Museum, Collection of Mary Emery

UNFINISHED SKETCH OF PHILIP II IN THE
CINCINNATI MUSEUM OF ART

LA GLORIA, OTHERWISE KNOWN AS THE TRINITY AND AS THE
FINAL JUDGMENT

nesses are executed with all Titian's unique and arresting skill in combining vigorous observation with color no words can adequately describe, and characterization so perfect the live man seems before us. If it be objected that both portraits could scarcely be true, we should be willing to admit that expressions change with thoughts and desires, and the painter transferred to his canvas with complete truthfulness exactly what he observed in his sitter at the moment of taking his likeness. There is no question of Aretino's mental brilliance; his published work demonstrates that amply; and there is equally no doubt that when, as at the moment Titian immortalized in this second portrait, he was thinking soberly, the planes of his face, the look in his eyes, the whole impression given out by the man would be nobler and more consonant with the spirit of his painter.

The portraits of the Empress Isabella to which reference in passing has already been made may properly be counted among Titian's most astonishing achievements. One of them disappeared long ago, but the other still hangs in the Prado, to which it was removed after the Emperor's death in the monastery of Yuste, in Estremadura. Only a monumental genius in art could take an insipid and inferior portrait of an unknown hand and from it produce not only a masterpiece but a remarkable likeness. So dear to Charles was it that he took it to Yuste with him, and as he lay dying asked that it be placed before him.

Titian had never seen Her Majesty. While he was at Busseto the Emperor gave him the presumably Flemish original, and after the portrait was accomplished sent word to his painter that the likeness was excellent. Gronau says of it that it is "a work of art of the highest rank." The Empress in Titian's work, which varies antipodally from the photograph of the Flemish original inspected by the writer, is seated beside a window through which appears a typical Titianesque landscape of rolling country and shattered hills seen in what is evidently a late afternoon haze that blends the soft greens and browns of nature. The imperial lady is surpassingly lovely and every inch the Empress. Her elaborate gown of crimson velvet and satin over white, with its slashed sleeves and rich gold embroidery, throws into striking prominence the exquisite pale and aristocratic features and the red-gold of her simply dressed hair. Her jewels are few and modest: she did not need them. Her left hand holds open a priceless Book of Hours, as indication of her devout nature, and her right, treated with all the artist's profound understanding of the importance of hands in a portrait as indices of character, is delicate and beautiful to perfection. The far-away expression in her face carries both resignation and sadness, and no one can look at this astonishing masterpiece without wondering compassionately what her short life may have given her in compensation for the heavy burdens she carried without complaint. We somehow feel a deep sympathy for the gentle little lady who, though her thoughts are so far away, perhaps on holy things, we are sure would talk to us if only she could. Perhaps she does not only because she is an empress.

It was during this period that Guidobaldo of Urbino had made his brilliant court the principal resort of the élite in art, letters, politics and arms. When he and the Duchess were not kept at Pesaro or Urbino by affairs of pressing moment or bad weather, they enjoyed themselves in the ducal residence in Venice and held open house for everyone of importance who might be influential in helping the Duke to secure command of the armies of the Republic. Detailed records of many of these meetings of the elect can be found in the essayist Sperone's *Dialogo d'Amore*. It was at one such discussion, years later, in which Tasso himself took part, that the poet rebuked Tullia for an opinion unjust to Titian. "Not at all," was the reply. "I hold Titian to be not a painter, his creations not art but miracles." The Master painted half a dozen or more of the personages who took part in these memorable conversations, besides doing splendid likenesses of Guidobaldo himself and Duchess Giulia Varana.

Though a somewhat troubled peace settled over Europe in 1545 the domestic political pot in Italy still boiled furiously. The Duke wished to keep Titian's genius at his command, and as he was a lavish patron with a regal taste in art, he could not be disregarded. At the same time the Farnesi in Rome wanted Titian to enter their service. It seems probable that he would not have risked taking such a trip and offending the Duke but for the urgence of his friend Girolamo Quirini and the fact that he persuaded the lord of Urbino to entertain Titian at Pesaro for a while and then voluntarily send him on to Rome.

It all worked out beautifully, thanks to Quirini's diplomacy. Titian and his son Orazio joined the ducal suite in Venice, accompanied it to Ferrara and then to Pesaro. After a short stay there, the two left, with a strong escort of honor the Duke magnanimously ordered to accompany them all the way. No artist had ever enjoyed such princely courtesy or been so loaded with gifts. His arrival at Rome was a triumphal entry. His seven mounted escorts, his attendant son, his baggage train, all combined to make the city turn out in honor of this majestic figure everyone knew and honored. Cardinal Bembo received him with his habitual cordiality, and Pope Paul III made him the Church's guest in sumptuous apartments in the Belvedere, with the Florentine painter Vasari detailed as his special guide to the city's treasures. We know much more of what happened from others than from Vasari, for that gentleman at his best was not a good narrator. He briefed the meeting drily in a single sentence: "There he found Vasari, who had then returned from Naples and was painting the Hall of the Chancery for the Cardinal Farnese, by whom Titian was recommended to his care, whereupon Giorgio kept him faithful company in his visits to the remarkable objects of Rome."

What a picture that makes! Guided by the young but more than a little stodgy Florentine who was an ingrained conservative, the great Venetian of infinitely more than ordinary artistic taste and judgment made the rounds, first of the galleries of ancient fragments which he studied with avidity, then of Raphael's tapestries, the various treasures of the Farnese palace, and finally the Vatican itself. There Titian made the one blunder recorded of his visit. During the sack of Rome, German soldiery quartered in one of the halls had damaged some of Raphael's work. Titian looked at the bad restoration of some of the figures, and turning brusquely on his old friend Sebastiano del Piombo, who was with him and Vasari that day, demanded to know what presumptuous ignoramus had daubed those visages. We can imagine the strained silence that followed Sebastiano's reluctant admission that he had done it himself.

Most of the letters Titian wrote from Rome have not come down to us, but Aretino's letters to him and about him are so numerous that we have a fair idea of how he spent his time and the work he accomplished. One letter we do have is the enthusiastic missive he sent Aretino declaring he wished he had come to Rome twenty years sooner. Characteristically cynical was Aretino's reply that caresses were the coin in which the Farnesi paid.

Titian's hasty expression opens a question that has exercised the critics for a long time. Crowe frankly doubts he would have gained anything more in 1525 than he did in 1545; that is to say, more than the natural broadening travel and experience give an already tempered and practiced genius. Lafenestre is dubious, and hesitates "to think" that the effect of all Titian saw in Rome would have "modified the direction of his genius to complete it more happily." To some extent Gronau agrees, yet he admits that we "must, I think, be grateful that fate did not take Titian from Venice to Rome in his earlier years. The art atmosphere there was dangerous to a nature impressionable to foreign influences . . . and we should never have seen the highest development of the art of painting in

Italy." Dr. Gronau may be right, but genius, if it be truly genius, has a diamond-like quality of hardness. Whether Titian had studied Rome or the art of other alien painters as a young man could hardly have made a whit of difference or swerved him from his obvious destiny in color. The painting of a Titian demands the genius of a Titian, and of no one else ever born into the world of art.

CHAPTER FOURTEEN

White Beard, Green Thoughts

TITIAN'S strong sense of the dramatic grew instead of decreasing with the years. He could exclaim cheerfully, as did Aretino: "The whiter my beard, the greener my thoughts!" His mind never faltered, his hand never grew unsteady, his eye untrue. Though he was approaching seventy, when most men if not actually in retirement and waiting for death to creep stealthily up on them are relaxing all their efforts, Titian was avid for work, proving in the first commission he undertook for the Farnesi in Rome that his imagination was as keen and inspired as his flawless technique was certain.

This initial picture was that amazing group of the Pope and his two grandsons, never finished, yet as brilliant an achievement in portraiture as ever painter laid on canvas. That it was "entirely to the satisfaction" of the three men who stood revealed in it for exactly what they were is an astonishing tribute to both painter and sitters; to him for unsurpassed mastery, to them for an appreciation of art keen enough to override personal feeling, or else for guile shrewd enough to mask their rage at being so ruthlessly discovered to posterity.

Although the picture is still in the condition of a sketch, its power is such as to place it as a full equal among the very first portraits of such masters as Rubens and Velázquez. Seated slightly to the left of the center—remember Titian's carefulness to dispose his principal figure just enough off-center to make the rhythm of his scene or setting more fluent and natural—Paul III appears as a peevish old man, muffled in his canonicals and cap. His head turns to his left, and he stares at his grandson, the Duke Ottavio, who bends toward him, his plumed cap held at his waist in his right hand, his left concealed behind him. The young man's posture is fawning, servile. His face wears a sinister expression blended of a malignant hypocrisy and cautious restraint. The only faces in the world of art known to this writer which wear anything like the same quality of expression are those of the old Infanta and the boy Infante in that masterpiece of revelation painted two centuries later by Francisco Goya, in *The Family of Charles IV,* in the Prado. There, as here, the artist has seen clearly and been able to make the souls of his sitters shine through the human integument and tell their true story for all time.

Titian's genius far outshone that of Goya, but the psychology of the two men as painters was exactly similar in certain respects: they exposed fearlessly the evil they saw regardless of the personages. Opposite his brother, behind his grandfather's left shoulder, stands Cardinal Alessandro Farnese, blankly noncommittal, perhaps even slightly bored by what he knows is occurring, and clearly in possession of his younger brother's plans. There is a chill in those forbidding lineaments that resides in their very expressionlessness. In the scarlet robes and cap of a cardinal Alessandro stands for the ruthless, silent, all but irresistible power wielded at that time by the princes of the Roman Church.

Between the two the seventy-eight-year-old Pope, querulous and irritated, grasps the arm of his chair as he turns a suspicious glare on Ottavio. Lafenestre's assumption that Ottavio's attitude was caused by his wish to be obsequious, and Gronau's that he desired merely to hear what his grandfather's low voice said, may be the explanation of the pose; but the historical record of the treachery of this pair of consummate rascals and the fact that they so conspired against their grandfather as to break his heart, seems to render that charitable belief dubious. No one knows why the painting was never finished, but Crowe's guess, antipodal from that of Lafenestre, is an interesting one. The Englishman says: "The canvas . . . was left to the very last unfinished, and we may think that the cause of this mishap lay in the dislike of the Pope to sit. Though the Palace of the Belvedere had been chosen as Titian's habitation because it was likely to facilitate his intercourse with the Pontiff, Paul was too old, too ailing and too peevish to visit the painter's room frequently. Titian finished the heads of Cardinal Alessandro and Ottavio Farnese carefully; he left that of the Pope incomplete." Lafenestre remarks: "Although, according to Vasari, the work was executed to the 'great satisfaction of these personages'—*con molta soddisfazione di que' signori*—the extraordinary truth of the action and of the physiognomies—might it not appear too audacious to one of the interested parties?" Paul III, it must not be forgotten, was one of the greatest benefactors of Renaissance art. He it was who charged Michael Angelo with the decoration of the Sistine Chapel. He it was who built the tremendous and magnificent Farnese Palace. He and his family it was who were responsible for so many works of art that the catalogue of 1680 of the Farnese Collection lists no less than thirty paintings by Titian alone. Many of these works have vanished, but enough remain to tell us of the terrific energy and purpose which animated Titian during his Roman visit of some eight months, one reward of which, of somewhat dubious value, was the grant to him on March 20, 1546, of honorary citizenship as a Roman.

Vasari tells us that the Venetian's next task was to paint a half-length of the Christ in the *Ecce Homo* tradition, as a gift for the

Pope. "But this work," says the chronicler, "whether it were that the paintings of Michelagnolo, of Raffaello, of Polidoro and of others had made him lose courage, or from some other cause, although a good picture did not appear to the painters equal in excellence to others of his productions, more particularly his portraits." At the same time he was painting this dolorous Christ, he was also working up as different a picture for Ottavio Farnese as could well be imagined: *Danaë.*

Paul III had convoked the Council of Trent, the agenda of which were the suppression of corruption in the Church, including simony and its attendant evils, and the endeavor to halt or exterminate the Reformation. Rome was crowded with the high-ranking delegates, princes of the Church. And in his studio in the Belvedere Titian turned from the tortured face of his mediocre conception of the Christ to the pagan expectancy and beauty of the exquisitely delicate and perfectly painted nymph Danaë as she watched Jupiter, in a brisk shower of gold, fall into her embrace. The entire combination spells Italy of the period. No one saw anything bizarre in the papal painter doing pagan myths to be admired by high churchmen who, for all their public laudation of Michael Angelo's stern concepts, nevertheless privately exhibited the admiration of normal humanity for the seductiveness of sheer beauty.

"Now it chanced," our gossip Vasari goes on in his relation of Titian's activities, "that Michelagnolo and Vasari, going one day to see Titian in the Belvedere, beheld a picture which he had just finished of a nude figure representing *Danaë,* with Jupiter transformed into a shower of gold in her lap . . . when, all having left the place, and talking of Titian's work, Buonarrotti declared that the manner and colouring of that artist pleased him greatly, but that it was a pity the Venetians did not study drawing more, 'for if this artist,' said he, 'had been aided by Art and knowledge of design as he is by nature, he would have produced works which none could surpass, more especially in imitating life, seeing that he has a fine genius and a graceful animated manner.' " It was this same grim Florentine who on another occasion, recorded by Dolce on page 23 of his *Dialogo della Pittura,* said after studying the portrait of Alfonso, Duke of Ferrara, and praising it warmly, "that he had not believed art could do so much, and that only Titian was worthy the name of a painter." *Tempora mutantur!* Titian's *Danaë* was produced in Rome, where Michael Angelo evidently considered he was supreme.

About fifteen years before this Correggio had painted his *Danaë,* a frankly voluptuous nude which, beautiful and compelling though it was, when compared with this new work of Titian seems both a little small and mannered. Titian had probably studied the Correggio, which for a time was in the collection of Duke Federigo Gonzaga before it went to Charles V. He had therefore seen the marvelously skillful solution of the difficult problem of *chiaroscuro* by the painter now dead, and appreciated the exquisitely balanced light and shade, the silvery rose of the flesh, the sensitive feeling. It is possible also that Titian knew the *Leda* by Michael Angelo. It was the great Florentine's one effort to make a pagan theme alive. Pontormo painted the picture from the original cartoon. Michael Angelo set upon the paper his cold, perfect, mechanical accuracy of anatomical design in both nymph and swan, but he might as well have tried to weigh a summer zephyr as to give his dead, soulless figures charm. The human spirit that vividly animated all of Titian's work was completely lacking in Michael Angelo's, and the glowing, transparent brilliance of color that produced the canvases of the former became gelid and unsympathetic externals in the hands of the man who, though he was painter and engineer and architect by turns, was in reality the sculptor, with mind and soul as gritty and chill and hard as the marble out of which he battered only one form of beauty.

It seems highly questionable that Titian learned anything practical from either Correggio's *Danaë* or Michael Angelo's *Leda* even if we admit he had seen them. All that Correggio had done he was already doing far better. He did not need the basic anatomical accuracy of the sculptor to make his work finer because he intuitively knew what Michael Angelo never could grasp: that art is never an accurate rendering of actual life or form but an illusion of it, an impression purposely enough incomplete to stimulate the mind of the beholder to complete the work. The Florentine left nothing to the imagination in line and forms; and as a result his later less gifted imitators and disciples produced only the Grotesque School. Titian left much to be imagined, and especially to be emotionally felt. When his conception of a subject bade him particularize, he could give us with stunning effect character delineation or scenery or action, all utterly convincing. In other terms Titian, besides giving us beauty that satisfies, compels us to think. Michael Angelo merely makes us admire his unerring skill in duplicating form, wonder that man can so successfully pit his genius against nature. But he does not touch the subliminal self or warm the heart as Titian does because the philosophy and dogma he clothed in tangible forms were only ideas, and their life was limited to the few who understood and chose to believe them. There was no universality inherent in any of them.

The *Danaë* painted for Ottavio Farnese, in the words of Lafenestre, was the superb sister of the great *Venus of Urbino,* but rendered with even firmer and loftier style. "This perfect creature," he cries, "so superbly proportioned, so healthy and alive, who, placed upon a couch in an attitude as supple as it is calm, develops with pagan tranquility harmonious movement in a rhythm of incomparable perfection. Never had the great colorist with more of both science and seduction played a light both so sweet and warm upon the tender flesh tints and the sumptuous fabrics; never had he given a picture more brilliance, more relief, more solidity . . .

he had realized in this sweet and powerful evocation the union of unequalled coloring and exquisite forms, all with a wise naturalism and warm poetic fervor."

Gronau does not especially like or approve of any of the *Danaë* canvases, of which Titian himself produced several at the commands of wealthy patrons, and he does not see in the Cupid of the original painting Titian's adaptation in painting of the principles of the statue of the god of love by Praxiteles, after he had studied the statue in replica in the Vatican galleries. While the painter was engaged with this canvas he also worked at a portrait of *Margaret of Austria,* daughter of Charles V and wife of Ottavio Farnese, another of *Clelia Farnese,* illegitimate daughter of Cardinal Alessandro, and a *Venus* and a *Magdalen* for Ottavio. The Farnesi, meantime, all of them, were scheming and struggling in their endeavors to further what Crowe calls truly their "dynastic interests," and subtly undermining the influence and power of the Emperor wherever they could. The artist paid no attention to what the man knew was transpiring; but the man Titian had so clear a realization of the odious intrigues and fundamental dishonesty of the papal court that he refused to yield to the Pope's urgence that he remain in Rome attached to it. Besides his wish to breathe the free and uncontaminated air of the lagoons again as his own master, Titian had a further good reason for wishing to go home as speedily as possible.

On December 18, 1545, after a heavy snow, followed by a thaw and a sharp freeze, the Grand Hall of the New Library, of which Sansovino was architect, crashed down into ruin. The weight of the frozen snow on the arched-over but not completed hall roof was too heavy for the supporting members. Fortunately the rare books bequeathed to the Republic by the poet Petrarch and Cardinal Bessarion had not been installed there. The crash took down with it all the ducats Venice had spent upon the Hall, Sansovino's reputation and his liberty. The ruins had scarcely ceased to quiver when the architect was seized and thrust into prison. Venetian justice was so stern and so swift in action that the unhappy artist was extraordinarily fortunate the charges of culpable negligence against him did not set him immediately between the columns on the Molo, with the headsman at his back. As it was, the authorities condemned him to pay a tremendous fine, serve a long term in prison, forfeit his status as city architect and lose all his other distinctions and privileges.

His legion of friends and admirers at once championed him stoutly. Cardinal Bembo, Emperor Charles V's Ambassador, Don Diego Mendoza, and of course the fiery Aretino did everything they could to get him out of prison. The Council of Ten received the pleas and maintained a grim silence. Sansovino stayed despairingly where he was. Then Aretino wrote a characteristic entreaty to Titian, busy in Rome. The news disturbed the painter greatly, but he reacted to it with all the power in which Aretino had expressed confidence, and by his intervention with the new Doge, Francesco Donato, whom he had painted as a Senator just before starting for Rome, procured the architect's release, remission of his fine and a final reinstatement, after several months of delay, in his post of official architect.

Interesting as that tribute to friendship is in itself, it is less compelling than the means which made it successful. The portrait of Senator Donato was left unfinished because of the necessity for starting to the Eternal City. But Senator Donato was an old and proven friend of the Triumvirate. When he was elected to the dogate, Titian wrote to pay his respects. The new Doge could have demanded his immediate return to Venice to paint the usual official portrait. Instead he returned Titian's compliments through Aretino and let him stay. On his own account Aretino wrote that it was a good omen the senatorial portrait was not finished, since it was clearly ordained by fate that Titian should depict him in the ducal coronet. The Doge was a kindly man, and Titian pushed his advantage to the extent of clearing their common friend and setting him back to work.

Since he was not ordered to come home at once Titian redoubled his efforts in Rome, not only in painting for the Farnese family but for Guidobaldo Duke of Urbino, and in striving to secure the release of the benefice of Colle for Pomponio, which had long been promised. All his efforts, however, were frustrated by the self-seeking interests involved, including the Duke of Ferrara and Cardinal Salviati, each of whom wanted Colle for a friend. Disappointed and not a particle the richer than when he arrived, Titian finally left Rome in May 1546, "enriched by many gifts," Vasari tells us without saying what they were, and instead of going direct to Venice broke his journey at Florence. Aretino tried to persuade Duke Cosimo to have his portrait done, but he refused, and Titian, after studying the art of the city, perhaps made another stop before reaching Venice, in Piacenza, where Pier' Luigi Farnese, a man now racked and wasted by anxiety and disease, was striving to maintain his jeopardous throne. The badly damaged portrait of him in the Naples Museum, Crowe thinks, may have been done from sketches made in Piacenza and finished later at Biri Grande, for Piero was not in Rome while Titian was there. The doomed man—he was stabbed by assassins under the orders of the Emperor through General Ferrante Gonzaga—in this final portrait is but a shadow of the favorite painted a scant three years before at Bologna.

Hardly had Titian returned to the Casa Grande late in July, to find Venice and its gay life unchanged, than the Papal Legate, Giovanni della Casa, gave him reason to think he would really secure the Colle benefice. The prelate introduced him to powerful friends, and the painter's hopes bounded up again. It was all futile. The Farnese brothers were much too busy to bother with such a matter. Cardinal Alessandro was on the eve of starting for Germany as Papal Nuncio. Ottavio was raising an Italian army to invade the

Danubian valley after crossing the Alps. So the painter turned back to his private commissions, and Vasari made a mistake when he said Titian finished the *Allocution* for the Marquis del Vasto at this time. The picture was begun in 1540 and in all probability finished in 1541 or soon thereafter. Crowe and Cavalcaselle declare, and Lafenestre agrees, that it was now he "composed afresh" that *Descent of the Holy Spirit* for the church of San Spirito to which reference has already been made, began an altarpiece for the church at Serravalle in Cadore, executed for Aretino the portrait from the death-mask of Giovanni delle Bande Nere, and had the Doge give him sittings for the official portrait which was overdue.

The likeness of the ferocious young Medici soldier was as remarkable an accomplishment as the two pictures of the Empress Isabella. Aretino, it will be recalled, was in Giovanni's suite when the young general had a leg shattered in battle in 1526, and told graphically in his letters of the last hours of his idol. Told that his only chance for life was amputation, and strong men were ready to hold him while the surgeons did their grisly work, Giovanni snarled back that twenty could not hold him, but that he was ready, so they could hack away. They did, and he died of shock and infection. Aretino then called in Giulio Romano and had a death-mask made. This later on was lent to several artists, finally to Titian. With supernatural skill the painter realized boldly with superb freedom the figure of the dashing *condottiere*. Here the artist had not even an inferior painting by which to guide his procedure. All the death-mask could do was to give him the size and form of the features; the rest he had to envision. So magically did he accomplish it that the resulting portrait looks, as Crowe remarks, exactly "as if it had been done from life."

It was also about this time that he painted the delightful and delicate picture of his daughter Lavinia, then about seventeen, called *Girl with a Fan*. It shows a shy, conscious young woman all in white, walking past with her flag-fan held stiffly erect, a slightly startled expression on her face, as if she had been made suddenly aware of intense scrutiny. The German critic Suida admits this picture to be the Master's work, but denies that it is Lavinia. He may be right, but there is a good deal of resemblance between the immature features and expression of the shy girl of this portrait and those of the portly matron of some years later admitted everywhere to be Lavinia after her marriage. Who the girl of this picture is really has small importance today. The quality of the work is what gives it its artistic significance.

Crowe calls attention to a curious mistake of some of the historians, who called Lavinia Cornelia. Ridolfi himself makes this error, with the words "said to be the painter's daughter, named Cornelia." The mistake undoubtedly occurred because, as von Hadeln points out in a note on the passage, Lavinia was married in 1555 to Messer Cornelio Sarcinelli. Ridolfi's manuscript was first published in 1648, and was written after the marriage, so his error is understandable. The Master was very fond and proud of Lavinia and painted her many times at different ages. He used her regular and attractive features in more or less idealised forms to grace various other canvases also, even, so some of the critics aver, giving her likeness to some of the nudes he executed for wealthy patrons. Going still further, according to Crowe, the painter permitted his studio assistants to use Lavinia's likeness for the *Salomé* in the Prado, in which she holds aloft the tray bearing the freshly severed head of John the Baptist. That a great master possessed of such astonishing delicacy of perception where color, light and shade and drama are concerned should be so little squeamish about the daughter who was closer to his heart than any other living creature is to us amazing. But again we must remember the times, and the totally different viewpoint of sixteenth-century Italy toward such matters.

Events moved fast as 1546 drew to a close. In November Cardinal Farnese, with his brother's army in camp near Ulm, suffered another attack of fever. While the southern soldiery died like flies from cold and dysentery, he fled south, stopped in Venice to see Titian, ordered another picture from him. Titian was glad to promise this, as Alessandro was bound for Rome, and Titian still hoped for his influence in procuring the Colle benefice. Then in February 1547 Giulia Varana died and the Duke married Vittoria Farnese, daughter of Pier' Luigi, at Rome on June 4. Not quite two weeks later Sebastiano del Piombo died, leaving vacant the office of the seals of the papal bull. All these events coming so close together prompted Titian to write Alessandro on June 18, offering his services and asking to be appointed to the Piombo now that his friend Sebastiano was dead. This was a diplomatic way of saying that he would be willing to change his residence to Rome and enter the Farnese service definitely.

While he was waiting action on this new turn of events, he painted the altarpiece for the church of Serravalle. The townsfolk had at first asked Francesco Vecellio to do the work. They did not approve his preliminary sketch, but did take his suggestion that they ask his brother to do something. While the painting was under way they apparently demanded that the figure of Peter be substituted for that of St. Vincent. The painter made the change as demanded—and charged them twenty-five ducats extra. The pretty little quarrel that resulted dragged on for six years after the painting was delivered, ending in 1553. The altarpiece is a splendid work, revealing the subtle influence Titian's study of the works of the Roman masters had exercised upon his own luminous art. Age, dirt and none too scrupulous care have considerably damaged the work, but it still reveals startlingly, through the serene strength of its principal figures, its masterly balancing of light with shadow, the subtle gradations of color and naturalness of the flesh tones, that the painter had learned from the best that Correggio and Raphael and Michael Angelo had left in the city on the Tiber. One evidence of this is Titian's inclusion in the landscape background of the miraculous draught of fishes which he must have observed in Raphael's cartoons for the tapestries illustrating the lives of Christ and the Apostles. The worthy church people of Serravalle little understood that the painting over which they raised a teapot tempest in regard to price marked, according to both Crowe and Lafenestre, a distinct advance over all the great painter's previous work as "one of the most brilliant specimens of his grandest manner."

While we cannot be certain of it, there are grounds for assuming that the beautiful *Venus and Adonis,* then an uncompleted study in the Casa Grande, was the canvas which Cardinal Alessandro saw and wanted finished for himself. Lafenestre believes also that the *Supper at Emmaus,* now in the Louvre, must have come from his hand at this same time because when the painter sold many of the paintings in his studio at the end of the year before starting for Augsburg to obey the command of the Emperor, a replica of this picture was purchased by a Venetian patrician, Alessandro Contarini, who promptly presented it to the Republic. The original, Lafenestre declares, without stating his authority, "had some time before" been sent to the Duke of Mantua. Crowe exactly reverses this statement. Lafenestre apparently is right. In its simplicity, beauty and strength the *Supper* reveals the steady progress the aging painter was making with the vigor of young manhood in uniting through the liberty of his conception idealized figures and mere supernumeraries: in this case the Christ and the two disciples, and the innkeeper and the boy. It is all the more noteworthy for that reason that Titian should have such small success as an animal painter. The little dog under the table snarling at a half-concealed cat hardly looks like a dog. Evidently the painter was not a real lover of animals nor was his observation of them close enough to be reflected by his disciplined brush.

As the summer of 1547 wore on into early fall Titian had about decided to accept the Piombo and transfer to Rome permanently. He went even to the extent of selling all but the very largest and best pictures with which his studio at Biri Grande was always crowded. But Charles V had defeated the Protestants at the battle of Mühlberg, taken the fat and unhappy Elector Frederick of Saxony prisoner, and was confident that he had crushed all armed resistance in Europe. Sure of his ground, he practically ordered Paul III to reconvene the Council of Trent, and gathered his own court at Augsburg in preparation for the meeting, sending word to Titian to come to him. The old painter was not too comfortable about the changed plans, for the Farnesi were not men to be offended with impunity by even an Emperor. So the letter Titian wrote Cardinal Alessandro on October 23, 1547, was a model of diplomatic hedging and caution. Still none too confident of its effect, Titian sent it not to Rome but to his friend and powerful protector the Duke of Urbino, who forwarded it with a covering letter equally diplomatic but urgent and giving the painter his full protection. We do not know what the Cardinal wished he could do when he read the two letters, but he had at least the good sense to know that a man of Titian's international fame, who had the solid protection of the ruler of all Europe and one of the strongest princes in Italy, could scarcely be molested without serious consequences. Also, much more important matters were at issue than paintings, and the temper of Charles, flushed with triumphs, was not such that he could safely be offended by being deprived in any way of his favorite painter.

So a little easier in mind, perhaps, and provided with the wherewithal for the journey by the Emperor, Titian started north toward Germany. Lafenestre says he previously divided the paintings in his studio into three groups, one of which he disposed of at public sale, one he left at Biri Grande to await his return, and the third he took with him to Augsburg, "perhaps to give as presents, perhaps to sell to the courtiers" there. Included among the canvases he took along was an *Ecce Homo* (today in the Prado) which he presented to the Emperor, and possibly two of the great *Venus and Love,* one of which now hangs in the Prado, the other in the Uffizi at Florence.

As we dip into the political history of that troublous year of 1548 we realize that perhaps Titian took these large, awkward but valuable paintings with him to court not altogether to create material patronage. Behind him stood the grim figure of a strong Emperor able to enforce his demands if need be with military operations. Opposed was a weak and vacillating Pope surrounded by intriguing relatives and sycophantic courtiers. He did not want the Council to be held anywhere but at Bologna. Charles insisted upon having his own way. While the suspicions, fears, jealousies and plots were increasing, Pier' Luigi Farnese was, as we have seen, stabbed by an imperial assassin, and General Gonzaga calmly gobbled up Piacenza. Titian was fairly caught between the two major contenders. He was a knight created by the Emperor, and a beneficiary and already almost official painter of His Majesty. He was bound by promises and his applications for the benefice of Colle and the Piombo to the Farnese family. No one was then wise and farsighted enough to know which party would eventually exterminate the other, what the effect of France would be in the imbroglio and, most individually important of all, to what extent the struggle would conveniently cloak or account for a number of long overdue private murders. In such conditions an artist might be snuffed out with much the same lack of effect on the troubled scene as a single candle beside a bonfire. But if the artist were canny enough to secure his relative safety by attaching powerful friends to his person through rich gifts, he would as least have a reasonable chance of escape if assassination threatened, as it easily might do. To go prepared was the essence of caution.

It is astonishing in the circumstances that Alessandro reacted as he did. Crowe seems to feel that Titian's added prestige in being sent for by Charles made him more desirable than ever, and as a result the Cardinal promptly saw to it that the painter was given the

long hoped for abbacy of Colle. Guglielmo della Porta received
the seals of the Piombo, and superficially Titian was to be envied.
However, for a man of seventy to set out early in January to ride
horseback across the Alps and then live for about ten months in the
very coldest Alpine cities in Southern Germany was not only a hardship but a very considerable risk. Even with the comforts of modern
hotels and inns, such frigid and cheerless towns as Ceneda, Innsbruck and Trent appeal only in the summer. Augsburg, nestling
inside its defensive walls, with one fine wide main street and frescoed houses, had little to attract the painter's eye. It made an ideal
setting for that very reason for the brilliant imperial court gathered
there for the Diet.

Charles had assembled everyone of importance, from the imperial family to the families of some of his prisoners. Titian also
had his own suite of attendants and assistants, among whom was
that *arrière-cousin* Cesare Vecellio who eventually wrote a book on
costume. At Ceneda, where he stopped *en route,* Titian received a
letter of introduction from Count della Torre to the Cardinal-
Prince-Archbishop of Trent which was an open-sesame everywhere, though he hardly needed it. He found on his arrival in
Augsburg that the town was full of old friends and patrons. There
were lords, courtiers who fawned upon him because of the favor of
his Majesty, ministers of state, prelates and, not least in importance
among the princes and German dignitaries, the millionaire bankers
of the famous Fugger family of Antwerp and the almost equally
wealthy Welsers. They all had their wives and families with them.
Charles lived for the moment in a splendid Fugger palace on the
main street. From it a bridge connected with the house occupied by
the captive Elector John Frederick of Saxony, his most valuable
prisoner. Part of the time the painter Lucas Cranach was also
there, and scattered about as close as possible to the imperial domi-
cile were Charles's brother, King Ferdinand, the latter's two sons
Maximilian and Ferdinand, his daughter Anne with her husband,

Duke Albert III of Bavaria, Queen Dowager Mary of Hungary, Emmanuel-Philibert of Savoia, Maurice, the new Elector of Saxony, the saturnine and courtly Duke of Alva from Spain, the Prince of Salerno and a host of others less important. Among them all moved the quiet but powerful figure of Chancellor Granvelle, the Emperor's main reliance and chief adviser, and his son, the Cardinal.

In such a group Titian was thoroughly at home and at ease. He knew he would paint most if not all of them. But his first charge, after being graciously received by Charles, was to paint the monarch. That first picture was the famous equestrian portrait of the Emperor as he rode recklessly forward toward the ford in the Elbe during the battle of Mühlberg. By April the picture was well advanced, and in May Titian sent Aretino a hurry call for more colors, especially for half a pound of lake. In a previous letter he told the poet he wished Lorenzo Lotto was with him to guide him by his criticism.

The battle picture of the Emperor was badly damaged by fire that swept the Prado in 1608 but was, when I last studied it, still one of the great pictures in that gallery of masterpieces. Mounted upon a chestnut Andalusian charger, His Majesty canters forward from a *massif* of lofty trees toward the ford in the river. He wears magnificent gold-damascened armor and a crested morion or open-faced vizorless helmet above which wave scarlet plumes. His legs are in close-fitting chain mail, and he carries his lance at the "ready." Behind him Titian has rather indicated the rolling landscape than painted it, but the result makes the figures of knight and horse stand out more resonantly in the harmony of colors.

The real mastery of the painting, however, lies in what Titian was able to do with so difficult a subject as the Emperor. Charles was far from being a well man in 1548. His always bad complexion was bilious and his usual expression gloomy, while the familiar Habsburg features were far from attractive. Without concealing any of this, Titian succeeded in investing his imperial warrior with a dignity and force approaching the truly heroic. Here indeed was the martial lord of Europe, the man delighting in war and at his best when with his soldiers, and showing, even through the tension he displays, the indomitable will that kept his none too vigorous body to its self-chosen tasks and its opportunities.

Not long afterward Titian again painted him, this time after dinner. The Emperor, who suffered atrociously from the gout, lay back in a large armchair to favor his throbbing foot. Here was no armored knight joyously tilting into the fray, but a very tired old man in a black velvet *béret,* doublet and hose. Beside him a window gives upon a pleasant landscape, and as the evening was cool on the balcony where the sitting was held, his Majesty wears one of his gloves and a voluminous robe with rich, thick fur collar and facings. His one ornament is the golden chain and pendant of the Golden Fleece. One does not need to look twice at this likeness to appreciate the power of both painter and sitter. Sombre thoughts, perhaps with unrealizable dreams, looked out from those alert yet wistful eyes. This is the man who for half a century held Europe under his potent spell, relaxed and allowing his trusted friend the painter to see him as he really was.

Charles was not ungrateful. On June 10 he signed an order doubling Titian's pension on Milan, which was to be paid in Venice, "regularly," warned Natale Musi, the Augsburg representative of General Gonzaga, governor of the fortress-city, as the Emperor really meant Titian to have the money. Lafenestre says of it drily that it was an "ideal pension, which to tell the truth he never enjoyed." Fortunate painter, to have so many private commissions which did pay, and such patrons as Chancellor Granvelle and his son the Cardinal-Bishop of Arras, who between them took at least three portraits and four great compositions. Time spent with these two was far from being wasted.

All through that summer, part of which was very hot, Titian

toiled with the energy of a man half his age. Portrait after portrait came from his brush with astonishing equality of excellence, leaving us an historical record of inestimable value. The period was one during which the Emperor imposed the famous edict of the Interim, the suppression of the great guilds, the restoration of the patricians to power, the installation of Maurice—who four years later in 1552 drove the Emperor pell-mell over the Alps by way of the Brenner Pass, a temporarily badly defeated man—as Elector of Saxony in the place of the monstrously fat John Frederick who was sweating mentally and physically as he sat to Titian not a stone's throw from the imperial chambers. Not only did Titian paint practically everyone at court, but he somehow found time to sit himself for the painter Lucas Cranach, who had long been attached to the Saxon court at Wittenberg. Excellent in many ways as a painter though Cranach was, his dry style and inferior quality of spiritual penetration made his likeness of Titian a record rather than a breathing impression such as the Cadorine gave of all his subjects.

Practically all the Titians were taken by orders of either the Emperor or of Queen Dowager Mary of Hungary to the Netherlands, where they remained until the imperial court went to Spain in 1556. There they were placed in the Prado and presumably were destroyed in the fire of 1608. Besides the portraits, the indefatigable painter filled in his spare time with four myths executed for Queen Mary—*Prometheus, Sisyphus, Ixion* and *Tantalus*. Sanchez Coello the Spanish painter made copies of *Prometheus* and *Sisyphus*, and these, with the engraving by Cort of the former, are the sole survivors to tell us of Titian's ability to turn from portraiture to mythology and back again under circumstances of such pressure and difficulty as would have daunted any other painter. Crowe reports the two surviving pictures as assigned to Titian, "though not without hesitation."

After the Emperor had left Augsburg Titian remained there to do as much as he could toward finishing his portraits while his impressions were fresh, and then started homeward to complete his tasks in the Biri Grande studio. In October he was in Innsbruck, where he painted, or rather sketched out in color, the children of King Ferdinand, secured a royal warrant which authorized him to cut timber in the forests of the Tyrol, not for commercial sale but for his own purposes, had the warrant balked by the royal ministers, and appealed over their heads to the King. The canvases of the royal children, which, damaged though they are today, still reveal traces of Titian's brilliance in the heads and hands, seem on the whole to indicate the work of Cesare Vecellio, already spoken of as in Titian's suite at Augsburg.

About the last week of October the painter returned to Venice, and the whole Academy gathered joyously to welcome him and listen to the thrilling stories he had to tell them of Emperor and King, princes and courtiers and churchmen, of the ceremonial masses attended by everyone, of the lavish entertaining and the gossip and scandal. Aretino has left us a somewhat nebulous outline of these gatherings in his palace on the Canal. But the Duke of Alva and Cardinal Madruzzi of Trent had gone to Spain to bring Prince Philip, Infante of Spain and heir to Charles's complex kingdom and problems, to Italy in order to begin familiarizing him with the intricacies of his inheritance and give him an opportunity by personal contacts to form his own judgments of the men and conditions with whose future he must work. The Infante was to make a solemn ceremonial entry into Italy at Genoa, and Titian, with his habitual foresight and wisdom in affairs, decided to go and present himself. He was the more anxious to secure the friendship and patronage of the future Emperor-King because, on the strength of his doubled pension, he had betrothed his daughter Lavinia to Messer Cornelio Sarcinello of Serravalle, and needed the money to provide the indispensable dowry. In addition to this, the profligacies and irresponsibility of Pomponio had made serious inroads

upon his reserves in spite of all he could do and of Aretino's letters
begging the young wastrel to behave himself. The faithful Orazio,
sent to Milan to collect the pension if he could, had failed to secure
a *scudo*. Titian wrote General Gonzaga stating all this and begging
for his good offices to remedy the default, but it did no good. A
personal appearance and the friendship of two such powerful and
highly placed nobles as the Duke of Alva and the Cardinal-Prince-
Bishop of Trent, which could be more readily invoked orally than
by letter, determined the weary and disheartened painter, and late
in 1548 he made the arduous trip northwest, but apparently to no
avail. While away he painted the Duke of Alva, and another portrait, that of Giuliano Gosellini, private secretary to General Gonzaga. This was sheer wasted time so far as influencing Gosellini
was concerned, for he happened to be a man of integrity who was
proof against such approaches.

Back at home early in 1549 Titian was more admired and popular than ever, and Aretino's letters are a mine of interesting gossip about the gay parties he attended and his flocks of effervescent
friends. Though we have practically no knowledge of his painting
during 1549, it is known that he sent to General Gonzaga a copy
of the equestrian portrait of Charles he had promised from Augsburg long before, hoping it might warm the governor's hard financial heart and bring the completely overdue pension. It was not
until February of 1550, however, that Gonzaga sent Titian's no-
tarized papers to the Milan Senate and asked that the statute of
limitations not be applied to his claim.

In the meantime the Emperor, upon the death of Paul III, called
a new Diet at Augsburg and sent for Titian to attend him again
there. The painter arrived the cold night of November 1, 1550,
and promptly gave his Majesty a letter from Aretino, who hoped
through his influence and the power of Cardinal Delmonte to become a cardinal himself. Charles was weary of the cares of state

:outier than ever, and in a very gloomy mood. Thinking more
bout abdication and spending the rest of his physically wretched
xistence in some religious retreat than of worldly affairs, he asked
`itian to paint him an allegory which should express all his dis-
llusion and his gnawing hunger for peace and repose.

The painter's response was to sketch out the celestial Court gath-
red about the Trinity. Darkly blue-robed and erect the Virgin
tands in the front row in the blinding glory emanating from the
wo thrones and the Dove, interceding with her divine son on be-
.alf of the penitent imperial family. Charles, in his burial shroud,
is crown beside his knee, behind him the Empress Isabella, and
ack of them Dowager Queen Mary and the Infante Philip, all
neel and plead forgiveness for their sins. Slightly to one side of
ie center of the bottom of the huge canvas Moses, a powerfully
iuscled old man with a beautiful tanned body, half reclines upon
cloud, his right hand holding aloft one of the tables of the law.
n front of him and partly concealed is the still darker Noah, both
ands high above his head supporting the Ark, with the messenger
ove perched upon it, the olive twig in its beak. Between Moses
nd the saint at the extreme left behind his back is the stark, grim
.gure of a black eagle with outstretched wings, head turned far
ɔ the left and open beak, looking at first glance almost as if it were
ying upside down. Opposite Noah with her left hand almost
ɔuching him, a typically Venetian and beautiful saint whose
olden hair is festooned with pearls, gazes toward the Trinity and
oints upward.

Vasari evidently never saw this picture or else he was more
han ordinarily remiss in describing it, for he has the Emperor and
impress on opposite sides, and says: "Our Lady is present with the
nfant Christ, who has the Dove over his head." Since the Christ
 adult and is enthroned opposite the Eternal Father, the Dove of
he Holy Spirit hovers between them in a golden nimbus of glory

and no infant is anywhere visible, the Florentine's inaccuracy must have been due to oral descriptions he received from observers who themselves were inaccurate.

Emperor and painter had many long and intimate discussions regarding the picture while it was being worked out. No artist of Titian's stature would have set himself willingly to such a composition, which called for its even moderate success upon supranatural powers. That it did succeed is a remarkable proof of the undiminished vigor and freshness of Titian's mind at the age of seventy-three in a task calling for the utmost that the world's greatest painter could do. Gronau points out that perhaps Titian kept in mind Michael Angelo's heroic figures in his *Last Judgment* to give scale and the general effect of the nearer persons in his canvas. "They too are of colossal proportions," the critic declares, "and yet as with Michelangelo's figures, we believe in their reality. Never has the Master's often criticised realism been more amply justified by success than in this picture. . . . It is especially difficult to give any idea of the colouring. The stronger details become merged in the general tone given to the picture by the wonderfully rich and graduated bank of cloud. . . . At the bottom . . . only one narrow strip remains free, and this Titian has filled in with a splendid landscape. . . . By the simplest process Titian here attains a high ideal."

Though this picture was a magnificent achievement, and today hangs in the Prado—not as the *Last Judgment,* the name the Emperor gave it, but as *La Gloria*—the main object of Titian's visit to Augsburg this second time was to paint the Infante Philip, then twenty-four, and enduring the trying process of learning the personalities and ways of his future subjects. Titian had not been at Augsburg a month before he had sketched the unprepossessing Prince. He finished the formal portrait probably by the following February. It is a picture of more than usual interest aside from its

being the first of the remarkable series of portraits of Philip executed during the next few years, which Crowe calls "the long
series of copies, the best of which adorns the gallery of Naples."

With so many demands upon his time and energy, the Infante
was probably a highly impatient sitter. Titian accordingly, with
his accustomed facility and speed in catching a speaking likeness,
put his entire energy and imagination into a swift approximation
of the head, a color sketch, as Crowe points out, "as it were his
own private memorandum . . . a thing that was neither drawing
nor painting, yet partaking of both, and sufficient for the reproduction of either:—a surface without the charm of rich tint or
broken modulation, but masterly as giving in a few strokes the
moral and physical aspect of his sitter." It showed the Infante life
size, seated close to a wall opening through which a landscape is
visible. His face was turned to the left but his eyes looked at the
beholder. Details of his costume are jotted down hastily: black silk
doublet with the white shirt showing at the neck; the white silk
jerkin or surcoat fur-lined and collared, with shoulder puffs on the
sleeves; the Golden Fleece on the breast; black *béret* ornamented
with small pearls; and hands merely hinted at roughly to give their
action without bothering at all to show the fingers. That was all;
but it was enough.

With these memoranda as his guide, the painter in his studio
could work up official and show portraits at his leisure, and he did
so magnificently. The first is the familiar one of the Infante in
Madrid, and it perfectly discloses the difference in Titian's methods. The sketch was for the single purpose of recording the true
likeness and form of the sitter in a furious drive against time and
impatience. The finished work represents the careful, often slow
carrying out of every resource of the artist's technical processes to
produce body, tone and substantial quality. In this instance, instead of having a sketch of one person or subject and a finished

picture of something entirely different to make the point clear, w
have the jotting and the finished work of the same theme for com
parison.

For a painter of Titian's uncanny skill and adaptability to trans
form a seated figure hastily outlined into a commanding prince i
resplendent armor standing erect, one hand upon his sword, th
other upon the plumed helmet upon the table behind him, was
simple matter. One could not tell that the Infante had not pose
for the portrait. In 1553, when Charles, following his wily custom
of years by trying through marriage to secure international peace
wished to betroth Philip to Mary Tudor of England, this canva
was sent to the Spanish Ambassador in London with instruction
to present it to the Queen, on the understanding that it must retur
to Spain when the live Prince had been substituted for the painte
image. "Bloody Mary," already flattered by the prospect of havin
a consort ten years her junior, was declared to have fallen in lov
with the picture; it may, indeed, have been the deciding factor i
the marriage of 1554, four years before her death.

Philip was even less attractive than his father, and his relativ
immaturity as contrasted with the Emperor's careworn visage mad
the dissimilarity the more striking. Nothing daunted, Titian gav
the sallow features with their displeasing Habsburg peculiaritie
of thick lips, prognathous jaw and unwieldy feet, a regal dignit
and rich dress. The haunting undercurrent of melancholy which
was Philip's unfortunate inheritance from his father, in the pain
er's experienced hands became the gravity and intentness of a ma
of high station and ancient lineage. One after the other Titia
produced from that original sketch portraits showing the Princ
later King, seated by a window in royal robes and wearing a *béret*
standing, in somber black trimmed with white fur; again, standing
in magnificent court dress; and so on. A year later, on February (
1551, Philip's treasurer sent Titian two hundred gold ducats fo
the first painting, and another thirty to pay for "*ciertas colores qu*

VENUS WITH A MIRROR

se han traido de Venecia para mi servicio—certain colors which were brought him from Venice for my service."

The payment when it came evidently jogged Titian's memory, for he promptly sent a tart letter to the incorruptible Giuliano Gosellini, General Gonzaga's secretary and man-of-affairs. After the usual compliments, the painter scornfully referred to his pension as his "passion," and said he would be willing to leave it in the hands of either Gosellini or those of Donato Fognana, his agent, 'provided it can be screwed out of the grasp of the treasury." As usual, this appeal accomplished nothing. And in May, when the Emperor started for Innsbruck and Philip began his return journey to Spain, Charles awarded Titian another, this time a Spanish, pension of five hundred *scudi* in the Infante's name. Three years later the painter wrote (September 10, 1554) to the Emperor to complain that none of the grants thus far made him had been paid, in either money from Milan or Madrid, or in grain from Naples. Like all the other letters, it accomplished not a thing. By August the painter so often pensioned, so little rewarded in fact, was back in Biri Grande and working as hard as ever, mostly for private individuals who both could and did make good their agreements.

CHAPTER FIFTEEN

Permanence in Change

TITIAN never saw the atrabilious Emperor again after Augsburg, though he was in communication with him at intervals. His direct relations now were with the Infante Philip, so soon to become King of Spain and one of the most dreaded of all sovereigns, as well as one of the richest and most powerful. Tradition cited by all the historians is that Titian followed Charles to Innsbruck, where he did a so-called imperial "family group" as an allegory which, if indeed it ever existed, has long since disappeared. Crowe regards the story as "an obscure and uncertain tradition" and questions Ridolfi's acceptance of it. Gronau does not mention it; neither does Lafenestre, so we may dismiss it as negligible.

With the change of his royal active patrons the nature of Titian's work for them changed correspondingly. For Charles the Emperor most of the requirements had been for historical portraits and religious subjects, several of which were more or less fully prescribed by His Majesty himself. For Philip the Prince and later King, though he was even more fanatically religious than his father—we cannot forget the Inquisition and its ruthless behavior during his reign, with the pitiless seeking out of all even faintly suspected of many other things besides heresy—Titian began by executing mythological themes. The choice of subject was fortunate for posterity, because it gives us greater insight for judging both the

292

painter's matured emotional quality and the methods by which he gave it expression. Both differed radically from the feeling and methods of his youth. Experience had deepened all his perceptions with the years. Now, instead of seeing just a little more in the pagan legends in which he had so delighted thirty or forty years before because they enabled him to paint the joy of living in all its youth and beauty, he roused to a loftier conception of his opportunity. Here was the stimulus needed to fire his soul with the passion of displaying his rare mastery. As Gronau happily phrases it: "His subject no longer interested him because it invited him to celebrate joy and pleasure and beauty, but because it offered him a splendid opportunity to display nude figures in a variety of movement in the open air, the play of light on human forms, the blending of contour into atmosphere. It is the glorious inauguration of Titian's supreme mastery of his craft."

The first of these new works was the *Danaë* already described and still safely in the Prado. Through the years this was followed by several others, some now lost, others still in existence and thrillingly beautiful. The best of his *Venus and Adonis* myths is in the Prado, and dates from 1554, Gronau calling it "pendant" to the *Danaë*. Then one by one came a *Perseus and Andromeda, Jason and Medea* (now lost), *Actaeon and Diana,* the *Rape of Europa, Tarquin and Lucrece,* and the canvas known both as the *Venus of the Prado* and *Jupiter and Antiope.* In his enthusiastic summation of these works Gronau declares that we cannot but wonder whether or not Titian personally observed the rollicking exuberance of strong sunshine on nude bodies, asserting that no artist ever painted such effects with a skill equal to that of this wholesomely young old painter whose soul and whose brush seemed never to grow weary.

Though Ridolfi tells us that Titian returned to Venice the richer by eleven thousand *scudi* in gifts as a result of his German contracts, the amount is probably as grossly exaggerated as his statement—called abruptly into account by con Hadeln in a note on the passage—regarding the length of his stay. In any event we know the painter's difficulties with almost all his pensions and promises of payment. It is not strange, therefore, that he should be anxious now, since he did not apparently intend to be absent from the city for any protracted periods again, to regain his broker's privilege in the Fondaco de' Tedeschi, which had been suspended because of his long stays outside the city since its restoration to him in 1539. If he could win back the *senseria* it would mean about 118 ducats a year income and remission of certain taxes, to say nothing of adding to his already matchless prestige. The eminence of his fame as a result of the very absences which had hitherto prevented his being considered for reinstatement now added weight to his petition to the Council of Ten, and on October 29, 1552, the longed-for decree issued. Titian promised to see that the last pictures to be done in the Hall of the Great Council would be accomplished in the time set under his direction. The Council accepted this arrangement, Titian instructed his son Orazio, his student Tintoretto and young Paul Veronese, and the decorations were completed within a short time. The devouring fire the year after Titian's death swept all this magnificence out of existence and the world is permanently the poorer for it.

The artistic records of the second half of 1551 and the first half of 1552 leave much to be desired. We know a good deal from letters written during that time about receptions, dinners, late suppers, and the viands that went with such festivities and "welcome home" affairs, but very little about what the painter was accomplishing. Crowe recalls in this connection a quotation Cicogna gives from the book of a Ventian doctor, Niccolò Massa, who recorded in 1556 that he had once, calling on Titian, asked him whether or not he felt any difference from day to day in his ability to work. The old painter smilingly replied that he did: one day he felt like work and could do much, and the next he was unable to accomplish anything. The surgeon explained it by a learned *obiter dictum* to the effect that it depended entirely upon the internal heat or chill of the body. Aretino put it more in our own way by exclaiming in one of his priceless letters that the painter had amassed a comfortable income by incessant toil; but, he added, "I would not exchange my ease for his wealth for any consideration."

One of the most puzzling and interesting of the innumerable lacunae in the story of Titian is the mysterious affair of the large packing case dispatched from Venice on October 11, 1552, containing, according to the covering letter, three paintings: a *Queen of Persia,* a *Landscape* and a *Saint Margaret.* The *Saint Margaret* is to this day in the Prado gallery, the *Landscape,* perhaps, in England under another name. But no one knows what the luckless *Queen of Persia* was or where she went. Titian's own words in describing the painting were simply: "A *Queen of Persia* recently come into my hands, of such fashion and quality as you will see, which I have judged worthy of examination in the exalted presence of Your Highness." Did he, as seems a reasonable assumption, paint her himself in gorgeous robes or nudity, using some particularly beautiful model? Until further research in thus far undiscovered source material can answer this question, it remains to titivate our curiosity.

The *Landscape* may be the picture in Buckingham Palace known by the title of *The Storm.* We know from contemporary and subsequent testimony that Titian was the first painter of note to execute landscapes as such in Italy, with figures, both human and animal, which were subordinate only. We know also that these paintings enjoyed immediate success. Lomazzo, cited by Lafenestre, told of the painter as being in this respect "a sun among small stars," and in another volume by the same author Aurelio Luini, the son of Bernardino, tells how, on visiting Titian, he asked how the latter was able to make the trees always suit his countryside and backgrounds. Titian showed him a mere sketch of landscape, in which nothing could be distinguished close at hand. Then he moved it away to the proper visual distance, and suddenly, as though lighted by sunshine, everything cleared up magically. "And Luini left the studio saying that he had never seen such a marvelous thing."

Pope Paul was dead, and the new Pope, Julius III, sent to Venice a new Nuncio, Ludovico Cardinal Beccadelli, Bishop of Ravello, to replace the former envoy, Giovanni della Casa. At the time he arrived the confessor of both Titian and Aretino, Fra Curado, the curate of the Minorites, had been thrown into prison because he rashly dared to deny or at least to question seriously the doctrine of confession and its divine origin. Painter and poet were exceedingly anxious about their friend, and Aretino immediately appealed to the Cardinal-Legate to extricate him from his perilous position. He did so, and the friends' joy took very practical form: Titian's in a perfect portrait, Aretino's in a sonnet. That a man of Aretino's character and habits should vouch for the saintliness of a priest who, while supposed to be charged with absolving a young woman from her peccadilloes was actually promoting a good marriage for her, was amusing to say the minimum. Cardinal Beccadelli must have had no small enjoyment in questioning the subdued priest who had languished for months in his cell, and then ordering his release.

The portrait is a magnificent example of Titian's style of the time, done with a full brush, and evidently, from Aretino's enthusiasm, must have presented a remarkable likeness. It shows a man with a noble forehead but a face on the whole weak and cunning rather than forceful. Gronau feels Titian had no particular interest in painting the man. In this the German differs from Crowe, who regards the work as an excellent specimen of the Master's current method. Crowe's statement, however, is slightly misleading in its implication of swift, free treatment with loaded brush. On close examination many touches are visible to testify to the careful working over with the minutest care in what the English critic has him-

ADAM AND EVE, OR ORIGINAL SIN

self called a "polishing" of the finish in other pictures. Also, a careful scrutiny of the document the seated Nuncio holds reveals that Titian painted with microscopic accuracy the lettering of a complete identification in the words: *"Julius P. P. III. Venerabile fratri Ludovico Episcopo Ravellen. Apud Dominium Venetorum nostro et apostolicae sedis Nuntio, cum annum ageret LII. Titianus Vecellius faciebat Venetis MDLII mense Julii."* The same delicacy and finish of touch is manifest throughout the canvas and the total effect is one of subdued brilliance.

Busy as Titian was, he had his share of domestic troubles to shoulder. Though he had betrothed his daughter Lavinia to young Cornelio Sarcinello on the expectation that the Emperor's treasurer would send him gold enough to provide the handsome dowry of fourteen hundred ducats he had promised, he could not make the necessary arrangements and the marriage had to wait. In 1549 his devoted sister Orsa died and left him without the attentions and capacity that had managed his big house and his entertaining since the death of his wife. Now Lavinia had to take over the domestic burden. Evidently the girl had been well trained by Orsa Vecellio, for the Biri Grande mansion continued to be the setting for many festivities, and patrons, sitters and guests were constantly coming and going. Activity was the secret of Titian's long life, work the salt that gave it savor, the gay reunions with his many friends merely the pleasant but not vital dessert.

By October of 1552 he had sent to Spain the works already referred to, among them the landscape which moved an English writer, Heath, to warm appreciation and to crowning the poet-painter with the title of "Homer of Landscape." But portraits, the allegorical works for Philip of Spain, and the finishing up of *La Gloria* for Charles V took most of the painter's time. The contrast between the Beccadelli picture and Titian's self-portrait painted at this time is striking enough. Lovely also is his likeness of Lavinia. The two canvases are very different, Lavinia executed with the tenderest care and minuteness, his own features brushed in with a vigorous disregard of limitations which make it seem as if the painter were impatient with himself, so that his technique could scarcely keep pace with his thought.

Lavinia he painted several times, always with the same evidence of deep affection and scrupulous regard for detail. Gronau remarks, in connection with the nudes her features sometimes completed, that "the truth is forced upon us that Titian in his portraits of women, with very few exceptions, does not altogether attain to the same level of excellence as in his portraits of men. Even the most celebrated, the *Bella,* for instance, are without depth of character, for the absence of which his usually perfect choice of colour in dress and accessories cannot always compensate. Titian's women are mostly without souls; they tell us nothing." Perhaps; but may it not be possible that even Titian himself could not paint what did not exist? While it is true that a few of his women sitters, such as Isabella d'Este of Mantua and the gifted Irene of Spilimberg were respected for their intelligence, and a few of the famous courtesans who were doubtless among his models for nudes were capable enough in both Greek and Latin, it is on the whole very doubtful that feminine intellect was either widely possessed or very keen. A Vittoria Colonna was as rare as a Michael Angelo. Hippolyte Taine remarked as he stood before the great Venus and Cupid in the Uffizi: *"C'est le sérieux vide et l'immobilité d'ame d'un animal en repos qui attend."*

Another year slipped rapidly by with the fast greying painter more than justifying Aretino's jest about the white beard and green thoughts by the mastery displayed in his work, when suddenly, on May 31, 1553, the Emperor sent a peremptory message to his Ambassador, Francisco Vargas, in Venice. It was written in Spanish and sent from Brussels. "They are saying here that Titian is dead. There is no confirmation, and it probably is untrue. Nevertheless, inform us of the truth, and whether he has finished certain pictures he undertook before he left Augsburg, or when they will be done."

Don Francisco answered a month later: "Titian is alive, well, and no little pleased to know Your Majesty had asked about him. He had spoken to me before about the picture of the Trinity [*La Gloria*], and on my inquiring again about it said he would finish it in September. I have seen it, and it seems to me that it will prove a work worthy of him, as is also a picture he has almost ready for the Most Serene Queen Mary [of Hungary] of *Christ in the Garden Appearing to the Magdalen*. The other picture, he said, is one of *Our Lady* similar to the *Ecce Homo* Your Majesty has. The reason he has not sent it is that he has not been sent any measurements. When he receives them he will proceed to paint it."

Before Titian could finish any of these works Doge Francesco Donato died and was succeeded on the throne by Senator Marc' Antonio Trevisano. The customary official portrait naturally took precedence over all other work. Though it was burned in the fire of 1577, a replica of it, doubtless painted from the artist's preliminary sketch, still exists in Budapest. This reveals, Gronau's disapproval notwithstanding, a strong-featured but kindly prince who seems full of vigor and human sympathy. The two portraits on which Titian was working during the summer, which figure largely in Aretino's letters, and which hung in the studio at Biri Grande during the winter of fifty-three and four, were one of the imperial Ambassador Don Francisco Vargas, the other of Protonotary Granvelle. Both have disappeared and left not a trace behind.

The happy connection with the imperial House begun back in 1530, enduring for almost half a century, absorbed all of Titian's time and best thought when he was not engaged upon an official assignment or an occasional portrait or composition for some private patron. During the summer of 1554 he made a shipment of no less than four canvases worthy of an imperial benefactor: *Danaë*, *Christ Appearing to the Magdalen*, the *Grieving Virgin* and *La Gloria*. There is no record of any other ruling family having ever collected anything like the number of Titians displayed by the Spanish Habsburgs in the Prado—forty-three portraits, and all the allegories ordered by Philip II. Here in a single gallery were the works gathered by Charles V, the family portraits sketched at Augsburg for Dowager Queen Mary, and not least in interest the painter's own image of himself with his painting of the King in his hand. The fire that swept the Prado destroyed some paintings, others were given to the visiting monarch Charles I of England and other personages of moment. According to Gronau the palace inventory dated 1686 listed no less than seventy-six Titians, though he doubts some of them were genuine. Notwithstanding all losses, today Spain still boasts the richest collection of Titian's works, even if "only half of the fifty mentioned in the catalogue are by his own hand."

"The letters of Titian on the subject of his *Danaë* and the *Venus and Adonis*," Lafenestre observes pithily, "edify us at the same time as to the generosity of Philip toward the clever painter who showed himself ready to satisfy the princely desires, and the facility with which the Prince, devotee and wanton, mixed with his practices of a superstitious piety a taste for provocative nudes." The artist assured his royal patron that he would like to paint "the likeness of my own heart, long devoted to your Highness," but as that was impossible, he would finish up *Venus and Adonis* in a form similar to that of the *Danaë*. He made it, as the Frenchman drily comments, not such as would "demand of painting serious encouragement of the marital virtues." That, it seems, was hardly its object. Vasari says the figures are "admirable; the Goddess is fainting as she sees herself abandoned by Adonis, who is accompanied by dogs, which are singularly natural." It is sometimes difficult to be patient with critic or commentator who ignores the facts that are evident to everyone in favor of his own empty words. The goddess as Titian depicted her was so far from fainting—by the way, did goddesses ever perform such a scurvy mortal trick?—that she had a passionate grip with both arms of the young huntsman's sturdy body, and her head is flung back upon her shoulders so that she can instantly see every change of expression in his uninterested face. Every line of both figures displays muscular tension and action, which is increased by the dreaming figure of Cupid under a tree in the background and the bored immobility of the impatient dogs on leash.

It was unfortunate for Prince Philip, to whom the picture was sent in London as a wedding gift, that when it reached him it had been severely damaged by a long wrinkle "in the beautiful middle portion" and would have to undergo exceedingly careful restoration. The royal dismay is easy to understand, for the chief charm of the canvas is Venus' exquisitely molded back and the brilliant contrast of her transparently rendered flesh against the rough sunburned body of Adonis. The disfiguring wrinkle still is visible, lying almost horizontally across the center and making the goddess look almost as if she had been beheaded. None of the critics esteem the picture highly, and Crowe feels it was merely a variation on an old theme which he and his studio had so often to repeat that both Master and students were tired of it, while the landscape betrays in color and lines that other hands than Titian's at least completed it.

The *Danaë,* now in the Prado, while more satisfactory than the *Venus and Adonis,* still suffers by comparison with the original painted for the Farnesi and later placed in the Naples gallery. The Madrid example has less delicacy, charm and transparence of color. In principle it is close to the original, though showing a certain loss of elegance and a more materialistic realism. It is entirely possible that this was due in part at least to the fact that Titian was working very hard and had much to trouble him. He felt also that he must continue to meet the demands of a Prince whose fleshly predilections were remote from his father's interests. Notwithstanding this, the Madrid *Danaë* gives as vivid a study of character contrasts as anyone could ask. The startled Cupid of the Farnese *Danaë* has here been replaced by an old hag of a servant of the gypsy type, with hard, drawn features, bony, muscular arms and bare shoulders, greedily extending her apron to catch as much as she can of the shower of gold pieces falling from the portentous cloud the placid nymph watches, almost as indifferent as the little dog asleep beside her. Was Titian a satirist, we wonder, that in this canvas he takes Love away from the waiting nymph and leaves as her only attendant the gutter harridan?

The Prado is a veritable Golconda for treasure and thought-provoking discovery. From the purely fleshly charms of Titian's nudes we may pass in a moment to the grave *Noli Me Tangere*, fragments of the picture Charles V so loved he kept it with him in even his cell at Yuste, the noble *Grieving Madonna* or *Lady of Sorrows*—rated by Lafenestre as one of Titian's "noblest creations" —and the imposing *La Gloria*, already described. With the shipping of these two latter works to the Emperor Titian sent him a covering letter, again complaining against the sticky fingers or grasping tactics of the imperial ministers, hoping that "the most christian Emperor that ever lived" would do something to relieve his painter's distress, and explaining that he would have sent the pictures sooner had he not been ill, and besides that married off his daughter. As an afterthought he attached a postscript: "The portrait of Signor Vargas has been put into the work. If it does not please Your Catholic Majesty any painter with two brush-strokes can change it to another."

The marriage of Lavinia that Titian related should be understood as a betrothal, for the marriage was not actually solemnized until the painter had been able to accumulate enough to hand most of her dower of fourteen hundred ducats to young Sarcinello. Moreover, that was only one of the worriments that harassed the painter. Pomponio had shown by this time definitely that he had no intention of reforming, and his father's reproofs and pleadings had accom-

plished no result, apparently, but to anger him. Aretino and Pomponio exchanged a lively series of letters, and Titian finally acted with
stern decision. In April he wrote to the Duke of Mantua asking
that the benefice of Medole, hitherto enjoyed by Pomponio, be
transferred to Titian's nephew. A few months later the painter was
given the income from the benefice of San Andrea del Fabbro, near
Mestre, just north of Venice, and he reserved that for himself. To
make his nephew the more welcome to his Medole parishioners,
Titian painted and gave to this simple little country church the
beautiful altarpiece of *Christ Appearing to the Virgin Mary*. It is
so clearly a picture painted in a devout spirit for the Master's artistic self-expression and satisfaction, and it so brilliantly displays
what the artist of the Venuses and Danaës could do when left to
his own wishes and imagination, that we marvel afresh at the power
and versatility of his genius.

He boldly chose Heaven as his field. In the foreground the
risen Christ comes forward, draped in His shroud, in a blinding
radiance toward His kneeling mother, who raises her hands in
adoration. Overhead a heavenly host of cherubim makes a tremendous ogival arch, the heads innumerable fading gradually into
the glory. Behind the Christ, Adam supports the great cross. Eve
is behind him, almost concealed, and behind this first human pair
are the grand heads of Abraham and Noah. Whether or not we
agree with Crowe that everything Titian painted at this period of
his later artistic life was determined by realism, we cannot but admit that the glowing canvas shows how he had profited by his
visits to Rome and Florence, and how the power of Michael Angelo,
the grace and beauty of the work of Fra Bartolommeo and Perugino, when filtered through Titian's own keen intelligence, emerged
in strength, grace and spirituality imposed upon a firm and substantial base of realistic impressionism. Injured and patched-up
though the picture is today, it is still in place on the high altar for
which it was painted, and invites all who see it to ponder the vision

of the man whose white beard never turned the fresh verdure of his thoughts to dryness.

On the last day of May 1554, Doge Marc' Antonio Trevisano died, and was immediately succeeded by Ser Francesco Venier. The new prince was a man not only of high character and purpose, but of vision and unselfish desires. He called on the painter promptly not only to paint the official portrait always required, but to execute the customary votive picture of his predecessor. The Venier likeness was completed early in 1555 and paid for by the Salt Office in March. Late in summer—August 19, 1554, to be exact—the Doge called Titian to the Palace, where he signed a contract to complete before September 1555, a picture in which Doge Trevisano in full robes of state would be shown kneeling before the Virgin and Child, to whom he is presented by Saints Mark, Anthony, Dominic and Francis. The contract, worthless until approved by the Council of Ten, called for a total payment of 171 ducats 12 *scudi* in instalments. It also provided that Titian should be fined, or that his heirs should suffer a like fate, if the picture were not completed within the time specified. What extraordinary people the Venetians were! When the contract, which everyone actually approved, was voted on in the Council, it was defeated. That was on September 5, 1554. Again the Doge tried to put it through on the 28th, and again the vote was negative. Titian had almost completed the work before a partial agreement became legal on January 7, 1555, when the Ten made an advance of fifty ducats and ordered a survey or appraisal of the work. It was in its place in a magnificent frame in the Hall of the Pregadi long before it was finally paid for in full. Both it and the Venier portrait were destroyed by the fire of 1577.

Busy and eventful indeed were the next year and a half. Doge Venier began, almost as soon as the votive picture of Doge Trevisano was authorized, to move toward a votive picture commemorating that hardly tried but gallant Doge of former years, Antonio

Grimani of the tragic record. Defeated at Lepanto in 1499, brought home in shackles, imprisoned, exiled, pardoned grudgingly, restored to a command, and finally, in 1521, elevated to the dogate, he had experienced almost every reverse of fortune humanly possible, to die at last rich in honor and esteemed by his grateful countrymen. No commemoration of him of the usual sort had been painted. Except for the customary official portrait in the Palace, he had become merely a name. So on March 22, 1555, Doge Venier convinced the Council that Titian should be ordered to paint a suitable votive picture by which Venice would testify to her appreciation of her son, whatever his early mistakes had been. Lorenzi says that by July Titian had made such progress with the canvas that an advance of fifty ducats was paid him. Then, with one of those sudden, mysteriously final occurrences that mark so many of the gaps in the Venetian story, for some reason the matter was dropped. Titian never finished the painting himself, and it was not until after he was gone that his students completed the remarkable picture today known as *La Fede*.

It is fortunate for us that the work was delayed, for it thus escaped the great fire that wiped out all the other Titians in the Ducal Palace. Today it radiates a golden effulgence through the Sala delle Quattro Porte. In the center a white-robed figure symbolizing Faith (La Fede) floats downward in a great aureole of light, surrounded by cherubim winging their way from the obscurity of rolling clouds. With her left hand Faith clasps the upright of a tremendous wooden cross whose foot is held by one cherub while another steadies the end of one arm. Opposite, another cherub touches the elbow of Faith's right arm, raising his little hand in a gesture calling attention to the great cup of sorrows Faith holds aloft. At the right Doge Grimani kneels, clad in shining armor under the golden robe of his office, his head covered with a white skullcap, his expression that of a man dazzled by a vision, his hands raised. Beside him kneels a richly dressed page bearing the ducal coronet, and behind both in the extreme right lower corner two soldiers in full uniform look on. At the left corner St. Mark gazes upward at the heavenly vision, while his imposing lion, with lashing tail, growls, and a distant view of the fleet at anchor and the city beyond completes the allegory.

Nothing could be clearer than that Titian attempted, with a degree of success that must be left to each beholder to determine for himself, to symbolize the late Doge's eventful history. In its technical aspects the picture moves the different authorities on painting to almost antipodal judgments. Gronau admits the striking qualities of the colors, the perfection of the work as painting full of fine touches, but is dissatisfied because it is "not a purely free creation of Titian's genius. Again we cannot help feeling that allegorical subjects were not his forte." Lafenestre takes an opposite view. The "ensemble of the picture is grandiose and arresting; we recognize almost everywhere in it the bold, free execution and intense coloring with intermittent heavinesses that mark the work of the latest period of the master." Crowe's feeling is the most clearly stated of all when he says this is worthy "to rank amongst the most magnificent and effective palatial pictures that Titian composed in his later years. Nor is there a single work of the artist which more fully confirms contemporary accounts of his style." Vasari merely mentions the canvas as one he saw in Titian's studio on his final visit to the painter in 1566, but he goes into detail regarding this later period of the painter's style so graphically and clearly the entire passage—adapted rather than translated by Crowe, and so lacking some of its original force— is worth repeating exactly as Vasari wrote it after he finished discussing several of the nudes we have already seen.

"It is nevertheless true that his method of proceeding in these last-mentioned works is very different from that pursued by him in those of his youth, the first being executed with a certain care and delicacy, which renders the work equally effective whether seen at a distance or examined closely; while those of a later period, executed in bold strokes and with dashes, can scarcely be distinguished when the observer is near them, but if viewed from the proper distance they appear perfect. This mode of his, imitated by artists who have thought to show proof of facility, has given occasion to many wretched pictures, which probably comes from the fact that whereas many believe the works of Titian done in the manner above described to have been executed without labour, which is not the truth, and these persons have been deceived; it is indeed well known that Titian went over them many times, nay, so frequently that the labour expended on them is most obvious. And this method of proceeding is a judicious, beautiful and admirable one, since it causes the paintings so treated to appear living, they being executed with profound art, while that art is nevertheless concealed."

Art so sublimed that it conceals art is the utmost tribute that can be paid an artist, for it is a tribute to the soul of its creator even more than to his technical accomplishments as an artist. It is difficult for the expert, accustomed to examining minutely every detail of a painting to assure himself that each is or is not evidential of the work of a particular man or period, sometimes to distinguish between his technical and his aesthetic opinions. There is a world of difference. The philosophy of the beautiful has nothing inherently to do with the details of material production, and that should be remembered on reading a criticism or comment unless one is sufficiently versed in aesthetics to be able to grasp the distinction without laboring it.

While Titian was hard at work on this and other pictures, he signed the marriage contract of his daughter and paid over to Messer Cornelio Sarcinello six hundred ducats on March 20, with the balance to be paid later in cash and jewelry. The young people were married on June 19, and the unpaid balance of the dowry was discharged in September. June 19 was a memorable day for

Titian because Messer Lorenzo Priuli was then elected successor to Doge Venier, and Titian found his affairs complicated by losing Lavinia as his housekeeper and incurring fresh obligations as painter of the new Doge, not to mention the flattened condition of the artist's purse after being emptied by the princely amount of the wedding dower.

Titian's international repute had become so high by this time that the Venetian Senate absolved him from the duty of painting portraits of the doges, and charged him with heading a committee, of which Sansovino was the other member, to exercise an important function. Sansovino had finished the great main hall of the Library of San Marco in 1553, and its ceiling had now been compartmented for frescoing. The Procuratori accordingly named the two foremost artists in the Republic as a committee to select the worthiest younger men to paint it, with the condition that each man so chosen should be paid not more than sixty ducats for his work, and the promise that whoever did the finest picture should in addition be given a gold chain of honor as a testimonial. By this time Titian's relations with his former pupil, that stormy petrel Tintoretto, were so distant as to exclude him automatically. Sansovino and Titian finally approved a group of several promising young men, one of whom was the newcomer Paolo Cagliari, or Paolo Veronese. He had arrived in Venice only the year before, and despite his youthful experience as a sculptor under his father, had acquired his reputation in Verona and near-by cities when he dropped his chisel and took to the brush instead. When the frescoes were finished Titian and Sansovino once more selected Veronese for honor, and he was launched on a career in the capital which almost immediately put him into competition with his benefactor and master.

Then it was that Titian's true greatness shone out clearly. Instead of crying down a mere boy of twenty-eight whom he had just made, the magnificent old Master competed with him on the

basis of achievement. In the meditative calm of the Biri Grande
studio he executed what Crowe calls "that fine and standard work,
The Baptist in the Desert. . . . It is not without reason that Vasari
and Dolce praise this fine creation as a marvel of design and
color. . . . No picture of the master gives note, as this does, of
the power with which Titian could set the example to his young
competitor in the conception and execution of form, realistic in
shape and presented in a plastic spirit." Painted with all the
bravura of which the eighty-year-old artist was master, and striking with unmistakable accents the true Venetian note in both
design and color, the Baptist shows a commandingly masculine
figure filling a full half of the canvas. Wild of hair and beard,
partly clad in skins, every line of his superbly muscular body revealing perfect physical condition, the Saint wears an expression
of mingled austerity and sweetness, force and tenderness. At his
feet lies a young lamb; behind on his left a foaming stream
chuckles its way over some rocks. The cliff at the foot of which he
stands and the characteristic landscape of the background add their
Titianesque touches of warm, transparent color as foils to the
sweetly painted tanned flesh and brilliant sky. It may not, as
Crowe suggests, differ to any marked degree from others of
Titian's later works except that possibly it is painted with a
keener realization of anatomy and a freer, more naturalistic design. For once none of the critics had anything to say about Titian's
harking back to Michael Angelo in his construction of the Baptist's figure, which is as convincingly normal for a large and powerful man as Michael Angelo's giants were merely ideas clothed
in astonishing if not impossible human forms.

As 1556 went into its fall season, one of the longest and closest
associations of Titian's life was abruptly terminated. On the evening of October 21, while entertaining at a late dinner in the mansion to which he came after his Roman visit—it was on the Riva
del Carbon, in San Luca—Aretino leaned back in his chair laugh-

ing heartily at a joke. He laughed so hard he lost his balance and fell backward, striking his head against the floor. At the same moment apoplexy struck him, and in a short time he was dead. The tradition is that he recovered consciousness long enough to confess and receive absolution. Then his irrepressible spirit flickered up for a moment, and he gibed: *"Guardatemi da i topi, or che son unto!*—Guard me from the rats now that I'm oiled!"

The man who excepted God alone from his slanders because he did not know Him apparently went out of life as truculently as he had lived it. Only Titian and Sansovino really mourned him. To practically everyone else his passing was a relief, for the world feared the power of his scurrilous pen and the malignity of his brilliant and unscrupulous mind. The general attitude of his victims is summed up perfectly in the letter written by Antonio Pola, a poor creature who had flattered the poet while alive and now turned venom upon him dead. "On reaching Venice I found that *mascarone* Aretino had surrendered his soul to the Devil. I think his death will not displease many, especially those who henceforth are relieved from paying the brute tribute."

CHAPTER SIXTEEN

The Gathering Shadows

IN NO MAN of whom we have authentic rec-
ords did the spark of life probably burn higher, more consistently
or longer than it did in Titian. The shadows that begin to lengthen
with most human beings at about the traditional three-score mark
never completely chilled him. After 1556, however, his activities
gradually decreased and his story becomes one more of repetition
than of fresh progress with but one or two notable exceptions. At
the age of eighty in 1557 Titian stood alone as the survivor of a
generation of painters and other creative spirits all of whom were
either dead or had ceased to be felt. Death struck about him on all
sides, and year after year he had to mourn the passing of some
friend or relative. Aretino was gone, and already forgotten by the
chattering world, when the painter's old friend and imperial
patron, Charles V, sighed away his life in the cheerless monastery
Yuste, in bleak provincial Estremadura, Spain, on September 21,
1558. Strangely enough, the worn-out Emperor's death resulted in
good for Titian. Philip II was at Ghent in Flanders when the news
was brought to him. He immediately went into temporary retirement in the monastery of Groenendaele. There, on Christmas Day
of 1558, he sent work to his governor of Milan, the Duke of Sessa,
to pay all the arrearage on the pensions his father had given the
old painter, his gesture of a belated clearing away of overdue obligations.

311

Titian felt himself too old to make the hard journey to Milan in midwinter, so he sent his faithful son Orazio instead—almost to his death. By March of 1559 Orazio was able to write back to his father that he had been in touch with the Duke and would soon have the payments in full, he hoped by Easter week. Once that was settled he intended to go to Genoa. With the help of letters to the King's ambassador there, he thought he could collect the overdue pension from that source. What follows is a sixteenth century parallel of many an American gangster tale.

Years before a fellow townsman of Aretino named Leone Leoni, a sculptor by profession, had appeared in Venice and established friendly relations with Titian and his family. Leone was a gifted rascal, unusually capable as a sculptor, especially in such small and delicate work as medals and coins. His record was very bad. Somehow he effected his escape from more than one city after having murdered citizens. In Rome he managed to become director of the mint, and used that opportunity, so the legend goes, to attempt counterfeiting. Escaping again when the law trod too close upon his skirts, he came to Venice. Again he had to leave hastily after a murder. Persuasive of tongue, with ample personal charm to cover a demoniac temper and the instincts of a ruthless killer, Leone by 1558 had found new friends, this time in Milan. By the time Orazio Vecellio arrived he was living in a palace he had bought, had servants and horses and maintained himself in style.

Orazio, carrying with him heavy, bulky cases of his father's paintings besides the documents for the governor, went to the Falcon Inn and was about to settle down there in very modest state when Leone appeared, demurred violently and insisted that Orazio should make his headquarters in the Palazzo Leone. Honest and straightforward himself, Orazio finally accepted the pressing invitation, and for some months enjoyed Leone's hospitality. By June 14, however, he became uneasy about abusing the tolerance of his host, and, since that very day he had received the two thousand ducats due his father, perhaps a trifle suspicious of the man whose evil repute he must have perfectly well known.

His mind made up firmly, Orazio booked accommodations at the Falcon. He told his host that he must leave, and Leone pressed him most cordially not to think of it but to remain indefinitely his guest. Orazio refused as graciously as possible, and during the evening came back to Leone's to clear out his baggage and paintings. Leone, accompanied by servants, attacked him with daggers in the house. But Leone, who struck the first blow, aimed badly, and instead of killing, merely dealt his victim a serious wound. Orazio fought his way out into the street, where he shouted to his servants for help, and was carried, bleeding, to the Falcon. Someone hastily notified the Duke of Sessa, who immediately sent his barber. That capable leech worked on Orazio so successfully that next day he was able to testify before a magistrate who was sent to him for that purpose. Leone was immediately arrested, but as Orazio could say only when asked the reason for the attack that he thought Leone was jealous of his standing with the Duke, the would-be assassin was let off with banishment and a fine. Orazio, on the contrary, went about for years in fear of the villain, who swore that next time—! Later on, when able to write his father about the affair, Orazio changed his story and said Leone knew he had the cash the governor had paid, and that the attack was an attempt to seize the money and dispose of any testimony at the same time. Titian wrote immediately to the King, and besides reciting the facts of the assault, preferred the deadly charge that Leone was a Lutheran heretic who had already been expelled from Spain. He added that later the fellow was condemned to the stake by the Duke of Ferrara on charges of counterfeiting, and banished from both Rome and Venice because of murders. A heretic to Philip II was as the crimson *muleta* is to the angered bull in the ring. For some reason not now clear this time the charge seemed without effect, and the long and terrible arm of the Inquisition was not invoked.

It is barely possible that the King was so displeased with his Apelles at the moment that he was indifferent. Some months before—November 1557—Titian had shipped him the painting of an *Entombment*. It reached Trent safely, and then vanished. Philip wrote the Count of Luna on January 20, 1559, from Brussels to report the loss, charging him in no uncertain terms to find and deliver the picture safely and lay the thieves by the heels. The letter closed with the royal mandate: "And inform me of whatever you do because I am anxious to know."

A few days after Orazio's attempted murder, but before his father knew of it, Titian wrote the King, referring to the missing *Entombment* and informing his royal patron that he had finished two "poesies" meant for him, *Diana and Actaeon* and *Diana and Callisto.* "When your Majesty wishes to have them, simply command me as to whom they shall be sent, so as to avoid what happened to the Christ dead in the sepulchre which was lost in transit." He added that he would, as soon as they were shipped, devote himself to finishing up a *Christ on the Mount* and two more "poesies" just begun, the *Rape of Europa* and *Actaeon Torn by His Dogs,* into which he promised to put all the talent God had given him. He closed by pleading again for fulfillment of the King's unmet promises of reward.

That letter was written June 19, 1559. Philip answered it July 13 from Ghent ordering the picture shipped to Genoa, asking for a second *Entombment* to replace the lost original, and assuring his painter that he had given such orders in regard to the pensions that there would be no further difficulty. Shortly after the royal letter had reached Venice, the Ambassador there, García Hernandez, wrote the King (on August 3) to say that it would take Titian twenty days more to complete the two "poesies" because he wished to put some finishing touches to them which no one else would consider necessary. At the same time he would have ready a second version of the *Entombment,* larger than the first, and a smaller fanciful picture of a Turkish or Persian girl. This letter is peculiarly interesting and important because it shows how anxious Titian was, at eighty-two years of age, to give his canvases the uttermost in finish, so that, as Vasari said, they would look as though they had been easily dashed off. García Hernandez closed his communication by reporting that with the pictures he was also shipping glass panes and drinking vessels for both water and wine. The factories on the island of Murano were already known throughout the world for glass without a flaw, which even mighty kings were glad to secure.

Late in September pictures and glass were sent off to Genoa, and both the painter and the Ambassador wrote the King. Titian had no reply, although the pictures reached His Majesty eventually and pleased him. These two myths of Diana are considered finer than the *Danaë* or any of the Venus canvases because these are both bolder and more delicately accomplished. In the one is the familiar legend of the young huntsman following his dogs and blundering in upon the chaste Diana bathing with her nymphs. The second shows much the same setting, but this time across the pool the luckless Callisto struggles in vain as one of the goddess's attendants strips away her robes and discloses her pregnancy by Jupiter. The goddess of chastity was almost as ruthless at times as Juno for, to complete the two legends, she changed Actaeon into a stag who was always hunted after that, and poor Callisto paid the penalty for attracting the king of heaven by being metamorphosed into a bear. Crowe's comment upon these two masterly canvases is eminently fair. He says in part: "It would be vain to look for the poetry and freshness of the Bacchanals in these late creations of Titian's brush. The flash and fire of youth were leaving the artist as they had left the man. . . . Titian was never more thoroughly master of the secrets of the human framework than now that he was aged. . . . His power was the outcome of years of experience, which made every stroke of his brush both sure and telling. But years had also made him a realist, and practice had given him facility; and both produced a masterly ease which is not always quite so like nature as earlier and more studied, though perhaps more timid labour."

Titian kept a sketch of the *Callisto* in his studio of the same size as the finished painting. Later his students finished the details and it is now in Vienna; but as it was completed by other hands than the Master's it does not bear comparison favorably with the original. During the year 1559 Titian's old bachelor brother and close associate, Francesco Vecellio, died at his home in the family house in Pieve di Cadore. Crowe declares there is no evidence to show that Titian attended the funeral or that he visited the town at that time. Lafenestre, on the contrary, says without qualification that he did go, taking the opportunity "to paint or to lay out the picture one still sees in the chapel of the Vecelli" in the parish church. Crowe's comment is that he may have designed the painting, "which has at least the merit of being Titianesque." It "displays some of the technical habits of Titian without his skill and force, and for that reason may be assigned to someone familiar with his style, which can be no other than Orazio Vecellio . . . an altarpiece upon which he [Titian] left scarcely a stroke, if indeed he touched it at all."

All through these earlier years of Titian's last phase runs a steady stream of paintings characterized by both astonishing variety of subject and brilliant treatment on the one hand, and increasing evidence on the other that the aging Master was coming to rely more and more upon his studio to do the heavy filling-in, concerning himself largely with the delicate blending of colors and finishing as none but him could finish. Religious themes, portraits, allegories flowed from his brush in almost undiminished numbers. In 1562, following a magnificent *Magdalen* sent to Philip II the previous December, we have the astonishing incongruity of a noble *Christ in the Garden* and the *Rape of Europa,* shipped together in

April. These were followed the same year by one of the most beautifully painted compositions Titian ever sent out, the great *Jupiter and Antiope,* usually known as the *Venus of the Prado.* The canvas measures approximately twelve and a half feet wide by six feet four inches high, and the main figures are almost life size.

The hard and enduring physical labor of painting these tremendous canvases set no brakes upon Titian's output. He very seldom painted a small picture. Both his conceptions and his industry were as heroic as his genius. His production, in the eighty-eight years between his introduction into the studio of Zuccato and his death, is incredible. If we believe what seems reliable evidence he produced at least at the rate of one picture a month during that entire time, a record no other painter in the world has ever remotely approached. And there were, besides the works we know, probably many others that have vanished unrecorded and still more so mutilated by time and patching that they cannot be identified.

For this greatest of all his mythological scenes the painter chose, with the daring only ripe genius could justify, to use the fable of Antiope merely as exculpation for painting a magnificent rendering of nature in two diametrically opposed themes, set against one of his most brilliant landscape backgrounds. To the right of the center—the picture is unevenly divided by a tree which supports both scenes—the almost nude Antiope is asleep on the grass. At her feet Jupiter, disguised as a shaggy brown satyr, bends forward, cautiously lifting off the light garment covering the princess' lovely legs. In the air above her unconscious head Cupid, as classic as ever the Greeks made him, shoots his implacable arrow down at the heart of the father of the gods, who glances up at his hunter.

That is the main scene which gives the painting its name. Directly behind, separated from the three main figures by the tree, another satyr with a floral wreath on his head squats on the turf beside a girl whose lap is full of wild flowers. Rushing upon this placid group a hunter with two large dogs on leash shouts to the companion who follows at his heels. The latter sounds his hunting horn as the hunter points toward the central background where, in the midst of as effective a landscape as the painter ever conceived, a noble stag has been brought to bay by dogs who converge upon him from all sides. So astonishing is the power of the picture as a whole that we are compelled to use reason before we can reject the absurdity of even a mythological princess calmly sleeping through being denuded by a predacious god, the ferocious barking of the hounds, the braying of the horn, and the shouts of the excited huntsman directly behind her. Yet the more we study the scene, with its perfect poise and design, the better we realize that not one figure, not one gesture or attitude can be spared from this perfection.

Gronau comments, and justly, that the painter cared little about concealing the fact that he used the fable only as "an excuse for a splendid picture of nature . . . the most splendid landscape of the many that we owe him." He goes on to inquire, because of the tender beauty that so strongly recalls the idealism of Titian's younger days, thirty years before, "whether an older picture, for some reason left unfinished and now taken up again, may not really have been the groundwork for this one. The sleeping Antiope has the attitude and form of Giorgione's *Venus,* which Titian as a younger man imitated in his *Venus of Urbino.* The treatment in color seems on the other hand to point to his later period, although we have some difficulty in connecting it with the technique in the other mythological works. In any case the 'Antiope,' from the softness in transitions and the artistic modelling of the figures, is one of the most perfect creations of the Master." Long afterward, when the Prado was burned, the first question King Philip III asked was whether this particular painting had been saved. Told it had been, he exclaimed that that was a comfort, because the others could be replaced, but this one could not.

The distinction made in the last chapter between technical and aesthetic values and opinions is clearly shown in what has just been said of this picture, and anyone interested in attempting to evaluate for himself this remarkable canvas in terms of pure beauty alone will find himself in difficulty the moment he begins trying to set a standard by comparison with other works of Titian. It is precisely at this point that the relative significance of the technical enters to affect the aesthetic, and the beholder is involved in a sort of philosophical chess whose rules presuppose the rationalization of taste. No careful student, moreover, can fail to consider when pondering the matter that while Titian painted remarkable landscapes, he was never a landscape painter in the sense that he depicted recognizable vistas, "direct studies from nature," as Berenson phrases it. Titian's landscapes were warm, lovely, appealing, decorative backgrounds, but pure synthetics. He meant their soft and subtle coloring, their splendid effectiveness of line and perspective, their general construction to be a rich harmonizing accompaniment to his main purpose. In consequence he fused such natural elements as proved coherent with that purpose, and made no attempt to reproduce veraciously what any given landscape disclosed. There was no real Italian landscape painter, in fact, until Bassano showed the beauty painting had hitherto overlooked.

Some two years before this, in 1558, Titian executed his first great night scene in the *Martyrdom of San Lorenzo*. The picture was painted for the altar of that saint in the church of the Crocicchieri, and Vasari displays for it an enthusiasm unusual for his cool temper. He says: "It represents the Martyrdom of San Lorenzo, with a building crowded with figures; in the midst of them lies the foreshortened figure of San Lorenzo on the Gridiron, beneath which is a great fire, and the executioners stand around it.

The time being night, there are two servants with torches giving light to those parts of the picture that are beyond the reach of the fire beneath the gridiron, which is a large and fierce one; but the light it throws, as well as that of the torches, is overcome by a flash of lightning which descends from heaven, and cleaving the clouds, shines brightly over the heads of the Saint and the other principal figures. In addition to these three lights there is that of lamps and candles held by those at the windows of the building. All this produces a fine effect, and the whole work is, in short, executed with infinite art, genius and judgment."

Let us look ourselves at this tremendous piece of drama which, though now blackened and disfigured, may have the power to move us to more adequate expression than it stirred in Vasari, whose blood seems to have been largely ice water. In the first place, sentiment conceived the picture but left Titian free to exercise his genius as he would. Messer Lorenzo Massolo, the son-in-law of Messer Girolamo Quirini, Titian's old friend and patron, died in 1556. His widow, the lovely Elisabetta Quirini, also an old friend and admirer of Titian, asked him to make a memorial to her husband in the form of an altarpiece for his patron saint. As the painter pondered the design it seems to have occurred to him that being burned to death by day, no matter how interestingly painted, could not compare for drama with the same scene by night. The church of the cenobite monks in which the picture was to be placed was already full of masterly works by painters ranging from Masaccio and Mansueto down to Titian's own day, with Tintoretto and Schiavone, both among his foremost pupils, admirably represented. Whatever he, the Master, did must accordingly not only shine in bright company but outdistance all the rest easily.

Agony and death are always more terrible in the darkness and mystery of night than by day. Peter Martyr he had depicted falling to the assassin in the full light of afternoon. Lorenzo he would show at the antipode of the light scale, enduring his tortures in

SELF-PORTRAIT IN ADVANCED AGE

EMPEROR CHARLES V AT THE BATTLE OF MÜHLBERG. SEE FACIAL
EXPRESSION IN DETAIL FROM THIS PICTURE ON PAGE 282

the glare of a fire that lighted up the grim faces of his executioners and with its lurid ferocity made even the glory opening in the heavens overhead pallid, the lowering clouds heavy and livid. Flaming cressets should add their weird light to the blaze of the fire under the saint, whose muscular body should be held by brute force over the flames as burly soldiers pressed him upon it. Far above, between the low-hanging clouds and the rolling billows of smoke, the heavens would open to send rays gliding down to illuminate the face of the dying martyr. Drama must inhere in every line, every motion, every nuance of color. Aside from its moral lesson of heroism in suffering, the picture must be such as to stop the breath of the beholder with its unrelieved terror. He must see the cruelty and malice of the brutal legionaries concerned in the murder, the callous indifference of the mounted officer in charge, looking on in silent approval of the hideous spectacle; the sadistic matter-of-factness of the men stoking the fire, of those holding down the writhing body. Most of all he must be made to feel in the saint's expression all the horrors through which he had passed alive, to come to this final scene and see, as his last vision in life, the benediction of Heaven falling upon him, unseen by his persecutors.

With such a setting, and such seeming confusion of figures, Titian had to exercise all his genius to handle his lighting so as to make the picture at once intelligible and graphic. He did this with consummate artistry, even in obscurity bringing out powerfully each one of his characters and welding them all, by means of his strength and delicacy of light and shade, into a coherent and moving whole. He knew, as few painters of any period have known, that even if the illusion of reality could be produced without completely adequate handling of the lights and shadows in a painting, the results would be shocking, even hideous. So with the unerring knowledge of unfettered genius he toned and blended and balanced his effects of darkness and light, detail and the merest suggestion, until the result gave the atmosphere vital to his theme.

All Titian's magic as a colorist is to be found even yet in the time-blackened nuances of red and grey. Crowe endeavors to show that he could hardly have painted this picture without having seen the earlier work of both Raphael and Michael Angelo, but after striking the balance he admits Titian to have been even more human than the Umbrian, and almost the equal as an anatomist of the Florentine, while excelling him easily in what was typically his own, that magical play of "tints and lights and shadows which mark the true Venetian." He adds as a final touch that Titian "preserved an individuality as unmistakable as it is grand and striking." Even if the grime of centuries and the patching and inexpert work of so-called restorers have damaged the canvas beyond recovery, we can still stand before it in the dim light of the church and feel the emotion of the painter who conceived and executed it.

It seems almost beyond belief that the author of such a work could, as Titian did, turn to grotesque caricature and ridicule the very classic forms which to some extent formed the groundwork of such a picture as the *San Lorenzo*. Perhaps this unsurpassed Master of the graphic felt that art was giving undue attention to the classic without understanding its forms and using them as they were meant to be used. Whatever his reason, he chose the group of the classic *Laocoön,* and with biting irony produced the three immortal shapes of the king and his two sons in the grasp of the serpents not as men, but as monkeys. We can imagine the horrified gasp his fellow painters and many of his patrons must have given when this incandescent burlesque was seen. Yet notwithstanding the caricature, Titian showed again and again in widely different compositions, that he, at least, understood and knew when and how to make use of classical form and intention without allowing it to interfere with the integrity of his own conceptions.

Such a master could afford to toss off the caricature we know only through Boldrini's print of it.

Apparently next in interest to Titian after his art and his family was his native town of Pieve. Again and again he went far out of his way to serve it in ways its less important sons could not. In 1555, which was a very hard year for the townsfolk because of crop failures that brought almost famine conditions which they had no money to combat, Titian lent them considerable sums and aided in procuring food. In 1562 he notified the town that he would like to get his money back. He also asked interest at the not altogether unreasonable rate of eight per cent. For some reason not now apparent, he and the town could not quite agree, and in the fall the dispute was adjudicated by arbitrators who decreed that the town should pay him almost a thousand ducats, but reducing the interest from eight to six per cent. We wonder if perhaps the sending of two pictures earlier in the year to Titian's relative Vecello Vecelli—a small *Venus and Adonis* and a *Madonna* for the town—was by way of making certain of his kinsman's good offices. Whatever the reasons, Orazio was in Pieve and elsewhere throughout Cadore toward the close of the year looking after his father's various properties and the family interests.

In July of 1563 Titian wrote one of his usual letters to Philip II, in part to inform him that he was almost ready to send him a *Last Supper,* on which he had been working for six years, asking instructions as to the way the King wished it shipped, and to whom, and again begging for the payment of his long overdue pensions. All the while he was steadily painting, and more than that, giving much thought and effort to composing the quarrels between the mosaicists of San Marco, which had become irreconcilably bitter. As some of the designing for the mosaic decoration and additions to San Marco came from his studio and was probably largely the work of Orazio, there was excellent reason for Titian's interest in the delicate situation. The quarrel and its development with all the attendant circumstances have no place here except as showing the many external interests which made incessant demands upon the old Master's time and energies.

It was apparently at about this time that Titian began work on the still beautiful *Venus with the Mirror,* now gracing the United States National Gallery of Art in Washington. The painter did not claim payment for it until two years before his death in 1576, and the canvas was one inherited by Pomponio and sold by him to the Barbarigo family. From that collection it went to the Hermitage in St. Petersburg. The late Andrew W. Mellon bought it finally, and it has, we hope, come to permanent rest in Washington, where its radiance and power glorify the entire National Gallery. Just when it was painted we do not know, or whether it was done for the artist's own pleasure or for a patron thus far unidentified. It makes no difference: the vital thing is whether the painter's work is both timeless in interest and beyond the change of times and fashions. If a painting meets that exacting test and can justify its existence after centuries have rolled over it with their widely varying canons of taste and liking, it may be said to have achieved mastery. This work does exactly that. Like all Titian's studies of the nude, it is ardent and highly sensuous, but nowhere in it can the most captious find the slightest trace of what the English painter Ricketts calls "the feverishness which such qualities would imply in a man of lesser faculties."

Even touched up as the painting is today, it remains a work of nobility, an outstanding masterpiece excelled by none of the painter's later works for the combined force and compactness of its composition, grand style of modelling, beautiful drawing, and an unsurpassed harmony of line and color. The partly nude goddess is so utterly natural in posture and expression, and the two Cupids are so ineffably her satellites we feel as though we were in their living presence and one or all of them might speak at any instant

THE LAST SUPPER, IN THE CHAPTER HALL OF THE ESCORIAL

JACOPO STRADA THE ANTIQUARY

in a tongue we should comprehend. Gradually the realization comes to us also that we are not looking at a mere painted representation of flesh, but at the sweet, warm, breathing flesh itself. No other master of his time compared with Titian in this ability, already pointed out in the case of St. Sebastian, to represent the beauty of a transparent and living skin. Here, as in so many others of his nude studies, Titian gives us an impressionistic reality so strong and so convincing we not only see the delicate blue veins under real flesh, but we know they are throbbing with blood, that the polished breast and throat expand to her breathing. This is the illusion of life as rich and warm as it is sweet and true.

The more the details are studied, the stronger is the hold this palpitating canvas exercises upon us. Venus is seated upon a striped couch whose vivid yellow and black so work into the general color harmony their violent hues do no profanation. The rich dark red velvet mantle she wears has slipped from one exquisite shoulder and is held together at her hip by one hand. Its dark fur lining and gold-embroidered edges make a matrix from which rises the magnificent shaft of her sublime form, and the left hand, lightly held against her breast, by its graceful, almost caressing touch, serves to accentuate the sensuous appeal of the lovely contours. Turning her head, she gazes into the mirror held up to her by a straining little Cupid who fairly staggers under its weight but holds his position with straining muscles beautifully delineated. This little god's back is toward us. It is so exquisitely painted as to make one wish to reach out and touch the satiny skin, for there is nothing sweeter in the world than the body of childish beauty and innocence. Behind Venus, Eros himself lays one chubby hand on his mother's soft shoulder and with the other holds out a garland of flowers to crown her. Everywhere there is wise contrast: the play of light and shadow, with the superb figure of the Queen of Love focussing the illumination against the dark background; the subtle colorings, symphonic in their harmonies, against the marvelously projected shadows and the muted reflections in the mirror. The painting is the concentrated riches of Italy at the full flood of the Renaissance. None of the various replicas and copies of it can compare with the original, patched and restored though it be.

We know from previous correspondence that Titian and his brother Francesco were interested in timber concessions in the Tyrolean forests, and that both were keen businessmen. It comes somewhat as a surprise, however, to find as 1563 drew toward a close both art and business in a letter to a single patron, in which Titian shows he is dealing with a customer as well as a princely art collector. The first letter asks the Duke of Urbino to pay for a painting he had ordered and evidently had sent as a gift to someone in Mantua, and for a set of designs which may have been intended for use in decorating the Duke's palace at Pesaro. In the second letter, dated January 4, 1564, Titian again referred to these matters, and mentioned business transactions which proved that he was supplying the Duke not only with paintings but with considerable quantities of timber in the shape of pine logs and planks, the latter, no doubt, from his own sawmill on one of the small properties he owned or leased close to the timberlands on the edge of Cadore.

Crowe retells from Cicogna and Bicchierai an interesting story apposite at this time because part of it leads into the second *Last Supper* sent to Philip II. Among the Titians which were very much worth preserving as the sixteenth century drew into its last quarter were a *Nativity,* which was placed on the high altar of San Marco, and a splendid *Last Supper* in the refectory or dining hall of the monastery of Santi Giovanni e Paolo. Both these pictures were burned up by accident. The *Nativity* caught fire from a blazing decoration after mass on January 19, 1880. It does not concern us. The other does.

The city of Padua, Cicogna tells us, was captured by the Venetians under the daring leadership of Andrea Gritti, Titian's friend and later Doge of Venice, on July 17, 1509, St. Marina's Day. In thanksgiving for the success, brought about largely by Gritti's strategy, the Republic celebrated the occasion annually after that and as a precautionary measure stationed troops at various points about the city where trouble might occur. General Gritti, to use Cicogna's own terse description of the fight—which Crowe does not mention—"recovered Padua, besieged by the armies of Emperor Maximilian, using the strategem of sending into the city certain peasants with carts of grain, among which were his own soldiers. Once inside, he burst out of the convoy and planted the Venetian standard upon the city towers." Gritti, besides being a noble of a distinguished family, had been thoroughly educated in the arts and letters as well as in the science of arms, so he knew all about the strategy at Troy and was adroit enough to use a modification of that ancient ruse.

On July 17, 1571, sixty-two years later, as the festival of St. Marina and the recapture of Padua were being again celebrated, the German troops who had been quartered in the storerooms beneath the refectory of the monastery of Sts. John and Paul held their own celebration, got thoroughly drunk, and accidentally burned up the buildings with all their contents. The *Last Supper,* in the long dining hall, perished with all the other decorations and treasures. Crowe, in telling the story in outline, hazards the opinion that we "may presume that the *Last Supper* which perished on this occasion was the original which Titian now copied for Philip of Spain." Since the painting of the *Last Supper* was delivered to the Spanish monarch late in 1564 and the monastery original of the theme was not burned until 1571, some seven years later, the impression conveyed by Crowe's statement is at the very least misleading.

Much more to the point is the correspondence between the royal envoy in Venice and the King, in which the Ambassador, García

Hernandez, told his sovereign of the monastery picture, which he said the monks would sell for two hundred *scudi,* but which he, Hernandez, could have copied by Geronimo Titiano, a distant relative and student of Titian's, at a cost of only fifty *scudi.* When the King learned of this he ordered the copy by Geronimo, telling his Ambassador not buy the Titian unless it differed markedly. Curiously enough Gronau, usually accurate, blindly repeats Crowe's blunder involving confused thinking when he tells of the delivery of the *Last Supper* in 1564, after seven years of work, which "repeated an older composition of the Master's which had adorned the refectory of San Giovanni e Paolo in Venice but had been destroyed by fire in 1571." Possibly the translator was at fault, and the original German may not have been so hopelessly bad as appears. Today we have the unassailable facts that the picture was delivered in Spain, that it proved too large for the space allotted to it, and that the monks of El Escorial, whither it was sent, used Procrustean methods to make it fit. Unheeding the frantic protests of the deaf-mute "Titian of Spain," the painter Juan Fernández Navarrete, the ruthless monks cut off a considerable part of the upper section of the canvas, mutilating the architectural background irremediably and completely destroying its balance and proportions. We wish we knew what the King had to say when he learned what had been done to the work of his favorite painter. Unfortunately the picture never quite justified Titian's written opinion of it as "one of the most difficult and perhaps most important works I have ever done for Your Majesty." In spite of its dramatic action, it seems conventionalized—a rare fault to find in Titian—and suggestive of Leonardo's better treatment of the same theme. It has been so worked over during the centuries that today there is relatively little for us to admire of Titian's personal touch beyond the design and the grouping of the figures.

During these later years gaps in our information and confused statements regarding work undertaken or finished leave only a partial picture of Titian's activities, with the year 1564 almost a total blank so far as reliable information goes. In the previous year Cristoforo Rosa secured the contract for decorating the vaults of the big town hall of the city of Brescia, but as so frequently appeared in such contracts, the authorities made reservations. The chief decoration was to consist of filling three octagonal spaces in the centre of the large square ceiling. Brescia was a proud city, and her authorities, while liking Rosa well enough to trust him with the rest of the work, demanded for the *chef-d'oeuvre* the finest works of the foremost artist of the Venetian commonwealth. Rosa probably was graceful in the face of the inevitable. At any rate, he agreed to the contract, and Titian signed it in his presence on October 3, 1564, promising to execute three canvases covered with such subjects and figures as the authorities might designate. When the work was done, a board of survey would examine the paintings and determine a fair price, in the meantime giving evidence of good faith to Titian in the form of an advance of a hundred and fifty ducats.

As usual in such matters, both painter and townsmen were leisurely. Time to think was not denied in those golden days to anyone, least of all to those whose creative work was meant to be permanent. The Brescians took six months to decide upon what they wanted, and Titian wrote his acceptance on August 20, 1565. September of that same year saw him in Cadore on his annual vacation trip. While there he laid out the decoration of the Pieve church in frescoes and mosaics to be executed by his pupils. December found him back in Biri Grande. Exactly what he did during most of the year we can only guess, but among other things we may suppose he completed at least the *Transfiguration* and *Annunciation* for San Salvatore in Venice, and perhaps the large figure of *St. James of Compostela* for San Lio, also in Venice, as well as the beautiful *Education of Cupid* for the Borghese Palace in Rome, if we may credit the careful research of Crowe and Cavalcaselle. For a tired old man almost ninety those four paintings alone would be a remarkable record; but we must remember that Titian's unflagging zest for life impelled him to engage in many things besides art. So it is quite within the probabilities that with the help of the faithful and industrious Orazio, an excellent painter and acute businessman in his own right, he was concerned with an unending series of affairs of many sorts that kept them both fully occupied all the time.

The *Transfiguration* was the one painting of that theme to come from the brush of the Master. It was a work of age, not youth, yet his conception of both theme and treatment is powerful and its color arrestingly rich and full. The noble figure of the Christ is shown rising with outstretched arms, gazing upward toward Heaven, while on the ground below three apostles watch Him in awe-struck attitudes, and Moses and Elias, at His sides, float in postures of adoration. Unfortunately these two, while strongly conceived figures, are on the clumsy side, and Crowe says flatly they indicate "the coarser execution of the master's disciples, and particularly the shallow technical handling of Marco Vecelli. Oily pigment superficially blended and a marked deficiency of bold contrast between lights and shadows are unmistakable evidence of this." Gronau feels and says firmly that this is by far the greatest of Titian's latest creations, fully worthy of comparison with the great Christ of the *Tribute Money* of younger days. "According to Vasari," Gronau says, "Titian himself did not think this work of much value, and it is mostly dismissed with a few words showing it aroused no special interest. In our judgment, this is one of the most powerful productions and masterpieces of painting that Titian has bequeathed to us. . . . No less a judge than Rembrandt has paid a tribute of admiration to the picture."

The brilliantly executed *Annunciation,* composed for a near-by altar in the same church, is the doubly signed picture that tells of the painter's wrath when told the purchasers did not regard it as worthy of him. No one who studies it and compares it as a work of maturity with the same theme, so often previously repeated, can avoid the conclusion that here the Master has captured a degree of spirituality combined with naturalness, all embodied in a striking new treatment of subject, which elevates the picture to a plane above that occupied by any of his previous renderings. Also, it sets the painter himself as close to the Florentine school of thought as it was possible for a true Venetian to come.

First of all as one studies the composition is the impression of the remarkable vivacity of Titian's imagination. Stereotyped as the theme was, the experience of more than half a century of painting shines out brilliantly in a conception entirely fresh and new. All the latent power of a lifetime is here unleashed; all the boldness and technical skill and, above all, the restraint of the finished craftsman completely at home in his medium, are displayed with the ease and spontaneity of certainty.

Again we note at once the off-centre balance of the composition, with all the lines focussing upon the figure of the startled Virgin, as she turns from her lectern at the lower right-hand corner of the canvas, and still holding the book she had been reading, raises the veil covering her hair and drifting about her. She fixes her eyes upon the angel in the opposing corner, who bows before her with hands crossed upon his breast. High above the Dove wings downward toward her in a blaze of glory surrounded by cherubim every one of whom breathes life and vigor. The face of the Madonna, faultlessly lighted by the glory and the rays from the Dove, is no longer the face of a young girl shrinking or at least subdued by her terrific destiny. It is an older, a finer and more delicate visage, "impressed," as Crowe states it, "with so much dignity and character that nothing more than the mould of the face suggests a point in common with these creatures of another world of thought." This is true notwithstanding the fact that the features, Crowe thinks, recall in some measure the *Venus of Urbino* and the Washington *Venus with the Mirror.*

In his younger days had Titian composed such a picture he would have relied for his effect upon a meticulous detail, as effective at close range as at a distance. At ninety he no longer painted for close observation but for the normal range, avoiding outlines and minutiae, instead balancing his colors in masses and effecting contrast by opposing lights and shadows worked in broad, sweeping planes. He was both angered and scornful at the feeling of the church authorities, who failed to understand the work, that it was unsatisfactory. With superb disdain he signed it boldly, TITIANUS FECIT FECIT—"Titian made it made it." No artist not entirely sure of himself would have dared such defiance of both patron and public. Vasari's statement that "these last works, though there are good qualities in them, were not much esteemed by the master himself, and have not the perfection seen in many of his other paintings," hardly seems justified in view of Titian's indignant insistence upon the *Annunciation* as his very own work. It is probable, everything considered, that Vasari misunderstood the painter, and applied to both *Transfiguration* and *Annunciation* the opinion the painter held regarding the first only.

From such a religious work to the beautiful but pagan *Venus and Cupid* of the Borghese collection is strange enough as contrast but typical of Titian's universality. The picture shows Venus, for once draped, with Cupid between her knees while she binds his eyes to blind him. Two Graces, one with the famous quiver of arrows, the other extending his bow, bend forward opposite the goddess, against whose shoulder leans another little Cupid, gravely watching the teaching of the boy god. Through the broad wall opening at the rear shimmers a mountain landscape culminating in a splintered crag at one side. No more striking example of Titian's later style could be asked, and the figures, built up of wonderfully impasted grey with black, blue and reds, are plasticity itself.

As the winter of 1565-66 drew on, Titian engaged the highly skilled engravers Niccolò Boldrini and Cornelis Cort the Fleming to reproduce selected examples of his choicest work. He applied to the authorities for what we of today call copyright protection of the prints thus made possible, and a decree dated June 4, 1566, granting him exclusive rights in all such work, issued from the Senate. About a dozen plates were made, which included the *Annunciation* just discussed, the Barbarigo *Magdalen, Perseus and Andromeda* and *St. Jerome.*

During the previous year Vasari had become convinced as an historian that to keep his *Lives of the Most Excellent Painters, Sculptors and Architects* up to date, he must revisit all the principal art centers of Italy and see for himself what his subject artists had accomplished since he brought out the first edition of his popular and highly important work. With remarkable speed and a comprehensive knowledge of what he sought, he covered the field fully, arriving in Venice May 21, 1566. After six days there he started home by way of Ferrara, writing of Titian in his usual cool vein: "Titian having decorated Venice or rather all Italy and other parts of the world with excellent paintings, well merits to be loved and respected by artists, and in many things to be admired and imitated also, as one who has produced, and is still producing, works of infinite merit; nay, such as must endure while the memory of illustrious men shall remain." The Florentine also lists the pictures he saw in the Biri Grande studio, twelve in all, ranging from the self-portrait of which we have no knowledge whatever to the three large octagonal pieces for the Brescia ceiling. The "picture ordered for Doge Grimani" probably meant the brilliant *La Fede*, today in the Ducal Palace, but several of the others were either destroyed, stolen or restored out of all semblance to their original appearance, and must be included in that melancholy roster of missing works the world so much needs in an era when the ugly, the sordid, the insincere are glorified, and the beautiful, sincere and inspirational seem largely forgotten or disregarded.

CHAPTER SEVENTEEN

The Last Decade

Few indeed and rare are the men in any age, laurelled by international fame, still vigorous under the weight of ninety years, who have possessed enough of the fire of youth and ambition to plan for a confidently anticipated future. Titian, magnificent old lion that he was, did so with the cool sagacity that marked all he did. With five of his strongest pupils he applied for and was immediately granted membership in the Academy of Painting in Florence, evidently looking forward to advantages to all of them from the new association. Death had taken all but one of his oldest and closest friends and associated artists, Jacopo Sansovino; and he, though no one then knew it, had but three or four years to live. The great old man stood gravely at bay against Time, whom he defied with a calm as unshakable as it was fine and courageous, painting still, always painting, always with eyes and hopes fixed upon the morrow.

So far as any published records are available, nothing seems to have disturbed his almost glacial calm seriously. When the Pregadi withdrew his immunity from taxation and ordered him to file a return not long after Vasari's visit in 1566 Titian, whether or not he employed a shrewd attorney or tax adviser, entered a report that is a gem of vagueness and half-truths that would do discredit to any corporation magnate in this age of income tax concealments. What is even more important, he seems to have been covered by the state-

335

ment which, to be euphemistic, is neither entirely frank nor complete. The return, much too long and detailed for reproduction here, was dated June 28, 1566, and witnessed by the Signori Bartolommeo Gradenigo and Sebastian Badoer, both of the Council of Ten. The account of his residence with which the statement begins is interesting.

"I, Titian Vecellio, son of the late Gregorio, living in the quarter of San Canziano in the mansion belonging to the Magnificent Madonna Biancha Polani, pay her as rent 60 ducats a year; and upon this house, garden and vacant land I have twice paid her 350 ducats, as appears in a contract before Ser Zulian Mondo, notary of Venice, on the 30th of April, 1555; I have also been obliged to rent from this Madonna, to the end that prostitutes do not dwell under my house, their lodgings for which I pay 32 ducats rent a year. In one of these apartments is Messer Zuan Andrea Ugon da Bresa, who pays me 14 ducats rent a year. In the other one lives Ser Pier Bonazza, and he pays me 16 ducats rent; by which I lose 2 ducats a year for these."

The painter then adds in the time-sanctioned melancholy of the reluctant tax-payer: "I must remark to Your Illustrious Signiory upon the small revenues I have with which to support my family, as will be plainly declared by me before the Illustrious Signori of the Taxes." The statement continues endlessly with what we suppose was a villa or cottage at least, set down as a non-productive shack; "morsels" of meadows that yielded no income; fields whose crops of hay or grain were scarcely enough to meet the taxes; dams and river embankments the cost of maintaining which far exceeded their returns; rents supposed to be paid in cash but actually discharged in cheese, wine, grain and even chickens; the Vecellio natal house in Pieve, lived in by his brother Francesco, who paid no rent; and a tumble-down little house on a meadow with only the walls and roof in place. Not a word anywhere does he say of the pensions given him by Charles V and Philip II; not a syllable about money lent at interest, the income from his *senseria,* the probably considerable profits of his timber yard at the Zattere, his gains from continuing quiet but thoroughly well-known transactions with antiquarians such as the renowned Jacopo Strada; most of all, not a sign anywhere about what he has for generations received for his pictures. As emphasis by understatement, the report is a model of reticence. He did not think it worth mention that the authorities at Pieve had just told him they were ready to receive his students and set them at the frescoes in the church, for which Titian was to be paid two hundred ducats.

The trade in antiquities was a flourishing one, with agents all over Europe eagerly chaffering with once wealthy nobles and private citizens over paintings, statuary, bronzes, silver, fabrics and whatnot which many an exalted family was quietly disposing of in order to maintain its position. Strada was so well known that late in 1566 he left Venice to take service under the Duke of Bavaria at Munich, disposing of his lucrative Venetian business to Niccolò Stoppio. Before he left the Republic Strada sat to Titian, who did a dashing portrait of him holding a statuette of Venus. The canvas shows the dealer standing behind a table, displaying the statuette to an unseen customer, at whom he gazes with his most ingratiating smile. The portrait discloses the painter's then current method in brilliant renderings of texture in both flesh and fabrics, and is distinguished by a treatment bold and free enough to make us instinctively listen for what the dealer is telling his customer.

The charges of avarice brought against Titian seem, on the face of such a clearly mendacious tax return, to be justified. Nevertheless, Titian had considerable cause for financial worry. We have seen all along that his eldest son Pomponio was a worthless and thoroughly dissipated man who not only squandered his own living but at least twice ran his father into debt. Orazio, though he was steady and dependable, an excellent second-class painter, good manager and devoted to his father's interests, had a wife and some very expensive tastes. Besides, he was privately much interested in alchemy, and that presumably cost him a great deal. Titian, though he had his moments of severity—as on the occasion when he petitioned authority to transfer a benefice from Pomponio to a poor nephew—usually was most indulgent to his children, and while he did at times receive considerable sums, he promptly invested the money and so froze most of his assets. He may indeed at times have been embarrassed to meet the demands upon him. We know he had to postpone Lavinia's marriage a year on that account, and that he could not, even when the marriage was celebrated, pay the entire dowry at one time.

In spite of this, all during the last decade of his life he continued to keep open house at Biri Grande while at the same time endeavoring in every possible way to arrange his current finances and investments to such sound purpose that he would leave his children comfortably provided for. As Lafenestre puts the situation: "We see him then on all sides regulating his affairs with the *sangfroid* and tenacity which are one of the traits of his character, as a man who calmly envisages and prepares for his coming disappearance."

It would be wearisome to recount much of his correspondence and efforts during these sunset years to collect payments, some of them years overdue. But one letter shows plainly the duplicity of the go-between, proves that Titian knew who was to blame, and reveals the guiltless patron as the Duke of Urbino. The brief note to the Duke was written May 3, 1567. It informs him that some time before Titian had sent him a picture of *Our Lady,* regarding whose receipt he had not had any official notice. He had learned, however, that the picture was a long time in reaching the Duke, so he recommends that it be exposed in the sun to remedy whatever damage it might have suffered in shipment. Six resultless months slipped past, and the Duke's Venetian envoy, Signor Agatone, put off the persistent painter with evasions and promises which finally wore out Titian's patience. So in October he wrote the Duke rather tartly to say that in the months since his last letter Agatone had done nothing to recompense him for the painting. As we hear nothing further of the matter there seems no reasonable doubt but that the Duke instructed the recalcitrant peremptorily to pay the bill.

Titian never forgot former patrons of distinction even when he had had no relation with them for years. Such a case came up now. Charles V had in a moment of generosity for Titian granted Spanish naturalization to Pomponio, which normally might be expected to produce a substantial income. In response to the painter's repeated letters about this through the years King Philip finally said coldly that he knew nothing about it, which was probably true. Realizing that further direct appeals to the King were useless, the wily artist turned to Cardinal Farnese, thinking by doing him a favor, to secure his official intervention, which Philip's crafty or greedy officials would not dare to push aside or conveniently "forget."

Assuring himself first of a favorable reception of his overtures by a letter, he sent a *Magdalen in the Desert* to the Cardinal in the baggage of Cardinal Facchinetti, Bishop of Nicatro, who was returning to Rome. The covering letter said in part: "Here is a figure of St. Mary Magdalen in the Desert in an attitude of piety and repentance. Since in former times Your Illustrious and Reverend Lordship has not disdained to manifest your approval of some other painting of mine, I am persuaded that this one will please you not the less, and since it is a painting of my extreme old age and painted for my own pleasure, I beg Your Illustrious and Reverend Lordship to receive it with benevolence in testimony of the devotion I bear you." The same letter requested the Cardinal to offer the Pope, Pius V, a *St. Peter Martyr*.

Two months of complete silence passed. With his familiar perseverance Titian recalled to the Cardinal not only the two pictures but Pomponio's matter. To this appeal was added Cardinal Facchinetti's kindly efforts. He made the indifferent Farnese understand that he could still, if he answered Titian, obtain a third painting. Deceitful as always, Farnese then, instead of replying personally, had his relative, Cardinal Alessandrino Farnese, write making beautiful promises and offering with apparent sincerity to "serve you in anything you may ask, and also will send you a present." In response Titian quickly sent him a *St. Catherine,* which the Nuncio at Venice carried in his train to Rome. "Nevertheless," comments Lafenestre in relating the incident, "neither Titian nor his son saw the color of the Spanish gold nor received the promised souvenir, as he states in a melancholy last letter written to this forgetful patron." It was after all King Philip II who was both the most approachable and the most generous of his benefactors.

As the *Martyrdom of San Lorenzo,* which we have seen already, was far enough advanced by this time to be a talking point, Titian wrote the King anew. After blaming the delay in sending the picture upon the illness and death of the Spanish Ambassador, García Hernandez, and the venality of officialdom, Titian said he understood the King desired a series of pictures illustrating some eight or ten major incidents in the life of the Saint, and asked for instructions as to size and lighting. When he knew what Philip wished he would proceed to work without delay, "and use the assistance of my son Orazio and another capable assistant." This is a clear intimation that the painter realized his physical powers were waning and he had to have pupils to perform the heavier part of the work under his direction. The entire latter half of the letter was a morose plea for the King's fulfillment of his and his father's promises. Not a penny did he receive, he complained, but that he had to spend half of it to pay all the ingeniously devised commissions, agents' fees and sundries greedy officials insisted upon from source to beneficiary. "The Chamber of Spain owes me pay for three years and a half," the despairing old man cried, "and the Milan Chamber for even more than that. . . . I should add that my claim on

Naples has never been settled." He closed by saying he would ship a *Nude Venus* with the *San Lorenzo*.

In due course the latter painting reached Spain in good condition and was placed above the high altar of the church at El Escorial, where it remains. The *Venus,* which Crowe feels may have been a replica of the *Venus with the Mirror* which was in the studio at the time of the painter's death and is now in the National Gallery in Washington, was never heard of again. It may have been among the number burned up in the Prado fire, or, like some others, have perished from mold and neglect in a storeroom, if not given to a visiting dignitary. In any event, there is nothing further known of it.

During the winter of 1567-68, while the *San Lorenzo* was on its way to Spain, Titian was kept busy finishing the three great ceiling paintings for the Brescia Town Hall. They were difficult subjects, for the Brescians knew exactly what they wanted and how it should be expressed. The central design was to show Brescia attended by Minerva, not as the goddess of war but of peace, Mars in full war panoply, and Naiads. The figure representing the city must not be shown as a queen, but merely as a beautiful female, simply gowned in white, holding a golden cornucopia in one hand while the other rested on her breast. Since Hercules was reputed to have founded the city, his lion-skin should be draped about her shoulders, his club placed at her feet. Every detail of design and of coloring—hair, eyes, helmet, olive branch, owl, crystal shield, and so on—was minutely prescribed for the painter. The central panel depicted Cyclops forging weapons in Vulcan's shop, with flames pouring out of it, and a lion roaring in the foreground. Third and last of the octagons showed Ceres, Bacchus and two river gods.

As the canvases had been under way a long time, the Brescians early in 1568 requested their old friend in Venice, the Procurator Girolamo Grimani, to press Titian for their completion. Evidently the painter was not satisfied with the advance he had had, for he wrote in June to announce the readiness of all three and made a demand for immediate payment. The Brescians apparently agreed, the pictures were publicly exhibited in the church of San Bartolommeo in October and subsequently were shipped to Brescia. Shortly afterward Orazio went there and was astonished at his hostile reception.

The city was seriously dissatisfied. The board of survey which had passed upon them declared flatly the pictures were not Titian's work, and set a total valuation of a thousand ducats upon them. Indignantly Orazio refused to accept any such sum and came back home. Titian was equally indignant, and a long and acrimonious dispute followed. The deputies of the town stood firm, however, and at last the painter grudgingly accepted the thousand ducats. As the Town Hall burned January 18, 1575, taking the disputed pictures with it, the city was probably relieved that it had not paid more, and Titian glad that the offending evidences that he had reached a point of needing assistance which impaired his work, had perished. It seems as though the Brescians, even if technically justified in their dissatisfaction, were a trifle severe. They must certainly have realized that a man of Titian's age could scarcely be expected to paint single-handed in a relatively short time three canvases each of which measured an hundred square *braccie*. A picture ten "arms" (*braccia*=arm) or roughly more than twenty feet on each side, with figures larger than life size filling it, was a considerable physical undertaking for a man in the prime of vigor. Crowe takes the position that if Titian with his own hand worked over the ground his assistants had previously covered, "the picture might properly be called his"; but if he did not—no.

One of these ceiling paintings, engraved by Cort in 1572, we know; not, perhaps, as Titian and his son, nephew and relatives painted it, but in the painstaking and laborious work of the highly skilled engraver, who left what Blashfield in his notes on Vasari's

Titian calls "memoranda of composition . . . their principal value is . . . an approximate reproduction of frescoes which have perished, or of pictures which have been lost since the engravings were made." Whether or not the finish of this picture in particular and presumably of its two companions betrayed the work of weaker hands than those of the indefatigable old Master, the fact remains clear that the daring of design, to say the very least, carries unmistakably the mark of the lion's paw. So the angry Brescians went distinctly far in their semi-repudiation, however technically correct they may have been in detail.

Titian's thought for his family appears nowhere more clearly than in his petition of June 19, 1567, to the Council of Ten, asking that his *senseria* be transferred from himself to Orazio. The decree issued in the spring of 1569, and two years later, in midsummer of 1571, Philip II authorized him to transfer or to bequeath to Orazio his pension payable from the Chamber of Milan. Similarly, in August of the previous year, 1568, the thriving lumber yard at the Zattere was registered for protective reasons in Orazio's name, though it remained effectively the painter's property. With the same business acumen that characterizes many men of large means today, he provided as far as he possibly could for the son he expected to survive and succeed him by a judicious combination of outright gift and legacy.

One blow Titian undoubtedly felt severely was the death of Sansovino on November 27, 1570, at the age of eighty-four, if we accept the baptismal registers in Florence. The architect-sculptor had taken to his bed six weeks before because he felt very tired. He had no illness, and often, as Vasari tells us, proposed to rise and dress himself, as being in perfect health, "but remaining thus for about six weeks, he felt himself becoming weaker, and requested to have the Sacraments of the Church administered to him; this having been done, though he still expected to live some years, Sansovino departed on the 2nd of November, 1570, and, notwithstand-

ing that the years of his life had come to their end in the pure course
of Nature, yet all Venice lamented his loss."

Vasari made a mistake in the date, according to that laboriously
careful research scholar G. Milanesi, whose *Scrittura di Artisti* is a
mine of information. As Vasari was not in Venice after his visit to
Titian in 1566, the presumption is that Milanesi's work in the Tuscan archives is more to be relied upon than the always more or
less haphazard statements of the painter. Sansovino's death was,
in the words of Lafenestre, "once more to compel him [Titian] to
dream of the Grand Departure." But it was more than that. As
Blashfield points out in his note on the architect's passing, this
man was not only the second member of the Triumvirate to go,
but he was a distinct loss to the world of art.

"If," says Blashfield, "variety of experience were the best of art-
masters, no one in the history of the Renaissance could have had a
better schooling than Jacopo Sansovino. . . . Taught by Florence
and Venetianized by adoption, this transplanted Tuscan left his
native city just as the decadence set in . . . he was able to assimilate
the Venetian freedom and gaiety and to enforce these qualities
with the science of his native city. The Libreria of San Marco was
the result." In his long life of more than eighty years (some accounts make it ninety-three years) he had seen practically all the
best of the Renaissance, and while faults have been found with his
works, both sculptural and architectural, he achieved to a far
greater extent than most men what is probably the divine plan, if
we may assume such a concrete thing, in that he left the world
richer and more beautiful by what he created for it.

Sansovino had been the last link connecting the arts of the sixteenth with those of the fifteenth century so far as Titian was
concerned. Now that Titian alone remained, and there was no enthusiastic publicist-friend to shout his fame into the ears of a world
already fast growing away from him, the painter turned with persistence again to Philip II in the endeavor to recapture the patron-

age that had practically ceased as the King of Spain became more and more internationally involved and had neither the time, the ear nor the funds to heed anything but matters of state. With the Low Countries in furious revolt against Alva's ruthless policies, the Inquisition producing an attitude among Spaniards everywhere of servile hypocrisy bred of terror, Franco-Spanish relations hardly better than unfriendly imbalance, the Turks again threatening Europe through their war against Venice, Philip had reason for paying no attention to his quondam favorite. Titian knew this, but the gritty fibre of the man would not recognize any obstacle, however great, and he hammered away at the King time after time. There was a good deal of justice in his complaints, as he showed in his letter of August 1, 1571, in which he complained that he had had nothing for many years from his Naples concession, "nor from any of my ordinary pensions." Plaintively he begs for help in his last years, in which he has "spent my all in the service of Your Catholic Majesty, without serving any other person, and not having received a single farthing for eighteen years in payment for the pictures I have sent you from time to time." In a special memorandum enclosed with the letter to Antonio Pérez, the Spanish Ambassador, dated December 22, 1574, he lists the pictures unpaid for. The dates as they appear are those given by both Crowe and Lafenestre, and for the most part concurred in by Gronau:

"*Venus and Adonis* 1556
  Diana and Callisto 1561
  Diana and Actaeon 1561
  Andromeda and Perseus (Crowe, 1556; Lafenestre, 1562)
  Rape of Europa (Crowe, 1562; Lafenestre, 1556)
  Christ in the Garden 1562
  Temptation of the Jews with the Coin to Christ 1568
  Christ in the Sepulchre 1561
  St. Mary Magdalen 1561

The Three Magi of the East 1561 (Not in Lafenestre's list)
Venus to Whom Love Holds a Mirror ———?
Nude, with Landscape and Satyr 1567
Last Supper 1564
Martyrdom of San Lorenzo 1567"

The last item is followed by the words: "with many others which I cannot remember." The second paragraph of the Memorial for the King reads: "The pictures sent to His Majesty at various times during the twenty-five years are these, but only in part. I therefore desire that Señor Alons [Alonso Sanchez Coello], his Majesty's painter, add those which are missing because I cannot remember them all." That final sentence and certain rather vague collateral evidence make Crowe feel that when, as we shall see in a moment, Philip ordered Sanchez Coello to sketch an outline memorandum for Titian of the battle of Lepanto and send it to him by the shortest route, the Spanish painter instead brought it in person.

That epoch-making sea fight put an abrupt termination to Turkish ambitions for European conquest for the next few centuries, lifted the terrible anxieties felt by all the Christian powers threatened by Ottoman expansion, and wiped out at one blow the entire Turkish naval armada. Venice and Spain had signed a treaty in May of 1571, but time was required to prepare for the undertaking, which all knew was vital. By August not a single Spanish vessel had appeared to join the composite flotilla Venice was preparing, but at last, late in September, Don John of Austria and no less than two hundred towering Spanish men-of-war toiled through the Straits of Messina to join the allied squadrons of the Papal States, Genoa and Venice. With oar and sail the combined forces made their slow way to the same field of action near the classical Actium, where Octavius crushed Antony in 31 B.C., and where centuries later Antonio Grimani was disgraced by his defeat. The vast Turkish armada lay at battle position, waiting at anchor for the "Christian dogs."

Lepanto was of extraordinary interest and importance, not only because it broke the Turkish naval power but because of the appalling slaughter and as the last sea action of major importance in which both oars and sails were employed. Only a handful of Turkish craft escaped. The rest were all sunk, burned or captured, with some twenty thousand men, while the Allied fleet lost at least eight thousand. As soon as possible after the fight was over and a messenger could be spared, Admiral Sebastian Venier, who with Admiral Barbarigo commanded the Venetian contingent, detached Captain Giustiniani and his ship to speed the news to Venice. About dusk on the evening of October 17, ten days after the battle, the Venetian cruiser entered the lagoon, the sailors shouting and waving Turkish banners, the men at the long sweeps, according to Crowe, "wearing the spoils of their enemies."

The city boiled over with excitement. Captain Giustiniani was carried in a wild outburst of relief and jubilation to San Marco. Doge, Council, Senate, foreign ambassadors marched to the Cathedral in state to worship with a solemn *Te Deum*. Up went the shutters of the shops all over Venice. "Closed for the death of the Turks" was scribbled on some. The doors of the debtors' prison swung open; the prisoners vanished into the roaring crowds, and nobody cared. Europe was safe—Venice was free! Time enough to think of the Venetians who had given their lives for the victory when the fleet came back. Now was the time to be joyful!

There is not a scrap of evidence so far as this writer knows to indicate that Titian heard, saw or took any part in the riotous festivities of thanksgiving. But it is impossible to think of such a leonine character and to imagine him quietly staying apart from such an occasion. Old as he was, with Orazio to lean upon, he probably contributed all he had to the universal exultation.

Whether he did or not, within two weeks the authorities decided the victory must be fitly celebrated by a permanent memorial in the form of a great canvas in the Ducal Palace which should forever keep the victory alive in the minds of the people. The heads of the Ten were authorized on November 8, 1571, to select one or more painters to represent the Battle of Lepanto in the main hall of the Library in the Palace. As a result of the deliberations of the three, Ridolfi says Titian was chosen, with his friend Salviati to help him. We know Titian's dramatic power from the engraving of his *Battle of Cadore*. As the old man would have had plenty of participants in the epic struggle to give him incidents and describe the terrific life-and-death, hand-to-hand fighting, he would unquestionably have left us a masterpiece. But for some reason, probably because he was busy with another subject, as we shall see in a moment, he declined, and Tintoretto finally received the commission, producing a canvas so striking and satisfactory that he was promptly given a *senseria* as his reward.

At this point in Titian's career there is a curious difference in the interpretations of confused facts given by Crowe, Lafenestre and Gronau. Without a special journey to Spain and a search of the voluminous archives at Simancas in person it is impossible to say definitely whether German, Englishman or Frenchman is more nearly correct. Lafenestre says plainly: "Nevertheless, the old master could not remain indifferent to this triumph of civilization and Christianity. If he did not feel capable of undertaking so huge and animated a picture as this one for the Ducal Palace, he yielded easily to Philip II's invitation. This monarch had asked him to preserve the memory of this great action by an allegory the *projet* for which he would send him." The sketch giving the King's ideas was commanded from the court painter, Sanchez Coello, who naturally had small liking for such a task. He performed it, nevertheless, and added another sketch giving the King's likeness of the moment. As soon as Titian had seen the two memoranda, he wrote to Philip declining the commission by saying that with such a painter as Sanchez Coello the King had no need to invite foreign artists to paint the picture, no matter how great their reputation at home. Philip insisted, and Titian painted the curiously misnamed *Battle of Lepanto* which may be seen in Madrid today, "a darkened painting, brushed in with evident haste, but in which the vigor of the old master shines out brilliantly in the spirited touch and the intensity of coloring."

Crowe tells much the same story but adds that Sanchez Coello, instead of obeying the King and sending the sketches to Venice by the shortest route, brought them himself. The Englishman contradicts himself flatly by stating first that Sanchez sent the sketches, and six pages later, referring to the letter and list of pictures sent to Don Antonio Pérez December 22, 1574, makes the assertion "that Sanchez Coello . . . did not 'send' it by the shortest road but actually took it himself." Gronau then enters the lists with the remark that "Titian did have relations with the above-named Spanish painter, whose brother, Hieronimo Sanchez, was in Venice in 1575 with a view to treating with Titian. At that time, however, the 'Allegory,' which the envoy from Urbino saw him painting in May, 1575, must already have been finished." Lafenestre completes the confusion by saying that the picture was "sent to Madrid Christmas Day, 1574."

The one sure thing we may believe regarding the time when this canvas was painted is that it could not have been executed before Lepanto nor after Titian died. That places its date within five years and fixes its style in the Master's last period. Anything else is superfluous. Unfortunately it is neither a very great work nor is it at all a real battle picture. It is exactly what Philip ordered: an allegory. It scarcely could be great when the King, who despite a cultivated taste was no artist himself, dictated its composition to a painter of an alien race whose forte was not that sort of forced imagery.

The King is shown in full armor, standing behind a table covered with crimson velvet richly embroidered in gold, holding up in very clumsy man-fashion his little son the Infante, born two months after the battle. A tempestuously acrobatic angel flies head downward from the opened heavens to hand the Infante a victor's palm, to which is attached a scroll with the bold inscription *Maiora Tibi*. In the lower left corner squats a dejected Turkish prisoner, half naked and shackled wrists to ankles, with trophies beside and behind him. The King's little spaniel stands on his hind legs at the right, head turned, as though he were fleeing from the vision of the descending angel. In the background is a confused maze representing a very impressionistic view of the battle itself. Gronau's comment will serve: "The picture betrays something of the distaste felt by the artist for this subject. Still, many parts of it are very fine, the pictorial treatment is broad and seems improvised; some strong reds in the foreground contrast wonderfully with the flames and smoke in the distance; the figure of the angel is full of vigorous movement. Titian's powers were not failing, but at his age even he was not able to cope with such a new class of subject." The German critic adds: "Titian had begun for King Philip with mythology; he was to end his work for him with allegories and pictures of saints. There is so much life and power in his creations, so far as he carried them out himself, that they bear eloquent witness to the unabated vigour of his hand as well as his devotion to the King."

In all probability this was one of the pictures King Henry III of France saw in Titian's Biri Grande studio when he visited the painter while in Venice in June 1574. Lafenestre toys with the idea that possibly Titian may have offered it to him. We know Henry offered the painter eight hundred ducats for the magnificent *Ecce Homo*—now in the Belvedere—which the artist refused, perhaps because it was the property of Giovanni d'Anna. When he finally shipped the painting on Christmas Day he sent a letter with it to Don Antonio Pérez in which he acknowledged the tardy receipt of eight hundred ducats as partial payment of the eleven hundred the Chamber of Spain owed him. Milan, however, seemed to be perpetually deaf to his appeals. "None the less," added the painter, "I shall continue to serve His Catholic Majesty as best I can, not only in the Battle but in other works commenced." Neither King nor Ambassador answered him for a full year, so again, and yet a third time Titian renewed his claim, once on Christmas Day, 1575, and for the last time two months later, on February 27, 1576.

These last letters are painful to read, they add nothing to Titian's reputation, and they accomplished nothing whatever. Regardless of anything the painter felt in his body and knew of himself in his heart, the dance of life was over for him. He was ninety-nine years old. His friends were all dead. All of his earlier patrons had died. Philip II of Spain had enough of his works already to stock a gallery, and the royal mind was burdened with many things more important to the State than adding to his art treasures. Lavinia, his beloved daughter, had died in childbed, his oldest son Pomponio was living a wastrel's life, and Orazio was all he had left. Undaunted, magnificent in his loneliness, the old man kept his eyes still on the future. And already in Venice was the insidious poison brought in the year before, to spread slowly and strike a deep root, strong and hot, in the very heart of the Most Serene Republic. The dread plague had arrived again.

Still completely unafraid, this man who had never been ill in his life except for the temporary attacks of fever from which almost everyone in Venice suffered from time to time, realized that he was old and lacked the vitality of his rugged youth. So he bargained with the Franciscan friars of the great church of the Frari, where already two of his noblest works were enshrined—the *Assunta* and the *Madonna del Pesaro*—for a grave in the Chapel of the Crucifix. In exchange, he would paint for them a *Christ of Pity* worthy to rank with its two fellows.

After some discussion the monks accepted the offer, and Titian began the painting. He had almost finished it by the following summer, but then some misunderstanding with the churchmen arose and he did not touch the canvas again. Angered, the painter changed his will, directing that his body be buried in the chapel of his family in the little country parish church at Pieve di Cadore. Many months later it was Palma Giovane who put the finishing touches to the painting, adding the inscription

Quod Titianus inchoatum reliquit
Palma reverentur absolvit
Deoq. dicavit opus.

CHAPTER EIGHTEEN

*Pretium non vile laborum**

THERE is an inexpressible melancholy in "the last leaf on the tree." Poets may sing as they will of death, of the beauty its cold breath pours upon the stilled features of even the least significant creature as the heart ceases to throb. The blunt prose fact is that no living thing, animal or human, wishes to die except in dire extremity. None truly enjoys even gradually growing old and being compelled to the realization of lessening force, the increasing swiftness of galloping years that race uncontrollably toward annihilation with flying rein. The greater a man's mind, the more is he frustrated and disappointed as the end approaches. Cecil Rhodes phrased it immortally as he sighed the words cut into his monument—"So little done, so much to do."

Titian had lived far past the normal span of the man of his day. One by one death had claimed his wife, his brother, his daughter, his most intimate friends, a host of his princely patrons and benefactors. Charles V, the once puissant emperor, had died out of the world, clad in the meagre robes of a recluse monk in his cell in the monastery of Yuste. Pope Paul III was long since forgotten, a handful of ashes that meant nothing to anyone. Dukes and prelates and soldiers, princes and great ladies, doges and poets and all the rest had trooped on into common oblivion, for the most part their accomplishments interred with them. But Tiziano

---

* "Not slight is the reward of labor."—Motto of the Order of the Golden Fleece.

353

il Divino, the Magnificent Old Master, undisturbed, serenely unafraid, more powerful of mind in some ways than he had been as
a student of genius eighty years before, worked tirelessly on with
the steadiness of a human heart.

It was March in the year 1576. Only a few days before, as we
have just seen, Titian had written to Philip II, for the last time
asking payment of claims we cannot but feel the monarch deliberately chose to ignore because he already had everything from
the painter that he wanted. Over silent, terror-smitten Venice the
thin, evil spirit of the plague mingled with the gauzy mists rising
from the lagoons and crept insidiously into the nostrils of high and
low in palace and hovel, hospital and church and office. The city
lay alone in its peril. Communication with the mainland was
cut off. Public affairs and private business ceased to exist except
for the barest necessities of life. Panic swept the city with its abject
fear and confusion. Every one of the hundred and ninety thousand
citizens who could fled as fast and as far as possible from the
danger that stabbed in the dark and mocked all attempts to drive
it away. Makeshift pesthouses and morgues were hastily opened
on practically every one of the islands in the lagoons. Every day
the soft and tender blue and white of the Adriatic sky was as-
soiled by greasy, menacing black *tourbillons,* as the goods and
garments of countless victims fed huge purging fires in every
quarter.

The still, cold, clammy horror of the Venetian winter was broken
only by the anguish of the dying, the futile, frantic prayers in every
church of those who could not leave town, the frightened under-
tones of those unfortunates forced to gather up and hastily inter
the thousands of dead who stiffened in every house, in every street
and byway. By turns the sun gloriously poured out all of its limit-
less gold upon the once gay and lovely city; but lordly architecture
and frescoed façade glared back, stony mockeries in its pitiless
revelation. By turns the moon, that transcendent, ineffably be-

witching and effulgent Venetian moon, soared majestically above
the silent islands of the city, that "Floating Republic" which, more
than any other, had given her back something of her own beauty
and significance. But no gay *canzone* lilted up, no mellow tenor,
no lyre or tinkling mandolin dared sing in silvery ripples that
matched the moonlight on the water. The few gondole that moved
were grim and black, silent and hurried. The grunted mono-
syllables of their oarsmen were profane and frightened; the pas-
sengers, silent all, covered from crown to heel, lay stacked, fag-
gots in endless cords not good even to burn.

One in every four Venetians in that ghastly year of 1576 was
struck down. Scores of thousands had fled. Of those who remained fifty thousand perished in agony, Titian and his son Orazio
among them. Why, one wonders, with life still vigorous, with
faculties and courage unimpaired, did not the greatest of Venetians
then alive flee the pesthole with his son, as so many thousands of
less importance had done, and seek the safety and beauty of his
mountain-guarded Cadore? Lafenestre asks: "Was it imperious
duties that held them in Venice? Did they remain merely to watch
over their house and property in the universal disorder? Or was
it perhaps that flight from Venice was interdicted at a certain time
by the frightened populace of surrounding lands?"

Winter dragged through its grim course. Summer came, and
brought renewed sultriness and heat, but no sign of relief. Venice
was almost deserted. It reeked of corruption and death. But still
the indefatigable painter in the Casa Grande in San Canziano
worked steadily on, beside him the ever faithful Orazio. Worthless Pomponio alone remained in the safety of distant Milan.

On August 27, 1576, Titian dropped his brushes. *Il Tiziano fu!*
Titian *was,* as the Italian idiom graphically expresses the end.
At the very margin of his hundredth year the great man collapsed among his unfinished works. Gronau alone among his
biographers declares, without stating any authority, that he died of

old age. The man who had done more for true progress, who had affected the world more, and more constructively, by the sheer majesty and beauty of his poetry of color and imagination than all the heroes and princes before or after him, had ceased. Two days later Orazio the loyal was struck down. The great Biri Grande mansion and its treasures stood soulless, undefended. Hoodlums, made desperate by conditions, scented their prey with the appalling prescience of vultures. Hardly was Titian cold before these vandals crept in, wary and predatory. Before Orazio or the authorities could prevent it they had partly looted the house. The smaller pictures, jewelry, money, decorations, antiques, rugs, tapestries, clothing, souvenirs, everything of a size they could carry off quickly and undetected, vanished. The mansion was stripped almost to the nakedness of a disused barn. The larger paintings the thieves could not possibly smuggle to secure places of concealment must have added the final note of the bizarre to that still shell of death as they glowed on against the walls, changelessly beautiful, rich with an immortality that had been denied to the genius which created them.

Although there is no record of it, we may well believe that Titian's bearded and now sunken visage wore an expression if anything more serene in death than in life. Disappointed as he surely was at not having been able to accomplish more, the painter nevertheless had the comforting consciousness as he felt the bonds attaching him to life dissolving that what he had done was good, that he had greatly enriched the world, giving it far more than it had given him, and so he could welcome sleep after toil.

Time and again had the plague visited Italy. Lawgivers and physicians alike groped in the blackness of superstition and ignorance in their efforts to combat what they could not understand and so could not fight intelligently. Regarding the visitation partly as a material condition and partly a divine correction for their sins, the Venetians mingled a ritualistic faith and valueless medicines

ALLEGORY OF THE BATTLE OF LEPANTO

LA PIETA OR THE CHRIST OF PITY, TITIAN'S LAST PICTURE,
COMPLETED BY PALMA GIOVINE

with a few sanitary half-measures that did accomplish a little. One of these was the decree that no person who died of the plague might be buried in the city, lest the contamination be further spread. Half a century before, in 1524, Perugino was ignominiously thrust into a field and hastily covered. Ghirlandaio's body was rushed off in the cold blackness of night in 1494 to a common burying-ground.

But should the greatest artist the Most Serene Republic ever produced be similarly treated? So magnificent was this man in even the untoward circumstances, despite the terror that stalked throughout the city unchecked, that solemnly the Republic reversed its ruling to honor him for the last time. What a meeting in the Palace that must have been in the muggy, sweltering heat of late August, as Doge and councillors, with black death sitting beside them in their deliberations and the stench of him in their nostrils wheresoever they went, decided that regardless of danger, Titian must be honored as befitted his achievements. As one man the painters and sculptors, architects and mosaic artists, wished to give him such a funeral as the Academy in Florence prepared for Michael Angelo; and reluctantly they abandoned the plan aborning, leaving to the city authorities the simpler but still impressive form.

On August 28, the day after Titian died, the canons of San Marco came to the mansion in Biri Grande and thence, with the highest dignitaries, escorted the body to its tomb in the Chapel of the Crucifix in the splendid church of the Frari, which the painter had selected as his burial place before his dispute with the Franciscans. The contemporary records do not give any details, so we do not know whether the ceremonies consisted simply of the Office for the Dead or a full requiem mass. We do know full well the danger such a public gathering entailed. It is enough that Doge and Senators, artists and people mourned so sincerely they were willing to place honor to the dead above risk to the living.

No monument was reared above the simple tomb for more than two hundred years. It seems very strange that Venice should thus officially have forgotten her greatest. Titian was spared the indignity of being memorialized by inferior talent, by a lesser genius than his own, until it no longer mattered. Even the *Pietà*, or *Entombment*, the picture on which he was working when struck down, was not in the Frari but in the church of Sant' Angelo until it was closed. And then from an alien and often bitterly fought race came the proof of immortality. By royal command of the House of Austria the sculptor Canova executed the great marble monument that honors him who honored his beautiful world.

"Titian," says Vasari in summing up his career, "has always been healthy and happy; he has been favoured beyond the lot of most men, and has received from Heaven only favours and blessings . . . to say nothing of his excellence in art he has always distinguished himself by courtesy, goodness and rectitude." Even in death he was fortunate. He never knew that Orazio, to whom he had looked with such simple faith and hope and on whose continuance of the family tradition of service with honor he so relied, was stricken with the dread disease two days later. Less fortunate than his father, the son was snatched up and taken to the hideous charnel house of the Lazzaretto Vecchio, the Old Pesthouse, where he died with thousands of other victims. The magnificent old lion was mercifully treated by death in that he never knew the treasures and the fortune he had laboriously accumulated through three-quarters of a century of ceaseless endeavor must fall into the hands of the greedy and conscienceless Pomponio, who disposed of everything in profligate living, to die himself, at last, friendless, alone, miserable and stripped of everything. Last of all, death spared Titian the blow he would have received the very next year, when flames burned out the Hall of the Great Council, taking with them the splendid *Battle of Cadore* and almost all the noble work he had officially executed for the Signoria and many a Doge.

Back in the first few lines of this attempt to create an impression of both beauty and skill by showing Titian against his backgrounds and his work, it was pointed out that the so-called makers of history are not the men usually who accomplish most for the world. The idea is worth pondering. Can more than a handful of us who have studied carefully and in detail Venetian history remember the names of the soldiers, politicians, prelates and others which resounded through the world as conquerors and glorious leaders during the century of Titian's life? Can we recall, except with considerable effort, anything notable that any of them did? Can we say, with the assurance of world development to confirm our statements, precisely how what they accomplished helped the world along? The whole Venetian dream and fabric crumbled with the Napoleonic era, and the men who had made the Most Serene Republic what she was in power and wealth, as far as permanent importance is concerned, might as well never have existed or wielded power. All they did in the aggregate was to lay the background, beginning with the oozy, pile-bastioned mud flats, from which Titian and his compeers drew a little to mingle with their native genius, and thus produce something of grace and harmony and delight that will endure as long as men have souls. It is needful only to step into any art gallery or museum in the world today to realize the truth of this, for whether a man be Solon, Croesus or Lazarus, he is to be found there, gazing at the radiant manifesta. tions of the souls of those great artists who, whether they were Italians or Spaniards or Dutchmen, spoke such truth so brilliantly that the man of every race today, centuries later, understands and responds from the heart.

Titian led them all, for no man ever influenced so many succeeding great masters of other lands. Spain's greatest, Velázquez, admitted his debt both in his own and in Titian's country. Rubens copied picture after picture by him and was perhaps Titian's most enthusiastic and studious admirer. His studio in Antwerp was decorated with these copies, which he cherished and looked to for instruction. Close akin to Titian in spirit, Rubens might almost be called his successor, though he never yielded so pliantly to the Venetian's influence as did his own pupil van Dyke. Rembrandt himself, though he had never seen Titian's best in either Italy or Spain, so thoroughly understood Titian's message that he kept in his studio as complete a collection of the engravings of his works as he could obtain, and more than once borrowed ideas from the Master. El Greco, still young when Titian died, also saw, because of his worship of beauty and color, the combined grace and power of the Venetian who was so far, far ahead of his time, and in his own magnificent portraiture owed not a little to the work he could easily study in Madrid.

No book intended for the enjoyment of the layman is the proper place for any detailed study of the painter's technique in a sense that would be acceptable to the serious student of art concerned with learning the Master's methods and how he might apply them. In consequence it is hardly necessary to say more than that Titian had no established routine procedure even within his various periods of development. His treatment varied with the subject and what he felt was the best means of approaching his ideal. In a general way, the underpainting course he followed to some extent throughout his earlier works was modified materially as he grew in both dexterity and mental power. His styles at different periods are a very different matter, for in style and the reasons that bring it into being are causes we can all understand without the close technical knowledge prerequisite to an understanding of method.

As we study selected paintings that marked steps in Titian's progress we can, if we will, follow the spiritual as well as the artistic growth of the man. Full of the divine fire of youth, intoxicated with the richness and variety of color all about him in city and country, lagoons and skies, Titian was predisposed by temperament to the lyricism of which Giorgione was the foremost example of the time. Symonds' comment upon the world he repsented is a very fair estimate of the motivating power of those early days which produced such canvases as the *Sacred and Profane Love* and the *Madonna of the Cherries,* probably the two most popular of all his works. The grace and spontaneity, the careful detail, the breath-taking smoothness with which Titian blended and harmonized his colors, have an irresistible fascination for the majority of beholders.

But the painter had not yet won the mastery with these, for in them he was not free from the lyric strain which to a certain extent saw everything in life through the same screen. Independence was slow in dowering him as one of the great Masters of all time. Somewhat difficult to follow closely in his great altarpieces, his growth is immediately evident in his portraits. The earlier ones sang, but all in the same key. They were charming, but they also lacked that force of character which is the sterling mark of portrayal. All men cannot possibly manifest the same emotion in the same general terms. In his progress, as he himself grew in mental stature, the souls of his sitters revealed themselves to his penetrating gaze, and for sweetness he gives that living eloquence which tells the story of the man before him as truly as a Roentgen ray reveals material things beyond the vision of the human eye. For emotion he gives us truth, and he does so by subtle means of expression in the sitters' hands, their eyes, the poise of their heads, in a thousand ways that vary with the nature of the subjects and his own mood of penetration. The sum total is his success in revealing to us the personality concealed behind the mask we all wear for self-protection.

This exchange of Giorgionesque lyricism for a strongly masculine veracity, with its consequence of little idealization, marked the development of his portraiture from handsome decorative souvenirs to likenesses of thinking men, creatures who manifest in an unforgettable manner that they have both acted upon their environments and been reacted upon sharply. Each face discloses to even the casual beholder what life has done to the man behind it. In other words, in the philosophical sense Titian had become a pragmatist, since his brush revealed him as believing the practical results of living were the essential truth he consistently sought to convey because it was both his duty and his privilege. He disclosed this not only in the portraits but in the brutally dramatic *Ecce Homo* and both the *Crowning with Thorns* canvases. Yet he never permitted himself to slip into pessimistic dejection or acerbity. His Latin sense of reality and his inherent self-discipline kept him sweet and always receptive to beauty, while in his least important efforts there is visible instantly that something we call genius because we cannot define it more adequately—genius, alas, that died with him.

It can be said of Titian with perhaps more justification than it can of most painters that the dividing line between his so-called periods is tenuous and not always discernible. His different styles, in a word, were much more the growing results of never ceasing observation, study and self-discipline than an abrupt change of conception and method. As has already been pointed out, his habit of painting in his later years practically without outlines and forming his impressions by spots of color cunningly juxtaposed or blended so as to produce at the proper focal distance images of startling beauty and harmony, was no sudden and revolutionary change. It was the deliberate outgrowth of his daily experimentation with color, light and shadow and balance, and as great a degree of simplification as possible. It is a broader, bolder, more majestic treatment. It demands of the beholder a greater degree of co-operation with the painter to bring out the full force and meaning of the work; and since it calls for that, placing part of the picture as a creation in the mind of the spectator, it is a long stride in advance. It marks, long before the studies of light made by the Impressionists and their followers of more recent years, such subtle analyses of the functions of light and shadow, such delicacy in the handling of color and building up of the body of his impasto, that much of the recent work is thin and shoddy beside his. And in his economy of landscape, which is so satisfyingly lovely despite its synthetic character, he reveals again and again the acuteness of eyes that never grew dim and the obedience of hands that never learned how to quiver. His fame is secure, though not a single one of his pictures has come down to us undamaged. Titian's conscientiousness of workmanship is not to blame for this. The carelessness of the owners of his work has been. Some paintings have been so blackened by the smoke of candles above altars as to be almost indistinguishable; some have been "restored" and badly patched; some mutilated arbitrarily or added to to make them fit wall or ceiling spaces; some gathered corrosive mold and decay in damp storerooms. "But," as Gronau remarks, "even from beneath this overlaying the art of the Master shines forth and victoriously asserts its ancient power." And that power, slow in developing its maximum, surged on triumphant to the end, leaving us an art so nearly perfect no other excels it in its total of effectiveness and charm.

When he studied the full splendor of Titian's maturer work Michael Angelo, grim, harsh old Florentine ascetic that he was, exclaimed that Titian only was worthy of the name of painter. Such a gift as his imposed upon its possessor the clear and inescapable duty to elevate humanity by leaving it enriched and ennobled by pure beauty. The poet probably has a vocabulary considerably inferior to that of the lexicographer. But the poet has a divine gift of sight to perceive and the divine skill to clothe his perceptions in words that stir or melt the heart as no lexicographer ever could. The Venetians and their fellow Italians could and did see with physical vision everything Titian saw. But they could not recognize its significance. Titian's lofty spiritual vision ran far above and beyond the power of the common eye and mind, his marvelous skill and indefatigable labor fixed forever in glowing color and luminous themes all his fellow men had seen without perceiving. He did his duty to his genius and to mankind.

Edward Hutton has well remarked of Aretino that he never was guilty of imagining words were things. So Titian, far greater Master in his field than was Pietro Aretino in his, did not slur detail nor was he ever guilty of vagueness or obscurity for the sake of an impression. His work carries its full, vigorous, thoughtful message and connotations in every stroke of his brush. Besides being the artist and "the prince of painters"—*Il Divino Tiziano,* as he was often called—he was the consummate craftsman in each of his different methods to the day he insisted upon remaining in the plague-ridden city to finish his work.

The great men of his age all contributed something to enrich mankind. By far the larger number of them produced nothing more substantial than material treasures, in the garnering of which whole peoples were enslaved, some were exterminated, empires made to wax and wane, and the dissemination of Christianity in whose name much of this was accomplished, forced to carry bigotry, persecution and unloveliness in its train. Far removed from all this, Titian created pure, radiant, glowing loveliness that not only worked no harm but that has blessed everyone who has had even the slightest contact with or knowledge of it for almost four hundred years.

Things commercial have a definite and easily determinable value: what they will bring in cash in the open market. That is their true worth. The higher their prices, the more men esteem that worth. But the greatness of art lies neither in the dollar value of it nor in the pride of individual ownership. Art is truly great only as it plants in the soul its miniatures of that divine creation we average humans are too far removed from Divinity to appreciate until the artist, be he musician, sculptor, poet or painter, reaches close enough to God to transmit to the inarticulate mass of us his fleeting contacts with Infinite Beauty and Infinite Compassion.

Titian the Magnificent did this.

INDEX

Index

171-